Communicating with Data
Making Your Case with Data

Carl Allchin

Beijing · Boston · Farnham · Sebastopol · Tokyo

Communicating with Data

by Carl Allchin

Copyright © 2022 Carl Allchin. All rights reserved.

Published by O'Reilly Media, Inc., 1005 Gravenstein Highway North, Sebastopol, CA 95472.

O'Reilly books may be purchased for educational, business, or sales promotional use. Online editions are also available for most titles (*http://oreilly.com*). For more information, contact our corporate/institutional sales department: 800-998-9938 or *corporate@oreilly.com*.

Acquisitions Editor: Michelle Smith
Development Editor: Sarah Grey
Production Editor: Daniel Elfanbaum
Copyeditor: Sharon Wilkey
Proofreader: Piper Editorial Consulting, LLC

Indexer: Judy McConville
Interior Designer: David Futato
Cover Designer: Karen Montgomery
Illustrator: Kate Dullea

October 2021:   First Edition

Revision History for the First Edition
2021-10-01:   First Release

See *http://oreilly.com/catalog/errata.csp?isbn=9781098101855* for release details.

978-1-098-10185-5

[LSI]

Table of Contents

Part II.   The Elements of Data Visualization

Part III. Deploying Data Communication in the Workplace

Preface

Communicating with data is a critical 21st-century skill. The demand for data skills from everyone in an organization has grown in the last decade compared to the initial need, which was for more data specialists. When you can use data to communicate, you can influence others' decisions and achieve your organization's goals. That's the first aim of this book: to show you how to understand, visualize, and present data clearly and effectively. Thus, this book will answer questions like these:

- What is communication, and how can you avoid *noise* interfering with your message?
- What is data, and where can you get hold of this precious resource?
- How can you visualize data?
- How can you make your data visualizations clearer and more effective?

My second goal in this book is to take you a couple of steps past that, so you can avoid some common pitfalls and conflicts that can arise when you use data in your business communications. My aim is to save you time and pain and help you ensure that your audience stays focused on your message. This book will also, therefore, answer questions like these:

- What aspects of data visualization conflict, and how can you balance them?
- What kind of context and presentation should you give your data visualizations?
- What sorts of communication challenges tend to arise in organizational departments (such as IT, HR, or marketing), and how can you overcome them?
- What should you think about when communicating with data in various formats, such as presentations or email?

The split of these objectives is to allow you to not just become familiar with the skills involved in communicating with data but to be able to use those skills in the organizations you operate in. As you become more skillful at communicating with data, you'll find that you are influencing those around you in a more powerful way than you could ever do with words alone.

Why I Wrote This Book

At my very first job in a large organization, I was assigned to a team that was preparing slide decks to report on the organization's operational performance and influence their peers and bosses. I was 22 and had never worked in an organization of more than 100 people. This company had over 40,000 people and operated in a completely alien manner to me. I sat next to the operational directors, so I had a good vantage point to see how the team worked. We compiled tables of numbers, insight, and commentary from other people's work with data to measure progress toward operational targets, determine future strategies, and analyze where previous decisions had gone awry.

We worked with aggregated data points from reports and charts used to run the various parts of the organization. These reports were formed from other people's work with data. I hated not being able to get to the raw ingredients of these compilations: the data. What frustrated me even more was that I didn't have the data skills to *see* that rawer data. I wanted to learn. So when asked about my next career move, I chose to follow the data and information back to its source and asked to work with the centralized data team. I haven't looked back since.

I haven't stopped working with data, so I've seen firsthand that the growth of data's influence on organizations hasn't stopped either. In fact, it's only sped up. Data now influences business decisions and economies in ways that are often too complex to fully wrap our arms around. Harnessing data has become an important part of organizational life across all industries and sectors. Data used to be the domain of specialists, but individuals across the organization are now being asked to communicate with data—whether you are a project manager, process improvement specialist, or team manager.

Skilled data professionals are thus in high demand, but our numbers haven't grown quickly enough to keep up with rapidly amassing data resources. Data work has traditionally been a centralized, specialist function, since it often requires coding in specialist languages or working with complex data reporting tools, but not anymore.

Over 15 years of working with data, those tools have changed more than any other aspect of the job. The new generation of data tools is far easier to use, with improved user interfaces and far less coding, greatly reducing the barriers to entering the field. More people are using data more directly than ever before.

This is especially true when it comes to data visualization. Tools like Tableau and Power BI from Microsoft have allowed subject-matter experts in all sorts of fields to showcase and share their findings through data. If that sounds like you, you're in the right place. Learning to use these tools still requires training and support, both in using the tools themselves and in the fundamentals of data visualization.

This book focuses on the latter. It is not a step-by-step guide to using any specific tool, but you might do well to read it in combination with such a guide. This book operates on a somewhat higher level, helping you understand basic data skills as well as how, when, and where to deploy them in your work life to get results.

My specialty lies inTableau, so if you want to learn how to prepare your data for Tableau, I recommend my first book, *Tableau Prep: Up & Running* (O'Reilly). Alternatively, if you want to visualize your data, I recommend *Practical Tableau* by Ryan Sleeper (O'Reilly) as a great starting point. There are many, many books on working with, analyzing, and visualizing data. So why write another?

Well, while *Communicating with Data* does cover those topics, it also takes you further into the working world. It will help you anticipate, plan for, and overcome many of the common challenges that arise when you begin communicating with data in organizations—from understanding the needs of different parts of the organization to making sure your audience actually views the communications you will make. This book aims to prepare you for what might arise and how to continue to deliver clear communications.

Who Is This Book For?

In a recent Accenture survey (*https://oreil.ly/Ij0er*), only 21% of employees felt comfortable with their own ability to read, understand, and work with data. This book is primarily for the other 79%.

No matter what your job, you need the skills to communicate with and influence those around you. In another study (*https://oreil.ly/BTAJn*), it was found that 84% of employers believed that communication and collaboration were important skills for graduating students. In response to the same question, data skills/literacy was recognized by 66% of employers as important. At school, you probably learned how to write and speak clearly but not how to work with data. This book looks to fill that gap.

If you're part of the 21% who *have* picked up enough data skills for you to work comfortably with data, this book should still be useful for you. Fundamental data communication principles are often missing in lots of the data communications I see, so this book will be useful to address any knowledge gaps you might have on the technical use of data. Soft skills also play an important part when communicating with data. In particular, you may find much helpful knowledge in the chapters dealing with situational challenges—that is, working with different people and departments.

Communicating with Data focuses on building your working knowledge of the terminology and foundational concepts required for working with data and using data visualization to communicate. These are the skills that can help you to be more effective in your communication, beyond language.

To make use of this book, you don't need to have any prerequisite skills beyond basic numeracy. What I'd like you to bring to this book is your expertise, your experience, and your questions so that you are thinking critically about what you read. By doing this, you will be able to use what you learn here to solve the unique challenges of your own workplace.

When you understand what is possible and what *you* can do with data, you can pose the right questions and answer them faster. Being able to quickly mix your subject-matter expertise with data is what will give you and your organization a competitive advantage.

Creating clear, insightful visualizations can help you find your answers and share them with others at all levels of your organization. Humans are great at spotting patterns in visual images but less so at analyzing data line by line. As you learn to create visualizations from your data resources, you will be able to communicate the trends and insights hidden within much more effectively. You'll be able to show what is truly happening in the data so that your audience can draw their own conclusions. Using data visualization to influence change is a powerful technique.

How the Book Is Organized

In my daily work, I teach people what data is, how to create influential data visualizations, and how to use them effectively. I've organized this book similarly to the way I organize my courses: we'll start out with important background information, dive into the specifics of working with data, begin working with visualizations, and then finish with a look at the social and organizational challenges of communicating with data in large organizations. The book is divided into three parts:

Part I, Communication and Data
> Chapter 1 starts with an in-depth look at what communication actually *is* and how communicating with data has changed over time. Chapter 2 dives into all things data: what it is, where it comes from, how to store it, how to prepare it for analysis, and how to gather the requirements for data work. This section lays the foundation for the skills you'll learn in the rest of the book.

Part II, The Elements of Data Visualization

This section begins with Chapters 3 and 4, introducing you to a key facet of data visualization: the most important chart types you are likely to come across in your day-to-day working life and the best practices associated with them. You will develop a sense of how to choose which chart best delivers what you need. Chapter 5 dives deep into the elements of a single visualization to show you how it all fits together. Chapter 6 takes you beyond the chart itself to look at other aspects that can help give additional context to your audience. The section concludes with Chapter 7, which explores how data visualizations work in various formats and methods of communication: the products you'll use to deliver your data insights.

Part III, Deploying Data Communication in the Workplace

The final section deals with how to deliver your findings in the setting of your specific workplace. It's common for data skills and their use to develop unevenly: some organizations use data better than others, and some departments within an organization will have stronger data skills than other departments. This unevenness will affect your communications: for example, how much does your audience trust your data? You'll need to tailor your approach accordingly. The first chapter of this section, Chapter 8, looks at how to find that balance. Chapter 9 concludes the book with a deep dive into several departments within a hypothetical corporation, illustrating the challenges that are unique to those departments and how to get past them.

My goal is to teach you the fundamentals of communication and data so that you can come away from this book able to visualize data, traverse organizational complexity, and influence others through communicating with data.

Conventions Used in This Book

The following typographical conventions are used in this book:

Italic

Indicates new terms, URLs, email addresses, filenames, and file extensions.

`Constant width`

Used for program listings, as well as within paragraphs to refer to program elements such as variable or function names, databases, data types, environment variables, statements, and keywords.

`Constant width bold`

Shows commands or other text that should be typed literally by the user.

This element signifies a tip or suggestion.

 This element signifies a general note.

 This element indicates a warning or caution.

O'Reilly Online Learning

 For more than 40 years, *O'Reilly Media* has provided technology and business training, knowledge, and insight to help companies succeed.

Our unique network of experts and innovators share their knowledge and expertise through books, articles, and our online learning platform. O'Reilly's online learning platform gives you on-demand access to live training courses, in-depth learning paths, interactive coding environments, and a vast collection of text and video from O'Reilly and 200+ other publishers. For more information, visit *http://oreilly.com*.

How to Contact Us

Please address comments and questions concerning this book to the publisher:

O'Reilly Media, Inc.
1005 Gravenstein Highway North
Sebastopol, CA 95472
800-998-9938 (in the United States or Canada)
707-829-0515 (international or local)
707-829-0104 (fax)

We have a web page for this book, where we list errata, examples, and any additional information. You can access this page at *https://oreil.ly/communicating-with-data*.

Email *bookquestions@oreilly.com* to comment or ask technical questions about this book.

For news and information about our books and courses, visit *http://oreilly.com*.

Find us on Facebook: *http://facebook.com/oreilly*.

Follow us on Twitter: *http://twitter.com/oreillymedia*.

Watch us on YouTube: *http://www.youtube.com/oreillymedia*.

Acknowledgments

When writing my first book, I learned how much support is needed from others, and this book has been no exception. *Communicating with Data* would not be the same quality as you read today without the considerable efforts from numerous people.

The content of this book has been shaped since day one by Sarah Grey, a fantastic development editor who added a lot of color to the characters you will find in many of the chapters. Hopefully, you will relate to these characters as much as I do and that they will help you relate to the technical details you will find throughout the book. My production editor, Daniel Elfanbaum, assisted me on my first book and took on the challenge of delivering this second one. Thank you both and the rest of the team at O'Reilly.

The technical review team members have all added their own perspectives and knowledge on the subject and made the text much richer than when they first read the initial drafts. Chris Love, Ryan Sleeper, Claire Reid, Jenny Martin, and Richard Silvester deserve a huge amount of thanks and credit, so please give them a high five in thanks if you ever cross paths.

An extra big thank-you goes to Jenny Martin, along with our fellow Data Prepper, Tom Prowse, for keeping our community-building challenges, Preppin' Data (*http://preppindata.com*), alive when I've had to bury myself in writing and editing. If you want to learn how to prepare data, the Preppin' Data website offers more than 50 free how-to articles along with more than 125 challenges to test your new skills. We genuinely just want people to feel the benefit of feeling comfortable with working with data.

My final thank-you goes to my support network at home. I took on this book—like millions of people across the world—as I was sitting at home during COVID-19 and didn't want to waste that time. Little did I know how mentally challenging that period would be. My parents, Janet and Trevor Allchin, have been encouraging throughout.

My partner, Toni Feather, deserves the biggest thank-you of all, as she provided day-to-day support but also the biggest motivation to get the book done by its deadline. We are currently expecting our first child, who just happens to be due at the same time as the deadline for this book. If you are reading this, the book will have narrowly been completed before the little one arrived.

I hope that by reading this book you will be more prepared for communicating with data than I currently feel like I am for parenthood.

PART I

Communication and Data

Communication

Trying to get anything done in an organization always requires more communication than you first expect. On any given day, you might be communicating with the following:

- The executive, to ask for funding to support a new project
- Your management, getting agreement to use their people's time
- Your peers, to deal with new challenges that arise daily
- Your customers and clients, to deal with their latest requests
- Your suppliers, to ensure that your logistics chain is ready
- Your team, to change priorities as needed

If everyone else in your organization is communicating this much, that's a lot of activity. Trying to make your points and questions heard—or even just reading, organizing, and responding to this onslaught—is a tough challenge for anyone. Any advantage you can gain will make you more effective at your job. This chapter shares the key aspects of communication by applying them to data visualization and shows you how understanding these basic principles can help you communicate more effectively.

You need to be heard, but you also need to ensure that what you say makes an impression. To help with that, this chapter also discusses the final, commonly overlooked part of the communication process: the receiver must retain the information you communicate in their memory.

The aim of this book isn't to teach you something new about your area of expertise but rather to help you share your knowledge more effectively. One way to do that is to combine it with data to validate your opinion. The engineer W. Edwards Deming is often quoted as saying, "Without data, you're just another person with an opinion."

Deming was one of the developers of Total Quality Management, a management framework that focuses on improving processes to create better and more consistent outputs. If you're suggesting ways for your organization to improve what you do and how you do it, you should back up your arguments with data.

If you are new to working with data, all this might feel imposing. The good news is that working with data is not as intimidating as it seems. Chapter 2 gets into the details of working with data, but first I want to introduce you to what makes data visualization so effective.

What Is Communication?

Good ideas are useless unless you can get other people to understand them. Getting people to understand your point of view takes careful communication. But what do I mean by *communication*?

The Communication Process

Communication is something you do without thinking about it every day. You share thoughts and ideas with others by speaking, writing, or just using expressive body language. What you are subconsciously doing with lots of your communication is creating a message and sending it to the person you hope receives it.

The act of sending and receiving a message is only part of the process: you *encode* the message in a way that you think will be clear to the receiver—that is, they will be able to *decode* it, or understand what you are trying to tell them. The sociologist Stuart Hall describes this process in his classic work "Encoding and Decoding in the Television Discourse" (*https://oreil.ly/qLhqh*). Hall describes how these concepts work in television media; you can apply a similar approach to your own communications. However you want to communicate with others, you are choosing how to take the information you have and share it. The method that you use to share it will require you to encode your thoughts. Therefore, your audience will need to decode the message to understand exactly what you meant.

Another factor in communication I often think about comes from a mathematician writing about passing messages through limited bandwidths. In 1948, Claude Shannon described communication in a way that's still relevant today, and ever since I saw it, I think about it in regards to data visualization. I've updated Shannon's original diagram here to focus specifically on personal data communication in the way that I think about it (Figure 1-1).

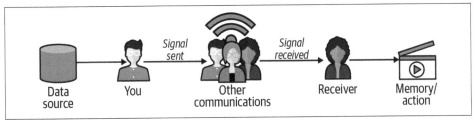

Figure 1-1. The data communication process in organizations

Let's look at how Shannon's model translates to everyday communication within an organization and why I think it applies to visual data:

Information sources and transmitters

In Figure 1-1, the information source is the data source, or others' reports formed from data sources, and you are the transmitter. You encounter many sources of information in the course of your job, whatever your role—everything from your email inbox to databases to your own experiences. You choose what information you pass on and to whom. This means you almost certainly need to filter or summarize that information in some way. You will definitely summarize or prepare the data if you are working directly with the data source. You'll do this when working with data too—more about this in the next chapter.

Receiver and destination

In organizational communication, your receiver is likely to be the destination. You have probably learned which methods of communication are particularly effective for the people you work with. For example, if you send emails to your boss constantly but get no response, you will probably stop sending them and look for another method. Perhaps you will start by speaking to your boss directly. Direct conversation is a much easier way to ensure that your message is received, because you witness it happening—well, most of the time. I'm sure there's been a time when you have spoken to someone directly, but they weren't paying attention and therefore didn't receive your message. In these cases, their body language will soon tell you whether you are being an effective communicator or not.

So why don't we always communicate in person? Simply, we can't, especially when working across different organizations or locations. The rise in remote working during the COVID-19 pandemic has shown the importance of in-person communication and how much harder it is to be heard remotely. After all, in a digital world you can't just walk over to someone's desk to ensure that the receiver gets the message you want them to. Video conferencing can help resolve some of those challenges. Still, too many video meetings can make it difficult to get someone's time and attention.

Getting Through to Your Audience: Context and Noise

Understanding communication isn't always easy, though. How many times have you been misunderstood? Hall describes how social context changes the way the audience decodes and interprets messages. The circumstances you are in when you receive a message makes a significant difference.

Imagine receiving a communication about average employee pay per grade. How you feel about your own pay would dramatically change the way you receive that information. If you receive less than the values mentioned, you would be unlikely to decode the message in the same manner as if you were paid considerably more than the values shown. The same would be true depending on how you grew up. If you come from a poorer background, you might be saddened by what you might consider excessive pay, especially to senior executives in large organizations.

Context is the background information and circumstances of a situation or event that help to provide meaning. Organizational culture, your location (in the main office, a branch, or remote), and seniority in the organization all play a part in setting the context for your work. To ensure that your receiver has the background information required to decode and understand your communication as you intend, you may need to provide additional context.

Let's look at an example. I'll use a mock retailer called Chin & Beard Suds Co. and its release of a new soap fragrance. You need to update the management team on sales. If you've sold 1,000 of the new product, you might be pleased and send a message that the product launch has gone well. Let's look at some of the context and noise factors that might affect your message:

Experience
Team members might have been through many new product launches and have different expectations of what good progress means in terms of the number of sales.

Other messages
The receiver might hear other information that you don't have. If the receiver hears that another product has to be dropped to be replaced by the new product, they might have different sales expectations if the older product sold in much higher volumes.

Market knowledge
If the receiver knows of an overall uplift in sales volumes for similar products, this might raise their expectations for the sales of the new product.

Some of the context you provide could include the following:

- Has the product met sales expectations so far?
- How has the product performed against its competition?
- What are customers saying about the new product?

Piecing all this information together is vital.

Another part of Shannon's system is still applicable today and may be becoming an even bigger challenge: noise. *Noise* is not always literal sound (though it can be) but refers to any interference that affects the communication being received. Trying to talk with friends is a much harder task that requires more concentration in a restaurant with loud background music than in a quiet environment.

Ensuring that your message even reaches your audience can be a challenge when it is competing with many other messages for attention. The popular writer and statistician Nate Silver, in *The Signal and the Noise* (Penguin Press), defines noise as elements interfering with clear understanding of a communication. This can include having too many data points or communications (such as a constant stream of emails), unclear or overly technical language, difficulty meeting in person or online, and personality conflicts in meetings. Contrary opinions, audible or not, can cause confusion for the receiver: their knowledge and understanding of a subject will alter how they absorb the information you are providing. Knowing about your audience is key.

Finally, communication is successful when the receiver not only understands the information but retains it and incorporates it into their decision making. It has to be memorable. (After all, communication is usually about persuasion in some way.) Next, I'll look at what we know about how the human brain retains information.

Don't Forget About Memory

What does it mean to retain information, and how long do you need the receiver to remember your message? There are three types of memory. You're likely to make use of them all:

Sensory
> As the name suggests, sensory memory is triggered by your senses. When communicating visual information, the sense you are likely to trigger is visual. You are triggering a sensory memory if the information can be retained within a second. Can you quickly remember which months met the £208,000 profit target, which would mean the annual run rate would lead to a £2.5 million annual profit (Figure 1-2)?

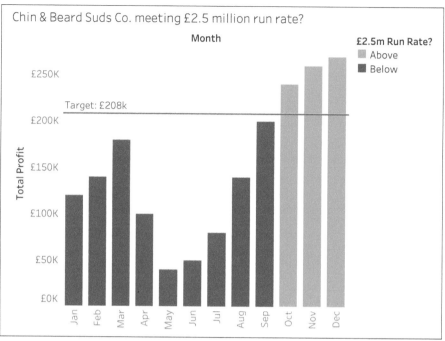

Figure 1-2. C&BS Co. monthly profit levels

Just glancing at this chart, you will likely be able to see that the target is being met in only the later months of the year. When communicating with data, you'll make particular use of a type of sensory memory called *iconic memory*, which stores visual information. This type of memory doesn't last long, but it can help your audience remember key bits of information long enough to put a much more complex message into other types of memory.

Short-term memory

Short-term memory lasts from a few seconds to about a minute for most people. It can help the receiver build up more complex pieces of information in their minds, from multiple data points.

Research in the 1950s found that the average person's short-term memory worked well for holding approximately seven items.[1] Newer research, however, suggests it might be only four items.[2]

---

1 G. A. Miller, "The Magical Number Seven Plus or Minus Two: Some Limits on Our Capacity for Processing Information," *Psychological Review* 63, no. 2 (March 1956).

2 N. Cowan, "The Magical Number 4 in Short-Term Memory: A Reconsideration of Mental Storage Capacity," *Behavioral and Brain Sciences* 24, no. 1 (February 2001).

You can enhance the length of your audience's memories by using a technique called *chunking*, or breaking information into small chunks. Because you are aware of how many bits of information your audience can easily retain, you can optimize the amount of information you show them. This reduces the risk of overloading them.

Long-term memory

As you'd probably expect, long-term memory is thought to last up to a lifetime. When communicating with data, we actively call upon this type of memory less frequently. You can make use of your audience's long-term memory by using themes that will remind them of long-held memories or information. There's a reason family kitchens are used so frequently in television commercials: many people relate that location to memories they formed as children.

Next, I'll show you how to use sensory memory to share key points through something called *pre-attentive attributes*. Without looking back at Figure 1-2, can you remember whether any months met the profit target? Hopefully, you can, and that is because of pre-attentive attributes that we will dive into deeper now.

Why Visualize Data?

Two words: *pre-attentive attributes*. This intimidating term simply refers to the ability to see patterns in images without having to think or consciously work to understand what you are seeing.

This ability evolved in humans to allow us to spot dangers, assess situations, and make instant decisions, without having to think about every little thing happening around us. For early humans, this was mostly finding food or avoiding being something else's food, while today it might be more like seeing a car, a falling object, or a hazard in our path. We still use this part of our sensory system even when we're not on the move.

Pre-attentive attributes can be used for more than just preventing danger. Data visualization relies on this pattern-spotting ability to communicate messages. By representing data in visual forms like bars, lines, or points, you can make use of pre-attentive attributes to grab your audience's attention and make sure they receive your message.

What pre-attentive attributes can you use in data visualization? Figure 1-3 shows a sampling of the possibilities.

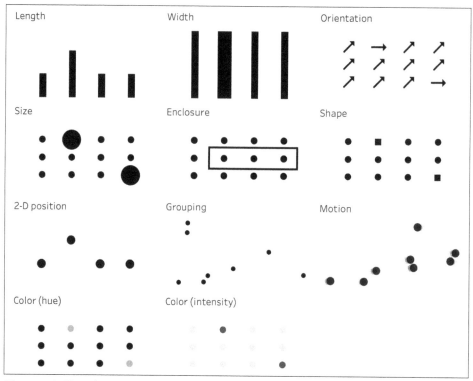

Figure 1-3. Visual representation of pre-attentive attributes

In this range of pre-attentive attributes, some are more effective than others. In *Now You See It* (Analytics Press), Stephen Few, an information technology innovator, highlights two in particular that humans are better at assessing precisely:

Length

Humans notice length at a glance, and we're also good at estimating gaps between different lengths. We can use this to our advantage with data by showing the greatest values as the longest. Length is frequently visualized as a bar chart.

2D position

Often shown in the form of a scatterplot (a chart type we'll explore in Chapter 4), 2D positioning places the greatest values at the top right of the chart. The 2D position is created by using two axes, one vertical and another horizontal. Comparing two metrics against one another is a common task in data analysis.

The other pre-attentive attributes aren't assessed as precisely, but don't disregard them. Precise comparison is not the only way to communicate data. For example, highlighting a key time period by using color or shape can capture your audience's attention.

In an analysis about air pollution (Figure 1-4), I used size, color, and shape to grab the reader's attention more than to communicate a precise message. The car visualization at the top is the first one you come across: it is designed to set the theme but also create intrigue. I used circles to demonstrate the volume of certain pollutants. The size of the circles increases with the ratio of the particulates in the air.

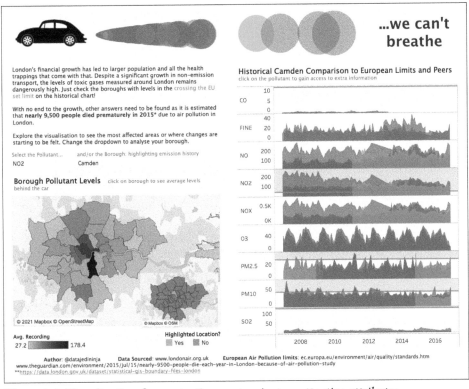

Figure 1-4. Visualization demonstrating nonprecise pre-attentive attributes

Look at the graphic for a moment and compare the size of the circles. Could you tell me the percentage difference between the largest orange circle and the second-largest orange circle? I know I can't, and I made the visualization!

But that isn't the point. I used orange to highlight the London borough of Camden and allow the reader to be drawn to the relevant metrics and compare them against the city's other boroughs. It's imprecise by design but still draws upon pre-attentive communication techniques. I was designing this view for a broad audience and therefore needed to use these techniques to share the insights I had found. Knowing what your audience will comprehend and how much work they are willing to put into decoding your message is a key factor in communicating well.

Pre-Attentive Attributes in Action

Let's take a typical table of numbers and see how we can make its message clearer by using pre-attentive attributes. The table in Figure 1-5 shows the number of bikes sold in the first half of a year.

Bike Shop	Jan	Feb	Mar	Apr	May	Jun
London	358	118	769	636	196	293
York	557	404	533	115	989	309
Leeds	564	540	112	633	606	961
Manchester	525	278	196	596	119	693
Birmingham	509	378	325	699	592	927

Figure 1-5. Table containing bike sales for stores in the United Kingdom

You are clearly an intelligent person (you have chosen to read this book, after all), so here's a challenge. How many seconds do you think it will take you to answer the following questions?

- What is the largest value in this chart?
- How many stores beat their target of 450 bikes sold in a month?
- Which store's sales fluctuate the most?

Did that take a few more seconds than you were expecting? It probably did, and it was probably slightly frustrating too.

The amount of effort a reader must use to interpret what they see is called *cognitive load*. You will come across this term a lot in this book; it is a key factor in measuring the effectiveness of your visualization choices. Making your audience think about what you are showing isn't always a bad thing, but you need to make the cognitive load appropriate for what you are sharing. Tables often take significant cognitive effort to interpret.

So why do so many people in so many organizations still use tables of data to communicate the results of their analysis?

In "The "Right" Data" on page 53, I discuss the importance of capturing the questions your user might try to answer. Tables are a good fallback option for some audiences when you don't know what your user might ask or be looking for in your data set. But we know the questions we want to ask of *this* table, so let's look at how we could use pre-attentive attributes to make the answers easier to find. Let's start with this question:

What is the largest value?
Answer: 989

We could use so many techniques to help answer this question. A simple change in color, as shown in Figure 1-6, is a particularly effective method and doesn't require removing any other data points from the view. This approach has no subtlety but shows how effective highlighting can be to pick out a single value—in this case, the largest.

Bike Shop	Jan	Feb	Mar	Apr	May	Jun
London	358	118	769	636	196	293
York	557	404	533	115	989	309
Leeds	564	540	112	633	606	961
Manchester	525	278	196	596	119	693
Birmingham	509	378	325	699	592	927

Figure 1-6. Highlighting the highest bike sales

Highlighting the highest value draws attention to it. When trying to find the highest value in a table of numbers, often you'll be looking for the longest number (in terms of the number of digits), as that is likely to indicate the highest value. Here, the bike sales are all three digits long, so we need another method to draw the reader's attention. To visually communicate more complex insights, we have many methods to choose from, depending on what you are looking to share.

But how could pre-attentive attributes be used to share other answers to questions your audience might have about the data in this table? Let's consider the next question:

How many times did stores beat their target of 450 bikes sold in a month?
Answer: 17

This is a tough one! Without any visual clues, you are forced to read each number and assess whether it is greater or less than 450. You are not only assessing the value but also trying to count how many meet the target.

You could use a similar technique to the first question and just highlight the values that meet the condition set in a different color (Figure 1-7).

Bike Shop	Jan	Feb	Mar	Apr	May	Jun
London	358	118	769	636	196	293
York	557	404	533	115	989	309
Leeds	564	540	112	633	606	961
Manchester	525	278	196	596	119	693
Birmingham	509	378	325	699	592	927

Figure 1-7. Highlighting values above the target (450)

But other methods might be more useful here. For example, using colored bars to highlight whether values fall above or below the target might make a simple count easier (Figure 1-8).

Again, the consumer of the chart will need to count the orange columns, but this is much easier than assessing whether a value is above the target first. To remove even the challenge of counting, you could create a chart just demonstrating that count (Figure 1-9), but you would lose the individual stores' monthly sales values. As with any data communications, being specific about what question you are trying to answer can change how you visualize the data. More on that aspect in Chapters 3 and 4.

Once you solve the basic question, you might want to go further with your analysis. Other questions that could be asked of this data include the following:

> *Which store's sales fluctuate the most?*
> *Answer: York*

Now we're getting into some better analytical questions.

First, we must define *fluctuating sales*. I'll use a simple definition: the greatest variation—specifically, the store with the largest difference between its best sales month and its worst.

Assessing this data using just values is really hard. As your questions become more complex, good use of data visualization will make finding the answers much easier.

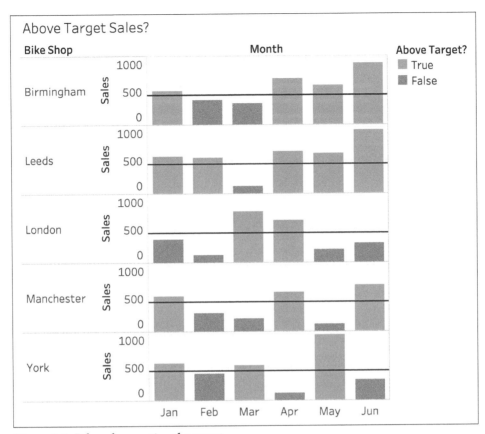

Figure 1-8. Bike sales meeting the target

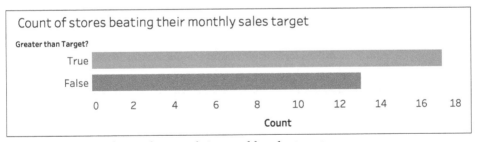

Figure 1-9. Count of stores beating their monthly sales target

My first instinct was to go back to our most effective pre-attentive attribute: length. Perhaps, I thought, a clear answer would appear if I drew a bar between the smallest sales value and the largest for each store. The result is Figure 1-10.

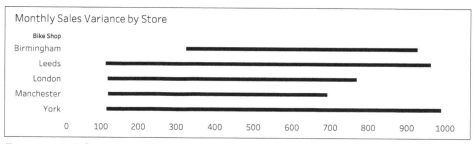

Figure 1-10. Sales variance shown as a Gantt chart

The bars in a *Gantt chart* don't have to start at the zero point, but the chart still uses length to represent the value being shown.

 The Gantt chart is named after Henry Gantt, who designed this type of bar chart in the early 1910s. Gantt charts are often used as project-management tools.

However, this chart still isn't the easiest to read: you have to pay close attention to where the bar starts. It's much easier to remove the minimum and maximum values and just show the difference instead of the actual sales value (Figure 1-11). To make the analysis even easier for your audience, you could sort the stores from largest to smallest difference.

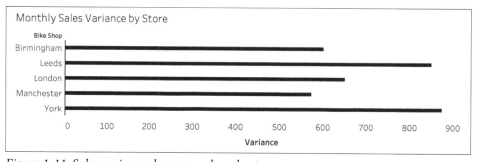

Figure 1-11. Sales variance shown as a bar chart

Now, seeing that the longest bar is York is much easier. Even though York has a similar sales variance to Leeds, having the bars start at the same place makes it much easier to spot the difference and interpret the chart.

In short, even when you're using pre-attentive attributes well, you still need to take care that the chart conveys the information clearly, that you're using the best pre-attentive attribute for the task, and that you're keeping the question in the forefront of your mind. When you do, your message comes across clearly, without forcing the consumer to think too hard. If you *don't* pay attention to these factors, you will create the opposite effect, and people will want to go back to tables.

Your understanding of pre-attentive attributes will help you make better choices about which charts will best communicate the message you want.

The challenges of communicating with data in your organization are likely to resemble the challenges of any other form of communication. You will need to find ways for your communication to be received, decoded, and remembered. This book will help.

Unique Considerations

What makes data communications different from other kinds of communication? First, as you might guess, they are based on a data source or data analysis. (You'll learn more on finding the right sources in Chapter 2.)

Second, data communication in the workplace is usually about meeting a stakeholder's requirement or answering a question. You'll need to know what those requirements and questions are and then analyze your data to find the answers.

Third, data communication, as covered in this book, is all about visual analysis. Chapters 3 and 4 will show you lots of options to analyze your data visually. The type of chart you choose is ultimately the signal you are sending, so you'll need to learn how to make the right choices for your audience.

Fourth, data communication is about trust. Your points carry more sway when you can show how they are supported by evidence. If data-informed decisions have failed in the organization before, you will need to work hard to build trust. Building trust with the receiver of your communications will reduce the noise of other opinions or messages that don't have the same level of supporting evidence. You need to be confident that your message will be heard; when it is, you can influence more decisions and get more done.

You will need to build trust in your data analytics skills. It's easy to manipulate data to support an agenda—filter heavily enough, ignore outlying data points, or use other tricks and you can eventually get the data to say what you want it to. Whenever data is used to support a political point or marketing campaign, you should look to the source to see how the data may have been manipulated. For your own work, your audience needs to know that you are showing a fair representation of the data points from the data source you are using. This level of trust will build as you continually provide fair, well-sourced, and useful data-based communications. As you spend time exploring data sets to see what stories are held within, remember to share what you were expecting to find as well as what you actually found. Telling a balanced story only enhances the weight of your opinion.

Another factor is trust in the data sources themselves. The rise of modern self-service data tools that focus on visualization has made it much easier for nonspecialists to access and work with data and to ask and answer important questions about its provenance and reliability (more on this in Chapter 2). If that's why you picked up this book, you're in the right place. Chapters 8 and 9 will get deeper into the specifics of how to help your audience understand and trust your data.

Chapter 2 will go over the fundamentals of working with data—what it is, what you need to do with it, and what's so important about it. Chapters 3 and 4 focus on the practical aspects of visualizing data, such as formats and chart types, and contrast traditional approaches with more innovative ones. Chapters 5 and 6 build on this by teaching you visual techniques for clarifying your communication. The communications philosopher Marshall McLuhan famously said that "the medium is the message," and Chapter 7 is a deep dive into how the medium and format you choose influence your audience and the way they receive your message. Finally, Chapters 8 and 9 get into the nuts and bolts of putting all this to work in a real organization full of real people with different needs and interests. Chapter 8 looks at the challenges of communicating in the workplace generally, while Chapter 9 zooms in on specific types of departments and teams for a practical discussion of their communication needs.

Summary

Communication is key to getting anything done at work. You will need to be clear so your audience can receive, decode, and remember your message. Making use of preattentive attributes will help you do this more effectively.

Data can help you communicate your message more clearly and explore the evidence for and against the points you are making, so you can confirm your ideas with evidence—or adjust them to fit the evidence—before sharing them with others.

CHAPTER 2

Data

Data is the fundamental building block of everything in this book from here on out. The visualizations in the following chapters require a solid understanding of data and how to turn a question into a data-informed answer. In my role as a full-time data analytics trainer, I frequently meet people who have worked with data for a while but need to brush up on certain aspects. This chapter covers those aspects to ensure that you have what you need on your journey to becoming an effective communicator with data.

This chapter will help you form and refine those fundamental skills by building your awareness of the following:

- What we mean by *data* and some of its key features
- The sources of data and how it is created
- Where you will find data
- How to structure data sources to make them easier to use for analysis as well as communication
- How to identify the correct data for your questions

Working with data can be intimidating at first because of the large size of data sets, or inaccessible data storage solutions you might have to use, or pressure to represent data accurately to your audience. However, you'll find that tasks become much easier once you've developed a set of fundamental skills with whichever technology you choose to work with. To answer your questions, you will need to sift through a vast amount of data from a plethora of sources. The core skills covered here will prepare you to work with data in your workplace, no matter the data's source.

Knowing your data is also important, as it allows you to validate your visualizations and describe the work to others. Imagine trying to speak a language without being sure what the words mean or represent. Often you won't have a perfect data set to answer the question at hand. Knowing more about what is possible, where the data is potentially stored, and how you want to receive the data set for analysis will allow you to work confidently and more efficiently with data.

What Is Data?

You hear the word *data* constantly, but what does it actually mean? *Data* can be defined as the facts or numbers collected about observations for the purpose of understanding the subject better.

Data collection has become a lot easier with the growth in digitalization. Technology has become intertwined with most facets of our lives, and thus we can measure those facets and store the subsequent data. With the volume of data points being captured, the new challenge isn't just finding the data points; it's also creating clarity around what they mean. For a long time, most organizations struggled to store the vast quantities of data being captured by their services, such as their customer-facing apps or call-handling systems. Advances in technology have reduced this challenge, so we can spend less time working out whether the data was stored and more time focusing on finding and using the data.

The volume of data created means it isn't always stored as you need it to be for your analysis, however. You might have others to provide data for you to work with in your role at your organization, but not everyone will be so lucky. Also, if you develop an understanding of what it takes to prepare data, you'll be able to articulate what you need more clearly. To understand how to turn data into something meaningful, you must first understand the key features of data so you can recognize what's useful and what isn't.

Key Features of Data

What image does the word *data* conjure in your head? I've worked with data for a decade and a half, and I still see the same image: a spreadsheet with columns and rows holding cells of data. Before we begin looking at the rows and columns, let's focus on the cells themselves and their contents.

Figure 2-1 shows an excerpt from a spreadsheet that I will use to talk about the importance of cells in a data set. This excerpt contains cells with different types of information.

Country	Region	Store	Sales	Target
United Kingdom	North	York	381511	306596
United Kingdom	North	Edinburgh	217350	358099
United Kingdom	North	Glasgow	318481	244420
United Kingdom	North	Leeds	140157	230293
United Kingdom	North	Manchester	389334	395410
United Kingdom	South	Bath	214770	216506
United Kingdom	South	Bristol	166261	289825

Figure 2-1. Basic spreadsheet of data

You'll need to recognize three main classifications of cells in order to work with data effectively.

A *header* is similar to a title for the cells listed underneath it. Each header should name what the values in the cells below it represent. If your data has been created for you, the headers should be clear. If you find that they're *not* clear, it's much more likely that the data set hasn't been prepared for you. In Figure 2-1, each cell under the Country header has a value that is a recognizable country. The more cells that contain a value you'd expect to see based on the header, the more confident you can be that the headers represent what you'd expect them to.

Categorical data helps us understand how to interpret the cells containing numbers. In Figure 2-1, the categorical fields are Country, Region, and Store, and the categorical data is contained in the cells beneath those field headers. If Figure 2-1 contained only sales and target values, the user of the data would have no way to understand what those values actually represent. By using the cells with categorical data, we can interpret that York, in the northern region of the UK, had sales of 381,511. The contents of cells containing categorical data are often regarded as the *categorical variables*.

Numbers are the final classification of cells to recognize early on. The numerical data points are often the element of the data set you are looking to understand. You can analyze numbers by aggregating the values or comparing the variance between them, among other types of analysis. In Figure 2-1, you might want to compare the sales to the target values to see whether each row's sales number is bigger than the target value.

You will use cells of data as the building blocks of your analysis. You will choose which ones to include; most data sets will also have many that you will ignore.

Just by getting up and going to the office, you've created a data trail. Companies utilize data about what you use and when you use it to shape their logistics flows. These data points require analysis to enable companies to make meaningful decisions. The next key feature of data is how we structure the data cells.

Rows and Columns

Cells of values mean very little on their own. I've used the terms *rows* and *columns* to describe how cells are organized. Being clear on how to interpret rows and columns in data sets will allow you to understand more about the values you find within them. Let's look at rows and columns in turn to understand their importance.

Rows

Ideally, a *row* of data should contain information about a single observation of whatever the data set is about. You need to look not just at the values generated by the observation but also at the different categorical and numerical values that are held in the same row. The categorical values will set the level of detail, or *granularity*, of the data.

Let's look at a basic data set (Table 2-1) to identify what each row represents.

Table 2-1. Basic data set

Weekday	Store	Sales value	Sales target
Monday	Manchester	1,000	800
Tuesday	Manchester	750	800
Wednesday	Manchester	400	900
Thursday	Manchester	1,350	1,000
Friday	Manchester	1,500	1,000

I trust you've noticed that this data set has only two columns of categorical values: Weekday and Store. Therefore, the data set's granularity is one row per store per day. Table 2-1 lists data for only one store, so each weekday sets the level of granularity that a record of sales value and sales target is made at.

Not taking time to recognize the granularity of the data set forming your communications is a mistake I see made frequently, even by experienced data workers. When working with a new data set, you must understand its granularity, because that will determine whether you need to aggregate the rows of data. *Aggregation* takes individual data points and groups them together at a less-detailed granularity. You can aggregate values in many ways, including by summing up, finding the average, or finding the maximum value of data points at a different level of granularity than exists in the data set. For example, in Table 2-1, if you wanted to average the sales targets for the Manchester store, you'd leave only one value: 900.

Using aggregation to answer the questions you are analyzing is a common task when communicating with data. Table 2-2 looks at some examples and the types of aggregation you might use based on the data in Table 2-1.

Table 2-2. Using aggregation to analyze data

Question	Aggregation technique needed
Which day had the highest sales value?	Maximum: You'd assess each sales value and return only the largest one.
What are the total sales for the Manchester store?	Sum: You'd add up the sales values and return the total amount.
What is the difference between the highest day's sales and the lowest?	Maximum, minimum, and subtraction: You'd find the largest and smallest sales values and subtract one from the other.

Most software used to communicate with data is designed to make these aggregations easy and intuitive to complete. When communicating with data, you must validate your results to ensure that your communication is accurate.

Columns

The final part of the data structure to understand is the *column*. Columns organize similar cells of data so you can make sense of them. In a well-structured data set, each column represents either a category or a numerical value, but not both. The term *data field* is commonly exchanged for *column*, but they mean the same thing. Software used to analyze data will frequently require each column to be uniquely named so the software can refer to the relevant values in a data set.

Sadly, the data sets you'll need to use when working with data are not always structured nicely. They frequently will require *data preparation* to form the necessary column structure. You may need to merge values or split a single column into multiple columns. Some columns might not be required at all, and you'll have to remove them to make your analysis easier to conduct.

You need a clear understanding of the questions you are trying to answer before you look at the data set. Table 2-3 doesn't show an additional column of data, but the Store column has a deeper level of granularity, as that column now contains a second value. If you are trying to answer questions only about the Manchester store, the additional value acts as a distraction to the analysis.

However, you can't simply remove the Store column, as the additional store, York, has added new rows of related data. The table's length has doubled, as the data set now covers two stores instead of one, with two rows of data for each weekday. If you removed the Store column, you'd no longer see which store each row's observations are about.

Table 2-3. Beyond the basic data set

Weekday	Store	Sales value	Sales target
Monday	Manchester	1,000	800
Monday	York	650	500
Tuesday	Manchester	750	800
Tuesday	York	400	500
Wednesday	Manchester	400	900
Wednesday	York	600	600
Thursday	Manchester	1,350	1,000
Thursday	York	650	750
Friday	Manchester	1,500	1,000
Friday	York	700	750

Additional columns of data aren't necessarily something to be frustrated with. They can allow you to perform deeper and more insightful analysis. Each question posed in Table 2-2 could be answered about both stores. Alternatively, the questions could look at which store had the higher sales each day or the higher average target. This is why it's important to be clear on the questions you need to ask; you want to ensure that your data set has enough granularity for you to answer the questions but not so much that you have to do a lot of work to find the answers.

Rows and columns work hand in hand; thus you need to understand the effect that changing one feature will have on the other. Each column should be a single data type, so let's turn to that concept next.

Data Types

This section provides more detail about each data type and the considerations you should make when using a data set with data types.

Numbers

Numerical values are at the heart of data and make up the majority of measures found within data sets. A *measure* is another name for the numerical values you've encountered in the example data sets so far, like sales and target values. A value made up of just 0s, 1s, 2s, 3s, 4s, 5s, 6s, 7s, 8s, and/or 9s is a numeric data type. When communicating with data, you often will aggregate these values if you're answering overarching questions, or you might still refer to each separate value if focusing on more detailed questions.

You may also find numerical values forming identification numbers, which are commonly used to allow data sets to be joined together. Identification fields also ensure a unique value for each categorical variable if the names of those values might change over time, as with a rebranded product. Most large companies will assign a customer an identification (ID) number to make analysis more anonymous.

Numeric data fields will be present in most data sets across all industries and departments. Consider the example in Figure 2-2, taken from the World Bank (*https://oreil.ly/RuA2W*), of the world's cereal yield in kilograms per hectare.

Data Source	World Development Indicators					
Last Updated Date	2020-10-13					
Country Name	Country Code	Indicator Name	Indicator Code	1961	1962	1963
Aruba	ABW	Cereal yield (kg per hectare)	AG.YLD.CREL.KG			
Afghanistan	AFG	Cereal yield (kg per hectare)	AG.YLD.CREL.KG	1115.1	1079	985.8
Angola	AGO	Cereal yield (kg per hectare)	AG.YLD.CREL.KG	828	830.3	798.4
Albania	ALB	Cereal yield (kg per hectare)	AG.YLD.CREL.KG	845.2	941.8	982.3
Andorra	AND	Cereal yield (kg per hectare)	AG.YLD.CREL.KG			
Arab World	ARB	Cereal yield (kg per hectare)	AG.YLD.CREL.KG	782.793101	1139.948023	1058.281005
United Arab Emirates	ARE	Cereal yield (kg per hectare)	AG.YLD.CREL.KG			
Argentina	ARG	Cereal yield (kg per hectare)	AG.YLD.CREL.KG	1410.7	1604.9	1511.2
Armenia	ARM	Cereal yield (kg per hectare)	AG.YLD.CREL.KG			
American Samoa	ASM	Cereal yield (kg per hectare)	AG.YLD.CREL.KG			

Figure 2-2. World Bank data on cereal yields, in kilograms per hectare

The main set of numbers comprises the values of cereal yield, the main subject of the data set. Although analyzing the numerical data is the key focus of understanding this data set, completing that task in this table alone isn't easy. Numerical data fields can also have *null* data points. A null represents the absence of data in a data field or row.

In Figure 2-2, numbers are also present in the form of years. The year would not be used as a measure, as it would never be added up. You'd never want to add 1961 to 1962 to get 3923, but you would want to know the cereal yield per year. The yield values are set at the level of country and year, despite other categorical data being present in the data set. The additional categorical data fields do not contain multiple values per country and year and thus do not add to the data's granularity.

The formats of numeric data types are important too. Whether a number is a whole number, or *integer*, or a number with a decimal place (sometimes referred to as a *float*) can affect how you use the value. Many data tools treat these fields differently. The format makes a lot of difference when it comes to the content of what the field represents. Take, for example, a column that has the word *percentage* in the header. If the data field is an integer, it might be represented with a value of 31, implying the value is actually 31%. If the field is being held as a float, the value might be recorded as 0.31. This demonstrates the importance of naming your headers clearly to indicate how each value should be used. After all, sales might have increased 3100%, or the percentage of survey results received might be a terrible 0.0031%.

Numeric data will be very important when you are communicating with data, so you'll want to check that you are using the values correctly.

Strings

String data is made up of alphanumeric data that can also include punctuation marks and symbols. Student names, university course descriptions, and course identification codes can all be forms of string data. Any field that is not just numbers can be held as a string. Any computer system that allows you to freely enter data will probably store the data as a string field, as the user might use more than just numeric values.

For new data analysts, string data is the data type that takes the most getting used to. This is because of the way string data is assessed by the tools that ingest it from the data source. Even if you are a more experienced data user, you might still regularly struggle to work with string data because of the number of forms it can take.

The string fields are going to be categorical fields in your data set. You might still use string fields as a measure by counting the number of rows that contain a specific value. However, most of your analysis will use the categorical data fields to break up the measures you are analyzing.

The flexibility of string data is fantastic but can cause headaches too. Tools read string data character by character. They also assess the *position* of each character in the string. In Figure 2-3, each character's position in the string value *Communicating with Data* has been denoted below the character. This demonstrates how business intelligence tools read from left to right, including punctuation and symbols such as spaces (characters 14 and 19 in Figure 2-3).

Figure 2-3. Character positions in a string value

If an extra space were accidentally added to *Communicating with Data* before the uppercase *C*, the position of each subsequent character would change, and thus the strings would be seen as completely different from each other by a computer, even if you, the consumer, might read the terms the same way. Therefore, for strings to be regarded as the same, they need to be identical.

When working with string data, you'll often have to *clean up* the values held in the data field to ensure that you are comparing similar string values correctly. Common cleaning tasks might involve any of the following:

Changing case

You might need to make a value UPPERCASE, lowercase, or Title Case (which capitalizes the first letter of each word).

Splitting names

Dividing names is useful for tasks like finding the city name in a full postal address or breaking up longer, amalgamated strings into separate columns of data.

Solving spelling mistakes

Finding and fixing typos can make analyzing data much easier.

String fields can be converted into other data types. By using string fields as a date or Boolean data type instead, you can complete specific analyses more easily.

Dates

Date fields can be the bane of many analysts' lives but sit at the heart of a lot of the questions you will try to answer. Date fields often must be precisely formatted for the date to be recognized in order for useful calculation functions to be possible. During the analysis phase, you might need many levels of detail from the same date field. Let's break down how much detail one date field contains, using the example in Figure 2-4.

Figure 2-4. British date value

Here are the basic parts of the date listed in the value:

- Day = 31
- Month = 12
- Year = 2021

But several inferred aspects are also present:

- Week number = 52
- Quarter = 4
- Weekday = Friday
- Day of year = 365

Getting these parts of the date involves using *functions*, or instructions to cause changes to a data field. Functions can extract part of a date (to form the values just given) or move dates forward or backward, but only if the software you perform that function in recognizes the data value as a date. If users have entered dates as strings, you can use functions to convert them to a recognized date format, enabling you to use date functions on those values.

Booleans

The *Boolean* data type seems like the simplest form, but using it can be anything *but* simple. Booleans come from *conditional calculations*, otherwise known as yes/no questions: either the condition has been met or it has not.

A Boolean data field holds just three values: *true* (the condition has been met), *false* (the condition has not been met), or *null* (the condition can't be assessed). Examples of conditions that could result in a Boolean field are as follows:

- Did sales meet or exceed the target of 100,000?
- Did the student pass the exam?
- Did the customer buy the product?

When you use a conditional calculation in a business intelligence tool, the tool creates a new data field with true or false values. If you'd like a more descriptive term or a simple yes/no answer, you can use *aliases* to change the true or false values to any term you like. A simple Boolean test like *Profit > 0* can be given aliases of *Profitable* if the test returns true or *Unprofitable* if false.

Because of their simplicity, Boolean fields can often be calculated quickly. Therefore, when working with large data sets, they can be quite efficient, especially compared to string data.

How Is Data Created?

Data does not just magically appear. It has to be created somewhere—and understanding where is important. To ensure that you're using data effectively and accurately, you need to evaluate its source.

Think of it like writing: writers often quote other works as evidence or to reinforce an argument. Without a source, though, a quote loses its validity and credibility. You should treat data without a source just as cautiously as a quote without a source. So where does data get created, and how can you know which sources to trust?

In your organization, you will discover useful sources of data—databases or files that are trusted by many and that will form the backbone of your analysis. Asking where your current reporting and data come from will lead you back to various sources. Not all of the stored data points will be shared in the reporting you use; understanding what other data points are available will enable you to ask more diverse questions of your data.

Some of the data required to answer all your questions will likely be created and stored outside your organization. By looking at outside sources of data, you can validate or challenge the data within your organization. These sources can take your analysis to the next level, and thus finding them is worth the additional effort.

Where Is Data Created?

Data is created in many places—far too many to cover in this book. Data can be created in many ways and is kept for many reasons. Everything we do creates data; understanding that can help us improve our lives.

Richard Silvester, founder of the data visualization company infogr8 (*http://infogr8.com*), talks about how much data can be produced by our daily activities. In Table 2-4, I've used Richard's "day in the life" concept to illustrate how you might create many data points during the first part of a typical day.

Table 2-4. How data points are created by everyday life

Action	Data created	Use
Waking up	Sleep-tracking data on wearable devices	Tracking your sleep on a wearable device can help you learn about your sleep patterns and what affects them.
Showering	Water/electric meter data	Energy companies can use smart meters to optimize production and understand high-demand periods.
Making breakfast	Data on products bought at the supermarket or ordered online as you run out of supplies	Your product-ordering data is fed back to suppliers to drive production levels and inform logistics companies.
Watching the news on your tablet	Usage data captured by streaming channels; app usage tracked by device provider	Production of programming can be modified in response to what people do or don't watch. Streaming services want you to keep using them and will recommend what you should watch next on their platform.
Checking social media for your informal news	Likes, shares, and app usage	Algorithms assess your interests and provide information on the content you interact with.
Traveling to work	Data from riding your bicycle (tracked on Strava), driving your car and filling up the gas tank, or buying a commuter rail ticket	The Strava file tracking your accelerations and routes helps improve cycling infrastructure. Satellite navigation systems are similar for roads. Ticket purchases show demand not only for trains but also for additional services like cafes that banks can support as new/expanding businesses.
Entering the office	Data from security badge used to access the building	This provides time tracking for employees and helps companies ensure that everyone is clear of the building in case of safety events such as fires. This data can also be used to determine space requirements and working patterns.

This section provides an overview of four types of data sources that you'll frequently encounter. These sources differ from each other in that sometimes data creation is a *by-product* of an activity, and sometimes it is the *reason* for the activity.

Data is considered a by-product when an activity occurs and data can be formed from it. Operational and transportation systems and the Internet of Things exist not to capture data but to enable processes and services to happen. Yet surveys are intentionally created to gather data to produce analysis and aid decision making in organizations. Let's look at each type of data source in turn to help you understand what you need to consider when data is collected from it.

Operational systems

Workers and customers of organizations all over the world use operational systems every day. The term *operational system* covers a multitude of systems, from manufacturing machines to registering an insurance policy.

Operational refers to allowing your organization to do what it is designed to do. For an insurer, the operational systems might include the computer systems used to create the insurance policies or the telephony system used to answer policyholders' calls. The *system* part of the term frequently refers to the computerization of a previously manual process. By using computers to complete the process, data can be captured at many points in time.

Drawing data from operational systems allows you to measure the duration of processes for the customer as well as measure where errors might have occurred. Another benefit is that data is produced without any extra effort from the system's operator, and thus steps aren't missed.

Banks, for example, now process transactions instantly, as technology links not only the bank's internal systems but also the global banking system. Movements of money, stock sales, and loan approvals now happen more quickly. Approvals are based on models and occur with more transparency to the client and customer than ever before. Data points enable rapid decision making but also can be used for analysis to make the processes even faster and more accurate.

In retail, the key operational systems are the cash register on the counter and the system measuring stock levels in the warehouse. Only over the last few decades have these systems been linked to other systems in retail organizations to seamlessly order new stock as products sell in stores. Every transaction and every movement of inventory or money creates data points in operational systems.

Figure 2-5 shows the flow of retail goods from manufacturing to distribution to the point of sale. Every step of this flow creates data points. The retailer can analyze these data points to learn how long shipments take, which items are most popular, and so on, and identify and correct any problems found.

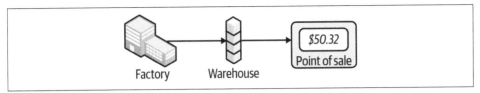

Figure 2-5. Operational process flow

These data points are increasingly stored in databases, whether they are used for analysis now or might be useful in the future. Operational systems are designed to do a job (whether that's manufacturing pretzels, validating tickets, or issuing insurance policies), not for data production, so the raw data they produce is rarely ready for instant analysis. The data must be carefully prepared to avoid losing or incorrectly manipulating the data.

Surveys

Organizations often use surveys to collect information directly from users, customers, and clients. These can be brief and broad or deep and narrow, as those being surveyed are unlikely to want to spend hours answering questions. The various types of surveys produce two main types of data:

Quantitative
> This data can be easily measured or calculated. It can come from counting responses or aggregating numeric responses.

Qualitative
> This data is more descriptive, collected from free-text-entry responses to survey questions or verbally in interviews or focus groups. It can offer rich insights, but these insights are much more difficult to find, especially within large volumes of survey responses.
>
> Qualitative responses are held as string data, which, as you've learned, can hold various characters and terms. These answers need to be readable by machines, so preparing them often involves breaking the strings into single words whose frequency can be counted.

Survey data doesn't just come in raw numbers or qualitative strings. Surveys can capture data in many ways, and this is a major factor in the data you will receive for analysis as well as in how comprehensive that analysis will be.

Radio buttons (Figure 2-6) and *single-value drop-down lists* (Figure 2-7) allow the user to choose only one answer from a list of options. Limiting the possible answers makes your analysis simpler. You have to set the possible answers before issuing the survey, so you won't discover new insights, but you can confirm possible preferences, for example.

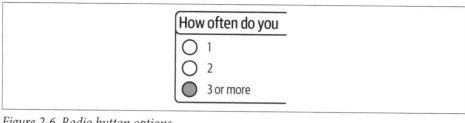

Figure 2-6. Radio button options

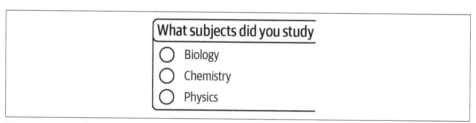

Figure 2-7. Single-value drop-down options

Multiple-choice questions, as in the multiple-value drop-down (Figure 2-8), give respondents more options. The answers are still predefined, so respondents must still pick the most relevant answers. Surveys can offer an Other answer option, but this free text entry makes analysis much harder because the answer introduces string data rather than set values.

What subjects did you study
○ Biology
○ Chemistry
○ Physics

Figure 2-8. Multiple-value drop-down options

Free text entry allows respondents to share their full feedback in their own words (Figure 2-9). The creator doesn't have to think through all potential answers before sending out the survey. Free text entry is a qualitative method, and it produces string fields that take a lot more work to process. Spelling issues, abstract phrasing, and sarcasm (especially among British respondents!) can all complicate your analysis.

Gaining opinions directly from those you are surveying is extremely useful and provides a powerful message to communicate.

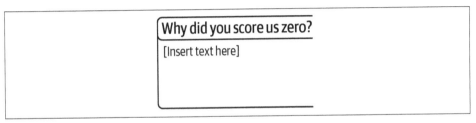

Figure 2-9. Free text entry

Movement/transportation

Our everyday movements create a lot of data. You can measure your own movement by using a smartwatch; gathering the movements of hundreds of thousands of people can provide unique insights into their behavior. Many people are nervous about sharing this information, so access will be limited to the company capturing it, or the data will be aggregated before it is shared with third-party organizations.

The Quantified Self technique was developed by individuals who began tracking elements of their lives by using data, from time spent reading email to the foods they eat throughout the year. The aim of capturing this data is the same as that of capturing data in organizations: learning from what happens currently to improve what should happen in the future. These types of measurements have become common in many personal devices, such as my iPhone telling me how long I have stared at its screen each day in the last week.

As the movement has grown and demonstrated more value, the number of devices (and sensors within them) that capture this data has increased. Strava (*http://strava.com*), an app that allows runners and cyclists to track their activities by distance and location, has been part of this development. As wearable devices have become more popular, their functions have expanded to tracking speed, heart rate, elevation, and more. The data can be useful for athletes who want to monitor their performance and determine the impact of their training.

Individual data is just the beginning, though; data collected from large volumes of runners and riders can be useful on a societal level. For example, local governments might use it to determine where to place infrastructure for safer bike routes.

The rise of satellite navigation for cars has led to similar data sets: measuring the speeds of vehicles using the system can help city planners monitor how roads are used and why traffic becomes congested. Strava's Metro project (*https://oreil.ly/nqOyu*) provides this data to transportation planners at an aggregated level to help them make decisions about future infrastructure.

Collecting and storing this data is a vast task that overtaxes traditional data storage solutions. Storing and processing data, especially in great volume, has become much cheaper over the last two decades, making such granular tracking possible. The ethical use of this data and of other personal identifiable information continues to be a sensitive subject that you will come across frequently as you work with data.

The Internet of Things

Data is also being created by our own homes through a series of devices called the *Internet of Things*. This often requires giving internet or local network connectivity to devices that traditionally have not been connected to the internet.

These devices can communicate with each other to create linked-up services, such as home appliances that you can control from your smartphone or farm equipment that adjusts irrigation levels based on predicted rainfall. Smart meters mean utility companies don't have to collect meter readings door to door and can determine usage on a much more granular basis.

Using data from these devices can be overwhelming because of the volume of collected data points, but unless you are the provider of these devices, you will likely receive aggregated records that reduce the data volume.

Data is being collected from more and more devices, which is both a blessing and a curse. Having more data to provide answers is useful—but if you need to form answers quickly, having so many sources to draw from can pose a big challenge.

Should You Trust Your Data?

You should treat data the same way you should treat words: with great skepticism. Before you trust someone's argument or believe something you read online, you should check the source, check whether the quote has been changed, and understand the wider context of how the words are being used.

The International Society for Technology in Education (ISTE) offers useful resources for checking references and sources (*https:// oreil.ly/ZKVLX*).

Data requires the same treatment. Starting with the source of the data allows you to identify potential bias. This is not to say you should ignore a data source just because it might be biased, but you certainly should use it with care and highlight to your audience any impact the source might have on your findings.

Table 2-5 lists our data sources from earlier in this section and assesses them for potential bias.

Table 2-5. Potential biases in data sources

Source of data	Potential biases
Operational systems	An operational system's developer specifies which data points are collected. Has the developer accounted for issues faced by people of other genders/ages/ethnicities and ensured that data that could support them is collected and not ignored?
Surveys	Quantitative data requires anticipating respondents' answers. Qualitative data requires much more cleaning before analysis, so understanding what preparation has occurred is key, as those producing the data can add their own biases, similar to the operational system developer in the preceding example. Surveys are often filled out by people who have a strong opinion, often with a negative slant. It's difficult to get responses from the moderately satisfied.
Transportation	Quantified Self services require technology and often subscription fees, biasing the data toward more wealthy individuals.
Internet of Things	Data acquired from this type of source can be biased toward those who can afford such devices.

The source is clearly important to the data's user. As the communicator of the data to others, it's imperative that you understand how the data is intended to be used. This can put a lot of pressure on you, as the author of the analysis, but as with anything else, critically appraising the source will help you understand potential issues. You can also work with other analysts to learn from their experiences.

Data as a Resource

Data comes from a lot of places; it's also stored in a lot of places. In this section, I'll guide you through the most common data storage formats, as well as one on the rise. Knowing more about these methods of data storage will enable you to ask clear questions and set better requirements with your organization's data owners.

This section also covers a key consideration in holding data: *security*. Before we dive more deeply into these topics, let's go over some important terminology, depicted in Figure 2-10.

Getting used to this terminology will make it much easier to work with data in your organization. When sourcing data sets, asking for the right level of data or source will be a big help in finding the right data for your analysis.

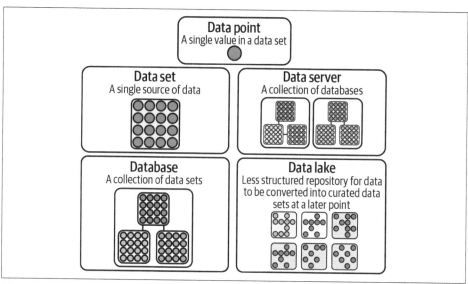

Figure 2-10. Data storage definitions

Files

Files and files and files of data are nothing new in the world or on your computer. Datafiles are created every day as a result of your work. This can involve taking data inputs from outside sources like market research, financial accounts, or internal sales records; adding your own logic through calculations or filters; and then creating a new file. Your files are likely to build up quickly and contain lots of data that you'll want to use over time.

The volume of datafiles poses a unique opportunity and a challenge at the same time. You will likely need to use not only your own files but also those of others across your organization. Keeping the files stored in a logical way that allows you and others to quickly find and access the information can be a challenge. Teams often have their own file management techniques, with little consistency among teams. Often only by collaborating successfully with others will you be able access the data required to answer your questions.

This challenge has become more pronounced, as files now are not just stored locally on your and/or your colleagues' computers but potentially are stored on cloud-based drives that many people can access.

Common file types

You will encounter various file types when working with data. This is due to the multiple software programs producing data outputs. If you can become familiar with these file formats, you will be able to work with more data from more diverse sources.

This will allow you to improve your work by using more sources to test your theories and validate your findings. The file type often defines how the data is stored within the file as well as the method used by a data tool to query the data in the file.

File *extensions*, the letters at the end of a filename that describe the format, identify the file types. The main file types you are likely to use are as follows:

Microsoft Excel spreadsheets (.xlsx)

An Excel spreadsheet is a "jack of all trades, master of none" when it comes to data in a business. A spreadsheet can be used to store data and may be used to *process* the data as well. The flexibility of using a spreadsheet to work with data means each solution is customizable; thus it may sometimes be difficult to pick up and work with the data inside a particular spreadsheet.

Comma-separated values files (.csv)

These are commonly used to export data from operational systems, databases, and website downloads, since many tools (including spreadsheets) are built to use them as input. The data fields are separated by commas (hence the name), and individual rows are shown by new lines within the file.

Text files (.txt)

These are even more simplistic than CSV files, as data fields do not have to be separated by a comma. Instead, they can be separated by any number of characters that can determine a new data field. If you plan to use the data within text files, you must first understand how the files are structured and how to turn the contents into rows and columns.

Portable Document Format files (.pdf)

PDFs are not necessarily only about data. PDFs often contain vast amounts of text as well as images. Tables of data found within PDFs can be read by a few data tools, making them a useful source of data if you can connect to the data within them.

Spatial files (.shp, .kml, or .geojson)

Spatial files contain exactly what they are named for: spatial objects. When you are working with data about locations, spatial objects such as points, lines, or polygons describe locations or geographical boundaries in a common manner. Shapefiles contain this information, so this file type is most regularly used when communicating data using maps; not all tools are able to visualize this type of data.

A plethora of other file types may be involved in your analysis, but many are unique to the tools that create them, and this book might be the size of an encyclopedia if all were covered.

Many data tools connect to files containing data by using a *driver* that allows the tool to query the data source. When looking to connect to more custom file types than those just described, you may need to download a driver to connect to the data set.

Common challenges

While the flexibility of the file types mentioned in the preceding section can be a good thing when entering data, it can pose significant challenges when you're using the data for analysis:

Control

The lack of rules or controls when entering data or adding data fields can create issues for those using the files. Most data analytics tools require data to be in a set structure of rows or columns, but files can have data added to them that does not meet these requirements. For example, a row could be added with totals for the rest of the data; if this isn't spotted, all the values will be double-counted in your analysis.

Adding data fields is easy to do in datafiles. If you don't set up the analytics tool to process these additional fields, you can create issues or even prevent refreshes of your analytical views. When you build useful analytics that people begin to rely on, you need to ensure that the views are available when the audience requires them. Unexpected data changes are a big reason for communications failing.

Origin

Even if a datafile is useful for analysis, it frequently will need to be updated to ensure that the analysis is based on the latest view of a situation. A file does not necessarily contain a link back to its origin showing how it was formed. Extracts from data sources pose interesting challenges in terms of whether the logic used to create those files can be replicated to produce a like-for-like result.

As discussed earlier, you need to understand the origin of the data to ensure that you assess any potential bias. If you can't trace the origin of the data in a file, understanding the potential effect on your analysis might be difficult.

Processing

Whether or not its origin can be found, a datafile does not necessarily retain the history of changes made to it. This creates challenges, as you will not know if alterations, calculations, or manipulations have been made to the original data. If changes *have* been made, false conclusions may be drawn from the data. Changes are not always made consciously either; it's easy to mistype or overwrite data values in datafiles, as there is little formal process behind writing the changes.

Size

Datafiles are not built for handling large volumes of data. As data becomes easier to capture, the volume of data to be stored becomes larger. Many file types have limits on the number of rows that can be stored. Although file types like Excel have increased the volume of data that can be held, the enhanced volume doesn't necessarily allow for *enough* data to be held. The datafiles are also slower to use when connecting the analytical data tools to the files, compared to databases.

Use

With all the unknown aspects just demonstrated, the use of datafiles can also be misconstrued because of a lack of context about their creation. A datafile may have been the result of research focusing on a specific group of people or a database query filtering out products. If this context is lost, an analysis of the data may draw poor conclusions due to the mistaken assumption that the data set is based on a complete population or set of products.

If you work with data, you will likely have to work with datafiles. The flexibility of data entry into datafiles can make them perfect for ad hoc analysis. However, if your analysis is set up to be *productionalized*, or run automatically, then you should look to provide more control on the input files to prevent errors in the processing of the data, as well as incorrect results being drawn from the analysis.

Databases, Data Servers, and Lakes

Databases provide more structure and governance with input and processing of data. Databases are built to ingest, process, store, and output data. The key differences from datafiles are that databases are more heavily administered and require a coding language to interact with the data. If you are new to working with data, this might pose a barrier to accessing the information required to meet your or your stakeholder's needs.

Database software is specially designed to work with data and handle many of the challenges that datafiles pose. Databases are often run on a computer, sometimes called a *server*, with much larger memory and more processing power than a laptop or desktop computer. A database is divided into tables of data. These tables might focus on elements of an organization such as these:

- Customers or students
- Products
- Sales
- Employee details

These tables often need to be joined together to answer the questions posed. For example, when analyzing sales, data on which products were sold and to whom must be factored in to provide a complete picture. Data tables can be linked together in commonly requested ways to form *views*. The mapping indicating how the tables in the database join together is called the *database schema*. Database schemas rely on using *joins* (covered in "One big data set versus many" on page 63 to tie tables together.

Common types of databases

Microsoft SQL Server is one of the most frequently used databases because many servers run Windows as their operating system. The most common database types use *Structured Query Language*, or *SQL* for short. SQL is a coding language that allows you to run queries on the database to return either data sets or aggregated values to help your analysis. SQL lies at the heart of other commonly used databases, including MySQL, PostgreSQL, and Teradata. Each has slightly different code requirements, making it difficult to use these sources without some training.

Database growth over time has led to a need for running multiple databases alongside each other. This is called a *data server*, which contains numerous databases. You might also come across the term *data warehouse*, which is a system that pulls together data from many sources within an organization for reporting and analysis purposes.

Many newer databases can still be queried with SQL, but they are more likely to be hosted on a cloud-based server than on a server run inside your organization, referred to as *on premises*. *Cloud computing* refers to the process of renting space on the servers of another organization that is likely to be a specialist in hosting content. The major benefit of using a cloud-based server is that you can increase the power and capacity of the server as you need it. Cloud-based servers are provided primarily by Amazon Web Services, Microsoft Azure, and Google Cloud Platform. Cloud-based databases are useful as information scales, as more data can be added without the server's memory maxing out.

The challenge of streaming data in vast volumes has created problems for SQL-based solutions. The data structure required to make SQL work effectively means that large inflows of data cannot be processed fast enough to push data into the structure of the database. This is where the newer solution of *data lakes* comes in. Data lakes are repositories of data often held in an unstructured state, to be processed later. Once data is identified as being useful and can be transformed correctly, it is processed into a more traditional SQL database.

Common challenges

You are likely to encounter challenges when working with databases. First, you'll face major barriers to accessing data by using SQL. In most organizations, employees have not been taught how to code in SQL. This means many people are unable to access the data source directly and have to rely on others to query data for them. This can make things difficult if the data you want to communicate is located only in a database.

It isn't just the coding language that limits access to data. Database access is much more controlled than access to datafiles because more important processes like regulatory mandated reporting are completed from such data sets. In most organizations, even if access to data sets is obtainable, the process requires IT teams as well as the business owner of the data giving access.

Although databases are designed for using much larger data sets, the analysis of data from databases can be harder if you are using basic analytical tools like Excel. Before analysis can even begin, determining the correct ways to join the tables and views from the database to form the data set often requires many subject-matter experts or hefty amounts of experience. To work with data from a database is difficult enough, but to complete this process when the source data resides in a data lake is an even greater technical challenge. Exploring and processing the data from a data lake can be quite time-consuming, often with many iterations required along the way.

Each of these elements creates hurdles to overcome, but the effort is worth it. Working with databases offers more powerful processing of a more tightly controlled data set. Your analysis can be made more repeatable and more stable if you use data from a database rather than using datafiles. Databases will frequently be updated with new or updated rows of data. If you use databases for the source of your data, you can more easily update your message with the latest information.

Application Programming Interfaces

The modern analyst has ever-increasing demands being placed on their skills. One area for growth for many analysts has been in coding skills because of the introduction of *application programming interfaces* (*APIs*) as a way to connect to more data sets. This set of procedures and functions allows users to build applications by using systems and data sources. The music-streaming service Spotify has an API (*https://oreil.ly/3fNSC*) that can allow its users to return information about songs, artists, and podcasts, or allow them to analyze their own listening behavior. An API not only is used for data analysis but also allows applications to write data points to a data set. For example, liking a tweet actually uses APIs to write a record to Twitter's database without giving you access to the database, which contains a lot of valuable information.

APIs have become more popular because of their ability to tie various data sources together in one place and standardize methods of access via website-based traffic (Figure 2-11). You will often see an API call as an entry in the URL window on your browser, as you are fundamentally going to a website address to fetch your data for analysis.

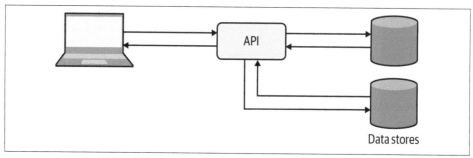

Figure 2-11. API layer between you and the data stores

Like any technological development, APIs have gone through distinct stages of evolution that addressed issues users found when working with them. Simple Object Access Protocol (SOAP) APIs were the original type of APIs but posed challenges, as the data was passed in Extensible Markup Language (XML) files, which are not the easiest to work with and have a structure that is hard to understand. Representational State Transfer (REST) APIs introduced a more human, standardized approach and allowed people to work with JavaScript Object Notation (JSON) files, which have a more logical structure. The newest form of API is GraphQL, which provides a more modern and easier way of working. You may still have to use all of the versions of APIs, so being aware of the potential issues is useful.

Services use APIs when communicating over the web, which is becoming the home for more and more data sources. Some differences exist between working with APIs and the files/databases covered thus far in this chapter. API calls often have limits on the scope of their requests to the underlying data sets and also restrict the amount of data that can be returned; the internet has varying levels of bandwidth, so APIs are constructed to keep data sizes small enough that information can be sent and received quickly. This can pose a challenge when conducting data analysis on large data sets, as you may need to make multiple calls to gather the information you require.

The challenges of working with APIs go beyond just the volume of queries you need to run. First, the coding required to send those queries can take some getting used to if you do not code in a computational language already. If you work in an organization, you may have a team that will support you with this part of the process and with the subsequent reshaping of data that many data analytics tools require.

Another challenge is that developers write APIs to allow users to access certain data sets in certain ways. This can create an inherent bias in the API as far as what data is available to answer your queries. As with any data source, you need to consider where the data originated from as well as what data has been collected and what has been removed.

Data Security and Ethics

Analysis of data can reveal trends around clients, products, and services. However, that same data can reveal a lot about individuals too, if used in certain ways. This makes the need to protect personal data from misuse very important. Misuse can take different forms, from identity theft to unethical use of the data.

When you work with data, it is important to ensure the following:

- The subject of the data is aware of how the data will be used.
- The data is kept secure, from its transfer from the source to deployment of the analysis.
- The data is deleted after it has met its purpose, and the supplier will no longer benefit from its retention.

The process of securing data through all stages of use is often known as *data management*. Having clearly sourced data, a defined purpose for the data, and a plan for deleting the data is important. Across the world, legislation has come into force that ensures that an individual's data is used only with their permission and is deleted when holding the data no longer serves the individual's interests.

Securing data is just as important. Merely having a good password on data isn't enough. Holding data-encrypted devices and using it inside secure networks means data loss due to hostile attempts to steal it will be less likely. Securing data means protecting the subjects of the data from potential harm or negative actions against them. After all, this data could be about you—how would you want *your* information to be treated?

Data security is not the only aspect that needs to be considered with regard to data use. Ethical use of data is becoming a more contentious issue as the power of data becomes more apparent. Being ethical involves more thought beyond just your own and your organization's ethics. As data points are often about human behavior, close analysis can reveal details of people's movement, beliefs, sexual orientation, and lots more besides. Ensuring that your analysis does not stray from the intended purpose for which the provider of the data gave permission should remain a primary concern.

Many books on data security are available, and even more on the ethical use of data, so this book does not attempt to explain all that is required to be compliant. Always keep in mind the potential impacts of data leaks or data misuse as you work with data. Data leaks can lead to your customers becoming victims of impersonation fraud elsewhere or being discriminated against due to sexual, religious, or political beliefs becoming known.

 For more information on data security, *Identity & Data Security for Web Development (https://oreil.ly/yfFYy)* by Jonathan LeBlanc and Tim Messerschmidt (O'Reilly) is an ideal starting point. If you're looking to delve into the ethical use of data, *97 Things About Ethics Everyone in Data Science Should Know*, edited by Bill Franks (O'Reilly), builds a broad awareness of key issues.

Easy or Hard? The "Right" Data Structure

A clear understanding of the constituent parts of a data set and where data comes from can help set the foundation for using data for analysis. However, the structure of the data, sometimes referred to as the *shape*, can make a huge difference in how easy the data is to analyze. An earlier section of this chapter covered columns and rows and understanding the granularity of a data set. This section covers how to shape and clean data for analysis.

The Shape of Data

Creating a data set that fits a certain structure can be the difference between hours of tough calculations or easy drag-and-drop use of the data. Whether your data set comes from a datafile or a database, the data will likely be in columns of some kind. What each column represents makes a significant difference in how easily you can form your analysis, or whether analysis is even possible.

Categorical data

The categorical data describes what each measure refers to. Having a separate column for each piece of descriptive data makes analyzing the data much easier, as you can simply answer questions based on each column. For example, to look at the average test score in the data from Table 2-6, you could find a value at multiple levels in the data set:

- Overall
- Per department
- Per subject
- Per course
- Per student

Table 2-6. Categorical data

Department	Subject	Course	Student	Score
Art	History	HI101	30957191	76
Art	History	HI101	52814935	92
Art	History	HI101	89620539	60
Art	History	HI102	30957191	66
Art	History	HI102	89620539	35
Social Sciences	Politics	PO101	30957191	58
Social Sciences	Politics	PO101	51123824	61
Social Sciences	Politics	PO102	89620539	75
Social Sciences	Geography	GE101	51123824	91
Social Sciences	Geography	GE101	63947347	82

Most analytics tools calculate these results by reading down a column of numbers to determine the values that meet the condition set. If the software you use doesn't work in this manner, you'll need to perform this type of calculation to answer the same questions. For example, let's work out each subject's average score (Table 2-7).

Table 2-7. Calculating the average score per subject

Department	Subject	Course	Student	Score
Art	History	HI101	30957191	76
Art	History	HI101	52814935	92
Art	History	HI101	89620539	60
Art	History	HI102	30957191	66
Art	History	HI102	89620539	35
Social Sciences	Politics	PO101	30957191	58
Social Sciences	Politics	PO101	51123824	61
Social Sciences	Politics	PO102	89620539	75
Social Sciences	Geography	GE101	51123824	91
Social Sciences	Geography	GE101	63947347	82

To work out the mean, you first need to determine the number of subjects. In this case, we have three subjects: history, politics, and geography. The analytical tool sums up the values that correspond to each subject and then divides by the number of records, with these results:

- History: a total of 329, divided by five students, means an average of 65.8.
- Politics: a total of 194, divided by three students, means an average of 64.7.
- Geography: a total of 173, divided by two students, means an average of 86.5.

Analyzing the data by department instead is simple, and similar logic would apply: instead of looking for each subject, the analytical tools would look for the different departments and then perform the same calculations for the relevant rows of data.

Measures

Just as each type of categorical data needs its own column in your data set, so does each measure. In Table 2-8, the measures are not in individual columns, preventing fast aggregations. In most tools, having values in separate columns makes analysis easier by enabling the aggregation of whole columns.

Table 2-8. Multiple measures across multiple rows

Department	Subject	Course	Student	Measure	Value
Art	History	HI101	30957191	Score	76
Art	History	HI101	30957191	Attendance	6
Art	History	HI101	52814935	Score	92
Art	History	HI101	52814935	Attendance	8
Art	History	HI101	89620539	Score	60
Art	History	HI101	89620539	Attendance	10

For this data, having separate columns for Score and Attendance would allow those values to be aggregated, as we saw in the preceding section. Being able to conduct calculations between measures is also important, and having a separate column per measure ensures that the calculations involve less complexity. The multiple measures within the Measure column in Table 2-8 also create additional challenges when analyzing the data set, as a row of data is no longer about a student's score in each course. To be able to count the number of students in the data set, you need to ignore each duplication of a student's reference number.

If the data set requiring analysis isn't in the form of a separate category or measure in an individual column, the data requires reshaping. Assessing a data set's structure is one of the first tasks you should undertake when working with a new data set or analytical challenge. A few techniques are available to achieve the required shape.

Pivot—columns to rows

Pivoting your data—changing its shape by turning selected columns to rows, or vice versa—is one of the most common methods of reshaping data. The technique should be used when you see data field headers that are actually useful for analysis. These headers often occur when adding data to a data set as a new column. In the case of Table 2-9, adding a new student's results to the data set creates a new column.

Table 2-9. Data requiring a columns-to-rows pivot

Department	Subject	Course	30957191	52814935	89620539	51123824	63947347
Art	History	HI101	76	92	60		
Art	History	HI102	66		35		
Social Sciences	Politics	PO101	58			61	
Social Sciences	Politics	PO102			75		
Social Sciences	Geography	GE101				91	82

The challenge in analyzing this data set is not simply aggregating a single column but updating the analysis as new students are added. This is much easier when student values are all in a single column and the measures are held in a separate column alongside it. The result of the pivot is shown in Table 2-10.

Table 2-10. Result of pivoting Table 2-9

Department	Subject	Course	Student	Score
Art	History	HI101	30957191	76
Art	History	HI101	52814935	92
Art	History	HI101	89620539	60
Art	History	HI102	30957191	66
Art	History	HI102	89620539	35
Social Sciences	Politics	PO101	30957191	58
Social Sciences	Politics	PO101	51123824	61
Social Sciences	Politics	PO102	89620539	75
Social Sciences	Geography	GE101	51123824	91
Social Sciences	Geography	GE101	63947347	82

The resulting data set does not have the nulls held as separate rows. Most tools remove those null records, as they do not contribute any values to analysis.

Pivot—rows to columns

As seen in "Measures" on page 46, having multiple rows for each metric instead of separate columns can create its own difficulties. Therefore, you can use another form of pivoting to correct the issue. Pivoting rows to columns requires a slightly different technique. In Table 2-11, which is the complete data set from Table 2-8, finding the relationship between Score and Attendance is much harder.

Table 2-11. Full data set of multiple measures across multiple rows

Department	Subject	Course	Student	Measure	Value
Art	History	HI101	30957191	Score	76
Art	History	HI101	30957191	Attendance	6
Art	History	HI101	52814935	Score	92
Art	History	HI101	52814935	Attendance	8
Art	History	HI101	89620539	Score	60
Art	History	HI101	89620539	Attendance	10
Art	History	HI102	30957191	Score	66
Art	History	HI102	30957191	Attendance	7
Art	History	HI102	89620539	Score	35
Art	History	HI102	89620539	Attendance	7
Social Sciences	Politics	PO101	30957191	Score	58
Social Sciences	Politics	PO101	30957191	Attendance	8
Social Sciences	Politics	PO101	51123824	Score	61
Social Sciences	Politics	PO101	51123824	Attendance	8
Social Sciences	Politics	PO102	89620539	Score	75
Social Sciences	Politics	PO102	89620539	Attendance	10
Social Sciences	Geography	GE101	51123824	Score	91
Social Sciences	Geography	GE101	51123824	Attendance	7
Social Sciences	Geography	GE101	63947347	Score	82
Social Sciences	Geography	GE101	63947347	Attendance	10

Pivoting rows to columns requires setting which data field will form the new headers of the columns for measures. The values that will fall underneath the headers can be selected from a column in the data set—in our example, the Value column. If multiple values exist in the same row in the resulting data set, the data being used for the pivot will often require you to select an aggregation. Depending on why multiple values might exist, you might want to pick the smallest, largest, or mean of the various values. The data set in Table 2-11 has no duplicates, so that won't be factored into consideration.

The result of the rows-to-columns pivot is a data set in which each categorical data field and measure has its own column, making analysis easier (Table 2-12).

Table 2-12. Clean data source resulting from the pivot

Department	Subject	Course	Student	Score	Attendance
Art	History	HI101	30957191	76	6
Art	History	HI101	52814935	92	8
Art	History	HI101	89620539	60	10
Art	History	HI102	30957191	66	7
Art	History	HI102	89620539	35	7
Social Sciences	Politics	PO101	30957191	58	8
Social Sciences	Politics	PO101	51123824	61	8
Social Sciences	Politics	PO102	89620539	75	10
Social Sciences	Geography	GE101	51123824	91	7
Social Sciences	Geography	GE101	63947347	82	10

Aggregation

The shape of data isn't just about columns of data; the number of rows also significantly changes the shape of data. In "Rows" on page 22, rows of data were identified as records of individual observations, but for ease of analysis, you can aggregate rows to make the data less granular. Often you'll leave data sets at the most granular level to ensure that you can ask a range of questions about the data. However, you can prepare data for specific purposes if you are aware of those questions. To raise the data to a higher level of granularity (i.e., less detail), the metrics that share common categorical values are aggregated. Here are some typical aggregations:

Sum
Totaling the values

Average: mean
Totaling the values and dividing by the number of records

Average: mode
Finding the most common value

Average: median
Ordering all the values and finding the middle value

Minimum
Finding the lowest value

Maximum
Finding the highest value

The granularity in Table 2-12 is at the student level: a single row represents each student in a particular course. To aggregate the measures up to the course level, the students' details need to be aggregated within each course. Table 2-13 shows the average (mean) score and average attendance for each course, as calculated from the student score and attendance data in Table 2-12.

Table 2-13. Averaged scores and attendance

Department	Subject	Course	Avg. score	Avg. attendance
Art	History	HI101	76	8
Art	History	HI102	50.5	7
Social Sciences	Politics	PO101	59.5	8
Social Sciences	Politics	PO102	75	10
Social Sciences	Geography	GE101	86.5	8.5

Aggregation can also remove granularity by determining the number of instances of a particular categorical value:

Count
    Adding up the number of instances of each member of a category

Count distinct
    Adding up the number of unique members of a category

Let's use a count, as we know the granularity of the data, to allow the user of the data set to determine its completeness. It's unlikely that all the data is in the data set, since only a few people are recorded for each course. Table 2-14 shows the count of students per course, along with the previous aggregations formed from Table 2-12.

Table 2-14. Count of students per course

Department	Subject	Course	Avg. score	Avg. attendance	Count of students
Art	History	HI101	76	8	3
Art	History	HI102	50.5	7	2
Social Sciences	Politics	PO101	59.5	8	2
Social Sciences	Politics	PO102	75	10	1
Social Sciences	Geography	GE101	86.5	8.5	2

Because of the ever-growing size of data sets, data aggregation is increasingly needed to avoid poor performance by analytical tools that must process billions of rows of data. Aggregating data to a higher level of granularity means the tools have to process fewer rows and can thus perform calculations more quickly. Having fewer rows to check against also allows you to validate data more easily. As previously mentioned, aggregating data should occur only when answering your questions doesn't require a deeper level of granularity.

Cleaning Data

As mentioned in "Rows and Columns" on page 22, a data field, or column of data, should contain a value describing a single element of the observation. Outputs from operational systems do not always come in an easy-to-read format or meet this "one data item in each column" guideline, and thus they require cleaning through splitting before analytical use. Note that data cleaning isn't required only for system-generated sources; manually entered file-based sources often require cleaning as well because of poor entries.

Splitting

Not every source will require you to create a well-structured data set. Determine early on whether this extra work will be needed, as you'll want to factor that into the time you have to produce your analysis.

The data in Table 2-15 could be split in a few ways. Note, for example, that the main data values are divided by hyphens.

Table 2-15. Log from security badge entry

Log
2022_10_13-08:31:47-30957191
2022_10_13-08:42:21-89620539
2022_10_13-08:47:19-52814935
2022_10_13-08:49:56-51123824

Splitting the log values at the hyphens would result in three columns containing the date, time, and student ID, as shown in Table 2-16.

Table 2-16. Result of splitting logic

Date	Time	Student ID
2022_10_13	08:31:47	30957191
2022_10_13	08:42:21	89620539
2022_10_13	08:47:19	52814935
2022_10_13	08:49:56	51123824

Splitting is a process that can be completed in many tools either with a few clicks or by writing a calculation. Whether you build the calculation yourself or have a tool with the automated option, the same logic applies. The logic requires the data processor to recognize the breaks between the data points to create a new column.

Depending on the type of analysis, you might want to perform a second split calculation on Date to produce separate columns for year, month, and day. To analyze whether students turn up later for classes in winter months compared to summer months, you could apply the same logic to the Time column to create separate columns for hours, minutes, and seconds. Analyzing the data held within the logs is much more difficult without splitting up the data. And with data updating continuously, splitting can become an arduous task unless the process is automated. Work out what you need from the data before trying to productionalize the data preparation to ensure that you have the required data fields.

Replacing rogue characters

As covered in "Rows and Columns" on page 22, each data field should be only one data type. String data fields can contain any alphanumeric character, but to conduct mathematical calculations, you will likely want only numeric data. Most software will not be able to process the analysis you want to do if rogue characters exist.

Data entry is rarely perfect, especially if values are entered manually. But if manual entry can result in mistakes, why do systems allow for manual data entry? The answer is simple: flexibility. When a system is being designed, restricting the data to be entered to a simple drop-down set of choices isn't always feasible. The flexibility of data entry is useful for the inputter, but the resulting data challenges can be tough.

Even the most careful data entry can lead to incorrect characters being added to data fields. For example, in Table 2-17, the Capacity data field should clearly be a column of integers, but the character *A* has accidentally been added to a value.

Table 2-17. Rogue character in a data field

Building	Room	Capacity
Roscoe	Theater A	470
Roscoe	Theater B	236
Simon	Theater A	A198
Simon	Theater B	330
Simon	Theater C	121

To return the field to being entirely numeric, you could manually remove the value. But this could lead to important values being filtered out of the data set, changing the resulting analysis. Alternatively, most data tools feature a calculation function called Replace that allows the user to replace characters. In this example, you could clean the data entry by using Replace to remove the *A* and leave the 198 value. If there isn't a clear pattern indicating where the rogue characters exist, you may need to use more complex functions like *regular expressions*. Look for what the data value should be before making any amendments to avoid leaving an incorrect value. The value 198 seems to be feasible within this data set, as it is within the range of other values in the Capacity data field, so it makes sense to retain it.

Learning to structure and prepare data can make your analysis easier and could even unlock other useful values in the data set. Remember, having each column representing a single category or measure will allow you to ask the questions you want to of your data. Each column should be a single data type to allow you to take advantage of forming calculations and aggregations that will be a constant demand when working with data.

The "Right" Data

Whether you have the "right" data to start your analysis is often determined not by the accessible data but by the question being posed. Without a clear understanding of what is needed, you'll find it's virtually impossible to provide the right answers.

Requirements are the questions and challenges you will be asked to resolve with data. As I've become a better analyst, I've learned how to identify what the stakeholder actually needs. Multiple factors often prevent the stakeholder from asking for their real needs. These range from the availability of data to the situation that the need has arisen from (Figure 2-12).

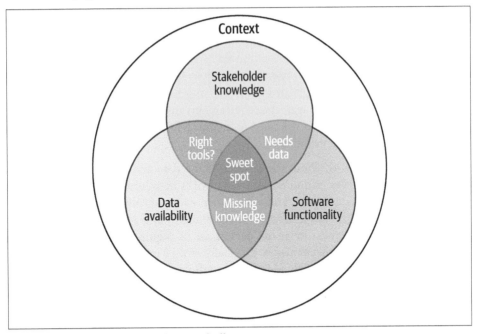

Figure 2-12. Requirement-gathering challenges

Details of these challenges are as follows:

Context

A person trying to find answers from data must always understand the context of the question being asked. For example, the answer to even a simple question like "What's happened to our profits?" differs greatly depending on the global macro-economic situation, the organization's stage of development, and even when the question was last asked.

The organization's context isn't the only factor to understand; the personal context of the individual asking the question is important too. Maybe they're under pressure because they're not meeting their targets and thus require a more analytical answer about their performance and how to improve it. Or perhaps the stakeholder is performing well and wants the analysis to demonstrate just how far ahead they are compared to expectations. Without clarity on context, you likely won't be able to use data to show what the stakeholder requires.

Stakeholder knowledge

The stakeholder's knowledge is a key factor in whether they will be able to articulate what they need. Knowledge in this regard has two components: subject-matter expertise and data skills. Subject-matter expertise is often why someone has the role they do in an organization. Is the individual highly experienced in their field? Are they renowned within the organization for their level of knowledge about how the organization works? Their level of expertise affects the level of detail the analysis might go into. If the stakeholder is new to their role or is more of a generalist manager, the requirements might remain at a higher level—in which case, the analysis will need to include a lot more contextual information rather than being deeply nuanced.

Simply knowing a lot about the subject of the data analysis isn't enough for a deep, technical review. Knowing how data works in an organization, what can be achieved with data analytics, and what data is even available for analysis can dramatically change the requirements. A stakeholder with low data skills and data awareness is unlikely to form the perfect set of requirements. Few people will openly highlight their weaknesses, especially as they move up in an organization. Therefore, you'll need to ask additional questions to deduce whether you should use your data skills to help the stakeholder ask for what they actually need.

Data availability

Obviously, you can't complete data analysis if the data doesn't exist. But just because you don't have access to the data now doesn't mean you can't *get* access. A valuable capability in an organization is knowing what data exists and where it resides. Being able to locate data quickly, or knowing who can, is a huge factor in being able to communicate with data effectively, because this knowledge can reduce the time it takes to find the data you need. With more data coming from external third parties or internet-based sources, being able to corral data for use in your analysis can change the requirements you are able to meet or promote. Without this knowledge, stakeholders are likely to ask broader questions for fear that the data won't be available or that they seem naive.

Software functionality

Even if you have all the constituent parts listed thus far, the software must have the functionality to meet the set requirements. Often tools can be manipulated to meet requirements, and the internet is littered with workarounds for software that doesn't have a specific feature. Software functionality is frequently underestimated when setting requirements. A stakeholder who doesn't know the capability of the software used in their organization often doesn't request its full capability, even when achieving it is relatively easy. Certainly many data visualization tools are much more interactive than stakeholders initially perceive, which is why they ask for more closed requirements. This means they want a particular answer and won't be open to the analysis being more exploratory.

The overlapping sections of Figure 2-12 also create challenges for you in trying to understand the true requirements and the data you will therefore need to answer them:

Missing knowledge

If you have the data and tools needed but have a stakeholder without knowledge, you will struggle to get clear requirements without a lot of iteration. They are likely to learn about the subject as you explore the data, so be prepared to work closely with your stakeholder. Your best course of action is to find others with experience who can help you refine the requirements earlier in the process.

Right tools?

If you have the data and a knowledgeable stakeholder, you will need to have software that can use the data to answer their questions. If your software doesn't have lots of the functionality you need, you will struggle to keep up with the stakeholder's needs. It can be a challenge to get new tools brought into your organization, so managing expectations about timescales is key.

Need data

If you don't have data, you can't communicate with data. This is a nice problem to have if you know where you might find the data you need. But not knowing where to find the data sets you need can be a frustrating experience, as you have no way to solve the challenges being raised. Knowing other data workers in your organization can help, as they might be able to share different sources they use or know of.

Often this mixture of challenges can make data work fail to have the intended impact or create frustration between all parties involved, unless time is spent on getting the fundamental requirements right. With so many challenges, how should you go about avoiding them and gathering requirements successfully?

Requirement Gathering

Requirement gathering is a task that can make or break your analytics project before you've even begun. With clear requirements from your stakeholder (or from yourself if it is a personal project), you can meet the needs of the project. Requirements do not necessarily have to be precise. One downside of absolute precision is that you may miss key insights. On the other hand, if the requirements are too loose, answering the questions being posed may be difficult.

With good requirement gathering, you'll be able to answer questions that your key stakeholders haven't even thought about yet. In many cases, you'll be analyzing data that has never been looked at before, and you won't know what it shows until you wrangle it together and start to conduct the analysis. Documenting the requirements and sharing them with your stakeholders will help validate that you're in agreement as to what needs to be done.

Asking the right questions

Getting to the real needs of a stakeholder is all about asking them the right questions. A stakeholder's knowledge of their subject and data can have a massive impact on whether you can form an understanding of their real needs. If you have a stakeholder who is used to requesting and using data solutions, you are much more likely to obtain a thorough understanding of what they need to achieve. However, if the stakeholder's knowledge of the subject or the data isn't strong, you will likely need to ask additional questions to understand what is really required.

Using the university theme of this chapter, let's work through an example.

Imagine you work at a British university, on a planning team responsible for ensuring that the university hits its capacity of students for the next academic year. In the UK, students gaining a place at the university is based on their high school grades. A number of students won't have made their grades, leaving spaces available in some courses. The planning manager, Vicky, comes to you to set requirements for a project that will help multiple teams understand the changing picture as results come in and places at the university get confirmed or otherwise open up if students don't make their grades.

Vicky's initial request is for "a dashboard to show how many students we have versus the places available across the university." When you first hear this request, it doesn't seem unreasonable and even seems achievable. You might need only to grab some summary numbers to measure:

- How many students have met their grades to confirm their spot?
- How many students have missed their grades?
- How many students have yet to confirm?

However, if you offer those numbers, you are likely to get back another set of questions. This is the great aspect of communicating with data: people are smart, so once you show them something, they learn and will often want to know something else building on that knowledge. A good data worker will try to get ahead of the subject by forming an understanding of where the questioning might go as they gather the requirements.

Rather than just saying yes to Vicky's request, you can ask a simple question that could help move you toward a better set of requirements: "What are you planning to do with those numbers?" Vicky's answer could guide you in adding to those initial summary numbers so that you can provide her with what she really needs. Some potential answers from Vicky are as follows:

- "We need to make sure we have enough classrooms."
- "We need to make sure we have the right number of professors."
- "We need to make sure we have sufficient on-campus housing space for the students."

At numerous times in my career, the answers have gone along the lines of all these points. Although this means more work to set up the initial views, effort will be saved down the line, as you're more likely to get the answers you require on the first try.

Another way to guide yourself and your stakeholders to the requirements they actually need is by using the *five whys* technique that was originally created by Sakichi Toyoda, who established the company from which the Toyota Motor Corporation was created. By channeling what I call your "inner toddler" and asking "Why?" in response to each answer to your questions, you will get to the real focal point of the requirements. Toyoda found that you should ask "Why?" up to five times in a row to find the answer you're looking for. Clearly, not asking "Why?" like an actual toddler is the key to not annoying your stakeholder.

Here is how your interaction with Vicky could play out using the five whys technique:

Vicky: "I need a dashboard to show how many students we have versus the places available across the university."

You: "Why do you need those numbers?"

Vicky: "I need to be able to tell the vice chancellor what capacity we might have next year."

You: "Why would the vice chancellor be looking for those values?"

Vicky: "She is looking to confirm the number of teaching staff that will be needed."

You: "Why is she looking for those numbers right now?"

Vicky: "She needs to know whether we need more large classroom space if we don't have enough staff to teach in smaller groups and rooms."

You: "Why the focus on classrooms?"

Vicky: "There are plans to refurbish all the lecture theaters in Building C, and that will affect capacity for social science courses."

Now you have much clearer insight into the information required for the analysis, and you needed only four *whys* to get there. The data needs to be more than just overall student numbers; it needs to be split by department too. Alongside that data set, joining a data set containing room capacity per faculty would allow you to compare the current student numbers against teaching space in case other courses are not full and could switch to alternate rooms.

The technique seems so simple—so why doesn't everyone just ask the right question the first time? Asking stakeholders challenging questions can be difficult. Stakeholders frequently are more senior members of the organization, and you might be nervous about challenging them. However, as discussed, stakeholders may not be used to working in this way, so posing these questions can be useful. Also, thinking through these questions with someone else can help you think differently about the problem in front of you and how you might want to approach the requirements.

Sketching

Understanding your stakeholder's requirements is not the only part of the puzzle you need to piece together before starting the work to ensure that you have the right data. Stakeholders often have specific charts, layouts, and formats in mind; not delivering those will reduce the likelihood of the stakeholder using the analytical products you come up with. If you deliver the initial work without checking the visual requirements, the stakeholder will likely ask you to rework your output, even if it answers the question.

Chapters 3 and 4 look at the most effective ways to visualize certain data points, but stakeholder requirements will not necessarily fit these best practices. The aim of these chapters is to give you the knowledge to articulate how data should be visualized, and why, to ensure that the message within the data is being communicated clearly.

The format of your communication is especially important when you're dealing with work that is for your stakeholder's management or for external third parties. Trying to get these details out of someone's head and into a requirements document is difficult for several reasons:

They are an experienced data professional.
Although an experienced data professional would score well on our stakeholder knowledge test, they pose separate challenges. They may expect you to match the way they would have approached the requirements they have given. Often they might have worked with different tools that have alternate options and strengths to those you use.

They're not the end user.
When you don't get to talk to the end user, it's difficult to understand how they might use the analysis and what they need it to answer. Even if your stakeholder has spoken to the end user, the requirements will be second- or third-hand. Each link in the chain will add their own interpretation and needs into the requirements, further convoluting the clarity around what is essential.

"I know what I want; I just don't know what it is yet."
This is a really tough situation to be in and not atypical in analytics, as questions can be hastily formed based on situational stimuli like meetings or seeing other projects. The situation is better when you have worked with the stakeholder for a while but can be challenging if it's your first interaction with them.

A nice approach to working through these challenges is to get the stakeholder to draw what they're thinking of. The drawing does not have to be a masterpiece; even the crudest rendering can quickly give you a sense of what the end product might look like. People are often hesitant to sketch out their ideas for fear of being bad at drawing. The quality of the sketch doesn't matter; I've even seen Post-it Notes stuck on a page with just a description of a chart type. Without the data, the focus instantly becomes what each sketched element adds to the work, how the user might interact with the work, and whose expertise you might need to complete the project.

Figure 2-13 shows a sketch based on Vicky's requirements, following the use of the five whys technique.

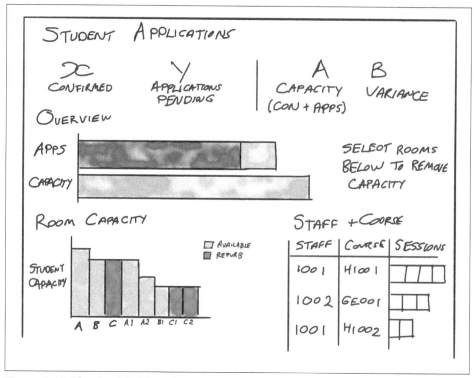

Figure 2-13. Sketch of dashboard meeting Vicky's requirements

The sketch can help drive you toward getting the right data by working out what data fields would be needed to form specific graphs (Figure 2-14).

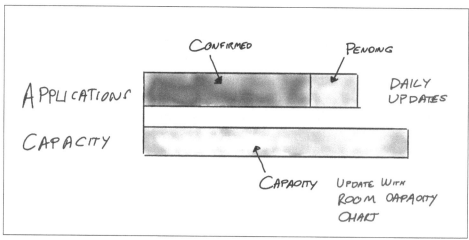

Figure 2-14. Detailed sketch of overview chart

Getting the right requirements can help guide you toward getting the best outcome the first time and ensure that you are collating all the necessary data for your project. Iterating a sketch on a whiteboard or on paper is easier than visualizing data in data software unless the user is highly experienced with the software. Faster iteration will allow you to find the best answer sooner and will likely increase the work's longevity, since it will be more relevant to users.

Use of the Data

Once you know the requirements, as well as how the data is likely to be represented in a data visualization, the next step is understanding the data flow from source to analysis. You need to consider multiple factors to ensure that you get the data you require when you need it, and in a usable format.

Frequency

As discussed in "How Is Data Created?" on page 28, data is created in many ways, but more data is getting captured with increasing frequency than ever before. For example, surveys are now conducted online rather than just in person or by mail, allowing results to be updated in real time. Thus you'll need to ensure that you can offer your stakeholder updated versions of the analysis without creating the challenge of continually maintaining the visualization. Depending on the tools you use, this can be easy, or you may need to revert to manual updates.

Being aware of when the data is "ready" is an important factor in ensuring that the data is suitable for answering the stakeholder's needs. Frequently, many stakeholders will be looking for certainty from their analytical products, and updating data will create confusion if they are not prepared for changing values. If your data is likely to change your visualization, the view clearly needs to show whether and when that might occur. However, updating data can be beneficial for stakeholders who want to start looking at potential results and emerging trends rather than waiting for the complete data set. Getting clarity on whether your stakeholder prefers to receive an early view of provisional data or wait for a solid, complete data set is key.

Volume

Along with access to streaming data sets, modern data sets are growing ever bigger. Many storage solutions are capable of storing huge data volumes, but using these data sets will impact the analysts' options as well as the performance of the visualization tool. These effects include the following:

Slower development
> Working with large data sets can slow everything you do with data. Data exploration is a key part of most analysis, since the way you visualize the data will likely change as you understand more about the data set. Each step of the exploration

will be slower because the data tool has to process more records. These steps include understanding what is within the data as data loads as well as building the charts themselves.

More difficult analysis

Larger data sets are harder to analyze, and not just because of the inevitably slower performance of the majority of data tools. Uncovering key findings and anomalies can become much more difficult. It can be easier to identify trends with larger data sets, as there are more data points to validate them, but analysis isn't always focused on that. Finding a data outlier can mean identifying a new high-growth client, a product whose sales are about to take off, or a musician who is about to have a million streams.

Slower performance

Slower performance is an issue for the end user as well as for the analyst. After working in financial services for nearly a decade, I've learned that people are not happy waiting for the loading icon to stop spinning and render their analysis. This can often mean the difference between them using an analytical view or just ignoring it.

You can take different approaches to working around these factors:

Sampling

Taking a sample of a large data set removes much of the difficulty in developing a visualization. Finding a large enough or representative sample can be a challenge. You may want to take a random sample of the data, or just the first thousand rows. Each technique has its own issues if you are using only this sample to form your analysis, but sampling will save development time regardless. Be careful not to miss extremes in the data that could dramatically alter the techniques you use to visualize the data. Replacing the sampled data set with the full data set before forming any conclusions is also key.

Incremental data refresh

Often data sets will require updating over time. When you're working with a large data set, the time spent refreshing the full data set can be significant. Powering your analysis with a data set in which only the new rows of data are added shortens the update time considerably. This technique does not work, however, if previously loaded records require an occasional update. For example, if a customer might return a product from a retail order, the data set should be updated to reflect the customer's actual order.

One big data set versus many

With data sets being created from an ever-growing number of sources, pulling data sources to get the right data set for your analysis is an increasingly common challenge. When pulling different data sources together, you should consider what the resulting data set is required for and whether you can alter it slightly to make it useful for others to prevent the proliferation of a single data source for each piece of analysis. After all, managing all these data sources can become quite burdensome.

Two common methods exist for merging data sources. One is *joining* data. Joining two data sources involves adding data fields from one data source to the other. Figure 2-15 illustrates the joining of separate data sets on the average grade per course and the number of students in each course to create the single data set required for analysis.

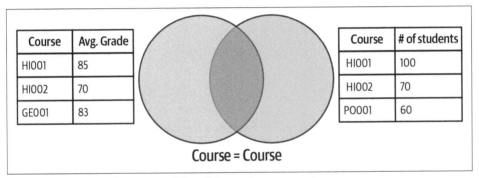

Course	Avg. Grade
HI001	85
HI002	70
GE001	83

Course	# of students
HI001	100
HI002	70
PO001	60

Course = Course

Figure 2-15. Join technique used for adding columns to a data set

To join two datasets, you need to specify two things:

Join conditions
> This logic specifies how two separate tables should be linked together. In this process, you match one field with another; for example, the course number in the first table matches up with the course number in the second table.

Join type
> Depending on the join conditions, you can choose whether to retrieve only records that match (this is called an *inner join*) or all records from each table in turn, regardless of whether a clear match exists.

The resulting table of data depends on the type of join you create:

Inner join
> The only values returned from either table are those that meet the join condition (Table 2-18). This is most useful when you need data from both tables to make a meaningful analysis. When the join condition is met, the data appears on the

same row based on that condition (in this case, where the course identifier is the same in both data sets).

Table 2-18. Inner join results

Course	# of students	Avg. grade
HI001	100	85
HI002	70	70

Left inner
All values are returned from the lefthand table, and data that meets the join condition is added from the righthand table (Table 2-19).

Table 2-19. Left inner join results

Course	# of students	Avg. grade
HI001	100	85
HI002	70	70
P0001	60	

Full join
All data is added from both tables, but when the join condition is met, the data is added to the same row (Table 2-20).

Table 2-20. Full join results

Course	# of students	Avg. grade
HI001	100	85
HI002	70	70
P0001	60	
GE001		83

The second technique, *unioning*, involves stacking similarly structured data sets on top of each other (Figure 2-16).

Whether to have one large data set that is suitable for many potential purposes or many data sets that are set up in a more custom fashion for each individual piece of analysis is a delicate balancing act. Your choice will often depend on the data tools you are using.

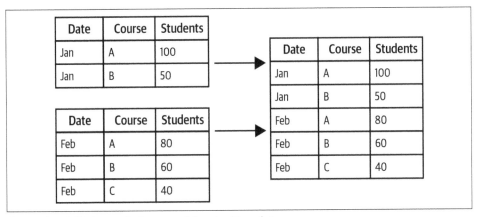

Figure 2-16. Union technique used for stacking data sources

Summary

Unsurprisingly, learning what constitutes data, where it comes from, how it is stored, and what you need to consider when working with it is a key step in learning how to communicate with data. The better your fundamental skills, the more effective your use of data will be. Many of these aspects can be daunting at first but are worth trying just to see what challenges you face.

Like the use of written or verbal language, trying to wrangle data to help convince others is a never-ending process. Different audiences and stakeholders will inevitably have different needs, so growing your skills with the fundamental building blocks of any form of communication is only going to be beneficial.

PART II

The Elements of Data Visualization

CHAPTER 3

Visualizing Data

In the first two chapters, you gained the fundamental knowledge we'll build upon for the rest of the book. In this chapter, we are going to look at the key to all data communications: the charts themselves.

Presenting data in the form of visualizations is a powerful and clear way to show your audience the story hidden within the data points. When you use charts correctly, your audience will easily receive the message you are sending to them. If your charts create ambiguity, your users are going to spend more time trying to decode the chart than thinking about the message you were trying to convey!

I am lucky enough to spend my work life teaching people how to turn the data sets all around them into analytical outputs. In many organizations, data sets are so big and unruly that sharing the stories within the data can be difficult—assuming you can find them. However, when analyzed well, this wealth of data can be a competitive advantage or challenge an organization's ways of thinking, which can lead to creating operational savings or new revenue sources.

How can you make sure the benefits of your analytical findings outweigh the effort of finding them? Much of this challenge has to do with the way you communicate your findings. In this chapter, we'll explore simple visualization techniques that will make this communication much easier and more effective.

When I first worked with data in Excel, I ran headfirst into this challenge. I was in my first managerial role. I ran a team that took database outputs, cleaned the data to create tables and charts in Excel, and shared those charts in Microsoft PowerPoint slides for reports to the company's leadership. I ran the team for three years, but we always struggled to get strong engagement with our work.

I couldn't have articulated it at the time, but we were working within a few simple scenarios. We were presented either good news or bad news; sometimes our audience already knew the news, and sometimes they didn't. Here's how that went:

Good news, already known

The easiest part of my role was to present good news to the stakeholders when they already knew to expect good news. The stakeholders had little engagement with our work, however, because they already knew the results from word of mouth or through other data sets that had already been shared. The stakeholders spent little time using the analysis; they felt that they already knew the outcome, so why spend any effort considering what the work was showing?

Good news, not already known

When we delivered good but unexpected news, our audience tended to shrug their shoulders, smile, and move on. They often asked whether we had calculated correctly or what caused the surprise. Because I didn't create the work, which was a static image, I could add little for consideration unless I had a strong briefing from the analyst on why the result was what it was.

Bad news, already known

A summary of poor performance can never be delivered well, especially when the leader of the team concerned is in the room. If we adapted our charts to explore why the news was bad, our listeners blamed the charts for "overexemplifying" the message. Their arguments often looked to blame the chart for showing the data in a poor manner rather than the poor process that had created the data points the chart visualized. If we stuck with the usual template that the team always churned out, we had little to explain the cause of the issue. The data didn't support or dispute any improvements, so it was difficult to add any value to the conversation about what needed to be resolved.

Bad news, not known

There's a reason for the phrase "don't shoot the messenger." Without a doubt, the toughest part of my role was communicating about my team uncovering unknown poor performance or another potential issue. In this situation, the audience should have felt the value of my team's hard work most keenly. Instead, they usually attacked "the data": *Why is the chart showing this? What data went into this? What calculation is this based on? There's obviously been a system error.* All these questions and points were fired, but again the tools didn't lend themselves to being able to give many of the reasons. Yes, I would prepare for these questions, but the tools didn't lend themselves well to explanation. Using Excel and PowerPoint meant I was presenting summarized data, so it was difficult to show the individual instances that had contributed to the issue. Tables of individual instances showing the issue would have been useful, but it was a tough challenge to capture the overall issue as well as the detail behind it on a printed page.

If I didn't know one answer, stakeholders often viewed it as a gap in the data. The data was right; the problem was that the message wasn't fully conveyed correctly.

It's not that charts weren't the correct answer for this situation—completely the opposite. Charts were the right option, but we didn't necessarily use the best ones for the messages we were sharing. We needed to be able to visualize the data in a more compelling and clearer manner. My team members were skilled in cleaning and transforming data sets into visuals but weren't experts in why they should favor one chart over another when demonstrating a particular trend they found in the data. To be fair to them, I didn't know this either at the time and wasn't able to guide them otherwise.

Just putting data into a chart is not enough. This might sound like a lot of pressure, but don't worry. Once you get the basics down, visualizing data can be a lot of fun. Once you know where you should use certain charts, you will become a much more effective communicator, and this will help build trust from your stakeholders— whether the message is good or bad for them.

Trust is an important factor that we struggled to generate when the messages weren't visually communicated well. If we had better communicated the message, we would have been able to generate more trust in the messages we were sharing, even if the message wasn't a positive one. We often relied on tables to provide the details that our charting lacked or to clarify our findings. Details in tables can be easily overlooked.

Using charts effectively is the focus of the next few chapters. They will form the backbone of your communication but can be made even more effective by using multiple charts together to tell different facets of the message. By adding interactivity to those charts, the message can be enhanced even further; you will read more about that in Chapters 6 and 7.

There isn't just one approach to take, though, even if you will read lots about best practices in the pages to come. Many of the people I teach say they have always enjoyed art or design but never thought they could use those skills in a paid job. Data visualization allows them to do exactly that. Designing data visualizations that convey your message in a clear, interesting way can be fun and satisfying. Once you feel comfortable working with charts and deciding when to use or not use each type, you will feel empowered to experiment with different styles.

This chapter examines some of the most important chart types in detail one by one, including how to read them yourself and when you should and shouldn't use each.

Tables

It might seem a little strange to study tables right after learning about the importance of reducing cognitive load. But if you are visualizing data, you can expect plenty of requests for tables. Knowing when a table is suitable and when it isn't makes a massive difference in your ability to help your stakeholders meet their needs.

Using tables to show views of data is far from new. People use tables at work every day to store and share data: in spreadsheets, reports, slides, and more. Why is the table so ubiquitous when it doesn't even make use of any pre-attentive attributes? Before we answer this question in "How to Optimize Tables" on page 76, let's look at the parts of a table and consider how they should be used.

How to Read Tables

The best way to read tables may seem obvious. You already know how to read a table as well as many of the other chart types in this book. I include this information because understanding the key elements of each chart type will help you use them more effectively.

A table is made up of *columns*, *rows*, *headers*, and *values*. To ensure that we're all on the same page, let's define them here. You can also see these terms illustrated in Figure 3-1.

Column
A table is split up into vertical sections called *columns*. Each column should represent one aspect of the data.

Row
A table is also split into horizontal sections called *rows*. Each row should represent an observation or set of observations about the subject of the table.

Header
The name found in the first cell of the column or row, referring to its contents.

Value
The details of the table. Each value is defined by the column in which it's located.

Columns and rows form the basic structure of tables, but depending on the use of the table, the columns and rows might contain different headers and values. If your table is the final output for your audience to use for analysis, you might find the headers become dates so the values can be compared next to each other from left to right. This style of table is commonly known as a *pivot table*. For tables that will be used as sources of data for visualization purposes, you will want a separate column for each measure in the table, with different dates being shown as separate rows, as shown in Figure 1-5 in Chapter 1.

	Column		
Bike Shop Header	**Sales Volume**	**Sales Value**	**Profit**
London	2370 Value	2844487	227598
Manchester	2407	2768049	249124
Row York	2907	3226770	-354944

Figure 3-1. Elements of a table

Categories

The first step in reading any table is understanding its categories. When you see a column that contains non-numerical values, like the leftmost column in Figure 3-1, it's likely to contain information that makes up this table's categorical data. (As you may recall from Chapter 2, *categorical data* is the data that allows us to describe our measures.) In this case, the table is categorized by the store where the bike sales and profit are generated.

When you're reading a table, ask yourself: is this data summarized, or am I looking at the original data set? Knowing the answer helps you begin to think about what questions you or others may want to ask about its contents. If the data is not summarized, it can be challenging for your audience to see the overall trends in the data set. The reverse is true for summarized data, in which the variety of data points is lost as they are aggregated into a single value.

If you don't see any of the categorical values repeated, you're probably looking at a summarized view of an underlying data set. For example, the data in our bikes sales table was almost certainly captured at the product or order level as each sale was made. It was then summed up, resulting in the table you see in Figure 3-1.

As you learned in Chapter 2, the granularity of the data (in this case, our table) is set by the unique combination of the categorical fields. These categorical fields will often be columns, unless you are working with a *cross tabulation*, or *crosstab* for short.

In the resulting table, each column is either a category or a measure. Many business intelligence tools used to build your communication require data to be held in this manner rather than in its pivoted form. Knowing how your table will be used is important to ensure that you are forming the data in the easiest way possible to use.

Crosstabs

Crosstabs use categorical values as column headers rather than just the names of measures. Figure 1-5 in Chapter 1, our original bike sales table, is an example of a crosstab: the dates are acting as headers for each column, instead of the name of the measure (such as "number of bikes sold"). If we *unpivot* the table from Figure 1-5, the resulting table would look like Figure 3-2.

Bike shop	Jan	Feb	Mar	Apr	May	Jun
London	358	118	769	636	196	293
York	557	404	533	115	989	309
Leeds	564	540	112	633	606	961
Manchester	525	278	196	596	119	693
Birmingham	509	378	325	699	592	927

Bike shop	Date	Sales
London	Jan	358
London	Feb	118
London	Mar	769
London	Apr	636
London	May	196
London	Jun	293
York	Jan	557
York	Feb	404

Figure 3-2. Unpivoted bike sales from Figure 1-5

Measures

After you have understood the categories, you can assess your table's measures. The name of the measure should be in the column header (again, unless you're working with a crosstab). Our bike sales data in Figure 3-1 has three measures: Sales Volume, Sales Value, and Profit. To find the measure for each bike shop, you read across the row from that bike shop's name to the relevant column.

 Many of the examples in this chapter come from a bike store called Allchains. The bike chain isn't a real set of stores but is formed from my experience of working with retailers. The examples and challenges related to Allchains are not just unique to retailers; they apply to a lot of organizations I have worked with across all industries.

Finding a measure is an easy task in a table as small as our examples. As a table grows, however, so does the challenge of finding the relevant value. As more columns and rows are added to a table, the cognitive effort for your audience to find the values they want increases too. Most data visualization tools allow you to add *row banding*, a way of shading alternate rows, to make it easier for the eye to follow each row across the table. In Figure 3-3, the table has alternate, light-gray row banding.

Table of Bike Sales

| | | | Month | | | |
Bike Shop	Jan	Feb	Mar	Apr	May	Jun
Birmingham	509	378	325	699	592	927
Leeds	564	540	112	633	606	961
London	358	118	769	636	196	293
Manchester	525	278	196	596	119	693
York	557	404	533	115	989	309

Figure 3-3. Row banding in a table

Tables have many elements, so reducing the cognitive effort of reading the table can make it a lot more likely your audience will be able to find the key points you are trying to communicate to them. You can use formatting to make individual values in a table easier to read.

I learned this lesson while taking data extracts from databases at a large bank. When you are handling values of nine or ten digits long, reading them is sometimes difficult. Which value is easier to parse: 32812749210 or 32,812,749,210? Both are large, but using thousand separators makes it much easier to know just how large the value is.

It's worth asking: does your audience really *need* to see the last few digits of the value? If they need absolute precision, use the full value. If not, consider summarizing the value by using *units*, such as showing currency values in thousands as *k*, millions as *m*, or billions as *b*. Financial reports often do this. Let's look at HSBC Bank's reported results for the third quarter of 2020, shown in Figure 3-4.

Key financial metrics

	Footnotes	Nine months ended		Quarter ended		
		30 Sep 2020	30 Sep 2019	30 Sep 2020	30 Jun 2020	30 Sep 2019
Reported results						
Reported revenue ($m)		38,672	42,727	11,927	13,059	13,355
Reported profit before tax ($m)		7,392	17,244	3,074	1,089	4,837
Reported profit after tax ($m)		5,164	13,732	2,039	617	3,795
Profit attributable to the ordinary shareholders of the parent company ($m)		3,336	11,478	1,359	192	2,971
Cost efficiency ratio (%)		63.5	59.2	67.4	66.4	61.0
Basic earnings per share ($)		0.17	0.57	0.07	0.01	0.15
Diluted earnings per share ($)		0.16	0.57	0.07	0.01	0.15
Net interest margin (%)		1.35	1.59	1.20	1.33	1.56

Figure 3-4. HSBC Bank third-quarter 2020 results (https://oreil.ly/ncRD4)

Without formatting these huge values by using thousand separators and using units of millions, this table would be challenging to read.

How to Optimize Tables

Now that you are clear on the elements of a table and how to make them as easy to read as possible, let's see when tables should be used.

I'll offer an initial answer to the question at the beginning of this chapter of why tables are still requested so much despite not leveraging the benefits of visualization techniques: because they offer *precision*. When someone asks a question like "How many?" a table can tell you the value.

In addition, the table's simple structure makes the values easy to find and refer to. You can make this even easier by simplifying your table through good formatting and by using units for particularly large values.

Tables can also show multiple metrics alongside one another without overloading the view with complexity (Figure 3-5).

Store	Bike type	Ordered	Delivered	Variance	Cost	Sold price
London	Road	973	948	-25	631	853
London	Gravel	355	355	0	316	427
London	Mountain	1,077	1,067	-10	1,299	1,564
York	Road	1,037	1,017	-20	716	968
York	Gravel	726	726	0	402	484
York	Mountain	1,154	1,164	10	1,367	1,775

Figure 3-5. Multiple delivery and sales metrics from the bike stores

This data can be visualized (don't worry—we'll get there soon, I promise). As a simple lookup reference, though, this table does the job nicely. Still, it could be better. Here are a few tweaks we could try:

- We could put negative values in parentheses (a common practice in accounting).
- We could also make negative values red, so the eye is drawn to an important issue: not all of the bikes ordered have been delivered.
- We could show Cost and Sold Price in thousands of pounds (indicated by "£ '000s") to simplify the values. Placing this unit indicator in the header means we don't need to repeat it in the table, making the values easier to read and compare.

Figure 3-6 shows the changes.

Store	Bike type	Ordered	Delivered	Variance	Cost (€'000s)	Sold price (€'000s)
London	Road	973	948	(25.00)	631	853
London	Gravel	355	355	0	316	427
London	Mountain	1,077	1,067	(10.00)	1,299	1,564
York	Road	1,037	1,017	(20.00)	716	968
York	Gravel	726	726	0	402	484
York	Mountain	1,154	1,164	10	1,367	1,775

Figure 3-6. Formatted table of multiple metrics

Another reason tables are still so popular is simple familiarity. In most education models, children are taught to read tables from a young age. Tables also clearly show individual values. Therefore, audiences trust tables more than they trust forms of data visualization that can hide values and that require more interpretation.

Here is where we run into the limitations of tables, though: while they can provide quick answers to simple questions, tables don't offer much to help you analyze trends or patterns and see the story within the data. For that, we have to look at forms like line charts and scatterplots. To analyze this data, for example, you'd probably want to start looking at ratios of income versus costs, or ask why administrative expenses increased dramatically last year.

Have I just made you read a long section on tables just to say you shouldn't use them? Not at all.

Tables will help build long-term trust in your analysis by allowing your audience to see the underlying values. The more your audience trusts your work, the more likely they are to listen to and act upon your message. Clearly showing the underlying values will allow your stakeholders to check your calculations, logic, and findings.

Highlight tables

As simple as tables are, you can use data visualization techniques to make them appeal to pre-attentive attributes. This helps your audience find and analyze trends and patterns without having to leave the table.

A *highlight table* is a data visualization technique that can add more context to the numbers in your table, highlighting peaks and troughs over time or across categories. Highlight tables allow you to add context to the values by offering the audience a means of comparing numbers without having to work out the variance themselves.

Figure 3-7 demonstrates the table of bike sales we first saw in Figure 1-5 as a highlight table.

	Month					
Bike Shop	Jan	Feb	Mar	Apr	May	Jun
Birmingham	509	378	325	699	592	927
Leeds	564	540	112	633	606	961
London	358	118	769	636	196	293
Manchester	525	278	196	596	119	693
York	557	404	533	115	989	309

Figure 3-7. Highlight table of bike sales

In Figure 3-7, I've used the number of bike sales as a sequential scale to represent the highest and lowest values visually. The lighter the background color of the value, the lower the sales number. The darker the background, the higher the sales number. Therefore, depending on what end of the sales volumes your audience wants to analyze, they can seek it out in the table quickly. Now, picking out those peak sales figures is easy, as well as which months haven't gone quite so well.

Nothing has been removed from the original table, but adding color lets us answer questions faster. The technique doesn't solve everything: you'd still have a tough time answering the question about which stores' sales fluctuate most. However, when a stakeholder wants a table containing a single measure, my default response is a highlight table. Even if they want just specific values, it doesn't hurt to show potential trends they might not spot otherwise.

When You Might Not Use Tables

Tables are not the right answer a *lot* of times. Of course, this book is about using data and visualization in new and different ways, so I'll encourage you to branch out. But in the following situations, you should shy away from using tables and use visualizations instead:

You need to find the overall pattern.
> Highlight tables don't work well with multiple metrics in the same table, or if your data includes extreme outliers. If you're looking for a variance analysis, a table is probably the wrong answer.

Your table has too many columns.

The more columns in a table, the more complex it is. If you are searching for a single specific value, finding it can quickly become difficult. How many times have you faced the challenge of scrolling through a wide table, trying to remember which row was the category you wanted?

Your table has too many rows.

Tables are hindered not just by too many columns but also by the number of rows. With too many rows, your audience might be scrolling for a long time to find answers. This is where filtering data to leave just the relevant information becomes important (more on that in Chapter 6).

Tables Summary Card

✔ Provides specific values

✔ Builds trust with users

✘ Shows trends

✘ Uses pre-attentive attributes

Bar Charts

The antithesis of many of the challenges we've seen with tables is the humble bar chart. Often when communicating data, the best answer will be a bar chart. This section covers the important elements of a bar chart and when to use them but also when you might want to move away from them as your method of communication despite them being so darn effective.

How to Read Bar Charts

Bar charts use humans' strongest pre-attentive attributes: length and height. Bar charts can be shown as horizontal bars or vertically oriented bars. Horizontal bars utilize length to show the values being represented, and vertical bars use height to do the same. Visually representing a measurement as a bar quickly clarifies the pattern in the data.

Let's represent our Allchains bike sales volumes as a bar chart (Figure 3-8). What conclusions can you draw from this chart?

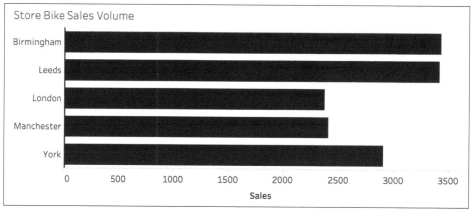

Figure 3-8. Bar chart of bike store sales volume

Here are a few things I noticed at first glance:

- The store with the highest sales was Birmingham (just barely beating Leeds).
- London had the lowest sales volume, but Manchester wasn't good either.
- York is clearly in third place, but equidistant between the leaders and the laggers.

That was easy! The chart could be made even easier to read, though, by sorting the bars by their value rather than alphabetical order as they are now. Figure 3-9 shows the effect of sorting the bars from highest to lowest sales volume to help the reader find the pattern in the data even faster.

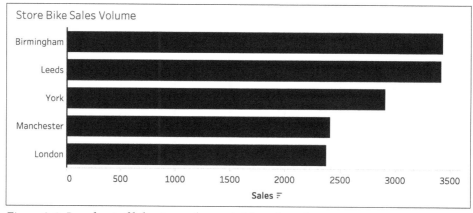

Figure 3-9. Bar chart of bike store sales, sorted by sales volume

Bar charts contain a few key elements that should be present: the axis, zero baseline, and headers. Without them, any bar chart will be a lot less effective and harder for your audience to read. If any of these elements are removed, you will need to offer the information they convey in other formats, like labels. Otherwise, your bar charts will not communicate the data clearly.

Axis

The *axis* is a key part of a bar chart that represents a scale against which each mark on the chart is measured (Figure 3-10).

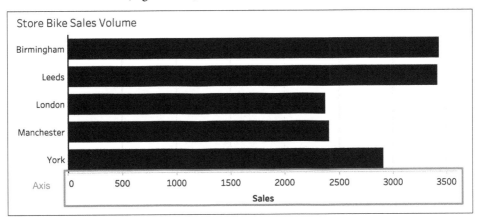

Figure 3-10. Axis of a bar chart

When I was a child, my parents kept a wall chart that looked like a big ruler. Each year, I'd press myself against the chart, straightening my back to see how much I had grown. (I won't tell you which characters were on my wall chart, but let's say I ended up a lot more Big Bird than Ernie.) Without knowing it, I was a human bar chart.

The axis is the bar chart's equivalent of the wall chart's ruler. Wherever the bar length ends, you should read across to see what value the bar represents. On the axis, you will find values marked in regular spacing known as *tick marks* that allow the reader to read the bar length against. Some bar charts have faint, regularly spaced lines in the background to guide the eye against the position on the axis. These are called *gridlines*.

An axis is frequently dropped from bar charts to avoid visual clutter. Edward Tufte, one of the most influential thinkers about data visualization, wrote about the need to reduce the overall amount of ink used in showing data, without removing any of the ink used to show the data.[1] This can be pushed to extremes as Tufte wanted the data to be the focus and not the icons, text, or logos that surrounded them. Many data visualizers have since removed the axis from their bar charts, thanks to Tufte and his

---

1 Edward Tufte, *The Visual Display of Quantitative Information* (Cheshire, CT: Graphics Press, 1983).

data-ink ratio, but this can be detrimental to the audience's understanding if the views become harder to analyze.

My personal preference is usually to leave the axis in place. Audiences look to where they expect the axis to be, to see what the axis represents as well as the values. If you do remove the axis, placing the labels for the bar inside the bar itself at either end allows the reader to still see the values. In Figure 3-11, I've added the values into the chart itself, left-aligned at the start of the bar so as to not affect how the eye perceives the bar's length.

Figure 3-11. Bar chart without an axis

Zero line

One thing that can't be dropped from a bar chart is the *zero line* (also called the *zero point*), which is where the bar length is measured from along the axis. You might do this in some other chart types, but *never* a bar chart.

 Let's talk about *never*. In some very niche use cases, data visualization experts may work out a way to show a nonzero-based bar chart, but I have yet to find a single good example. This book aims to give you clear guidance on what to do when you are first working with data—so, hopefully, when you see me use extremes like this, you will know that a rare exception may exist, but otherwise it's the advice to follow.

The reason for this absolute position has to do with the way your brain interprets the bar chart: by assessing the lengths of those bars. When you remove the zero point, you are removing the relative scale your audience is using to make that comparison. Let's take Figure 3-12 as an example.

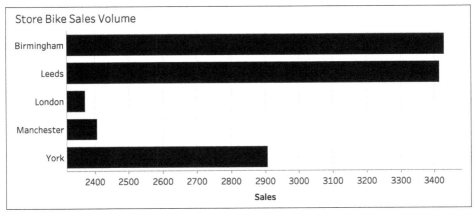

Figure 3-12. A misleading bar chart without a zero line

Wow, that's a lot of difference between stores. If the CEO of Allchains saw this chart without the axis, they'd at least *think* about firing the London and Manchester store managers instantly.

In the standard bar chart in Figure 3-8, London's bar was nearly 70% the length of Birmingham's. With the zero line removed, though, the bars start not at 0 but at 2,300. London's bar is now only just 6% as long as Birmingham's. The difference is exaggerated because our brains don't fill in the missing 2,300 as we assess the value by comparing the lengths of the bars. This difference shows the importance of pre-attentive attributes. When the audience sees this chart, they will assume a bigger difference in the values than there actually is.

Sometimes you will find charts with a zigzag on the axis showing a portion of the axis has been removed. This usually occurs when the author wants to highlight the differences between the values rather than just show the true proportionality. I'd avoid this technique, as it's possible your audience for your communication doesn't spot this and draws an incorrect conclusion from what they see.

Headers

Headers are as important to bar charts as they are to tables. They ensure that you are labeling the contents of your message clearly. In a bar chart, the headers are the labels identifying each *separate categorical member that has its own bar*, as shown in Figure 3-13.

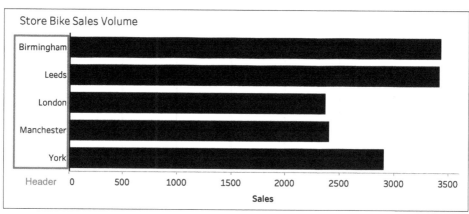

Figure 3-13. Headers of a bar chart

Labeling these elements clearly makes the bar much easier to read.

If you've used bar charts before, you might wonder why all the bar charts I've shown in this section are *horizontal bar charts*, meaning the bars go from left to right. The headers are the most significant factor in deciding how a bar chart should be oriented: after all, most people don't like to twist their head to read vertical text. Even text at an angle that you will find in Excel charts is unnecessarily hard to read compared to horizontal text. Try it for yourself with Figure 3-14.

Do you find yourself tilting your head to make the headers easier to read? Ben Jones highlights this point in his first book, *Communicating Data with Tableau* (O'Reilly), and I've noticed this in every vertical set of headers I've looked at since.

Vertical bar charts can be a go-to option when you have headers that fit in the space below the bar without the text flipping to be vertical. You may also want to use vertical bar charts when fitting the bar chart alongside other charts on a multiple-chart view.

The headers also help to set the space allocated to each bar. This space can help you to decide how wide the bars should be on a vertical bar chart or how tall on a horizontal bar chart. No hard rules exist as to the size of the bars; this will ultimately be a design choice for you to make. Having enough space on either side of each bar will help your audience differentiate them. However, if you add too much space, the bars will become too spread apart and hard to read. Finding a balance between these two is ultimately an aesthetic choice.

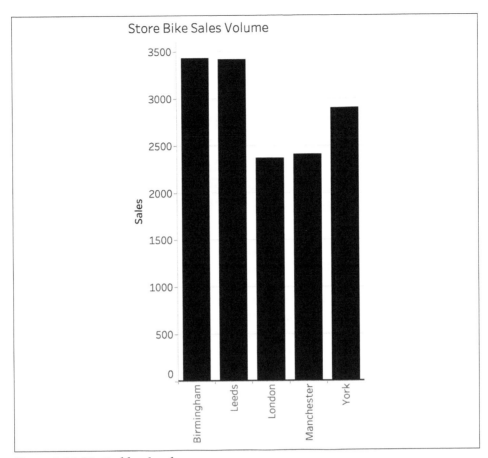

Figure 3-14. Vertical bar headers

How to Optimize Bar Charts

Bar charts can go beyond these basic elements. If not used with care, they can quickly become complicated. Let's look at techniques for taking bar charts to the next level without creating too much complexity.

Multiple categories

Some questions can't be answered with just one category; sometimes you'll need to use multiple categories in your bar chart. But before you do, consider the question you're answering. Making sure that the question is precise will help you design a chart that best communicates the answer to that question.

Maybe you are trying to answer this: "Within each store, how many bike types have been ordered?" In Figure 3-15, each store's orders are broken down by Bike Type, using the order of the headers. This makes it easy to see that mountain bikes are ordered the most in each store.

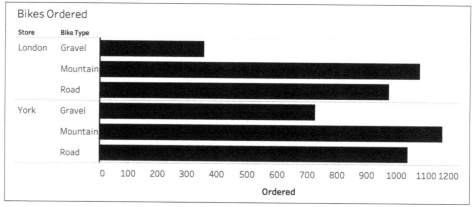

Figure 3-15. Bar chart with multiple categories

But what if the question you're trying to answer is "Which store orders the most of each type of bike?" Figure 3-16 shows the answer by changing the order of the categorical fields in the previous chart (Figure 3-15). Now we take the Bike Type and break it down by Store. That's just one simple change.

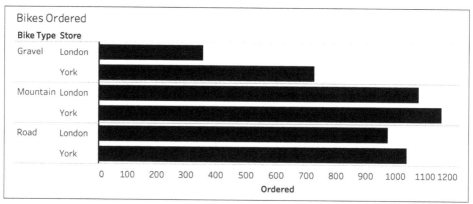

Figure 3-16. Multiple-category bar chart with alternate category ordering

With such a small data set, you shouldn't have too much difficulty using either chart to answer either question. You should notice, however, that the order of the categories *does* better position each chart to answer one of the questions. As the number of members of a category increases, the cognitive load of a chart with multiple categories can dramatically increase too. Be clear on the primary question you are answering when making choices about how to construct your bar charts.

Color

Using multiple colors in bar charts can make them a lot easier to interpret—or a lot harder. Color allows us to use multiple categories on the same chart without having to break down the categories as we did in Figures 3-15 and 3-16.

One technique is to apply color to show how a bar breaks down by an additional category. In Figure 3-17, the bar representing each store's orders has been divided by the type of bike ordered. This is called a *stacked bar chart* because the different-colored parts of the bar are stacked on top of each other like building blocks.

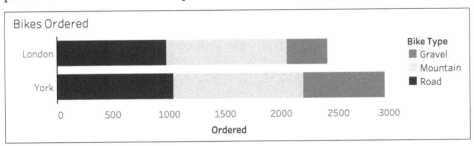

Figure 3-17. A stacked bar chart using color to indicate categories

Which store sold more road bikes? This chart makes it easy to compare the type between two stores.

Stacking bars isn't always a clear way to communicate the answer to the question posed, though. What about gravel bikes and mountain bikes? Which store sold more of those bike types? Since the bars do not start from the same position, comparing their lengths is challenging. (You've also seen this problem in the Gantt chart in Chapter 1's Figure 1-10.). One solution is to use a chart type in which stacking doesn't occur, like a dot plot; we'll cover these later in this chapter, in Figure 3-27.

My point is that you have to use color in a deliberate way. You also need to understand that just using color doesn't necessarily make the chart clearer.

For example, keeping color to a minimum reduces the chart's cognitive effort for the reader. You might have noticed that I haven't used many bright, bold colors in the charts so far. In fact, I've kept to grayscale wherever possible. This is an intentional choice. I want to make the data as clear as possible and not emphasize any particular part or value. Figure 3-18 uses color simply, to split bike type orders by the two stores.

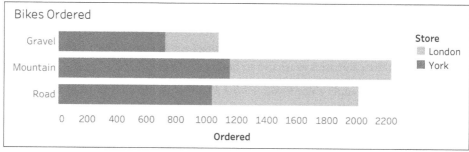

Figure 3-18. Two colors in a stacked bar chart

If I were to introduce color, the chart could become a lot "louder" than needed (see what I mean in Figure 3-19). As you flick over from the previous page, this bar chart drags your eyes toward it, doesn't it? It jumps off the page, especially in comparison to Figure 3-18.

But does all that color really help the reader? It doesn't help me. Yes, the color grabs the reader's attention, but if the chart isn't as easy to interpret as possible, how clearly does it communicate its message?

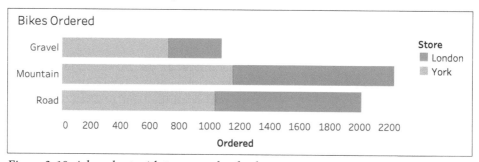

Figure 3-19. A bar chart with too many loud colors

You can use color more effectively by setting a theme (more on that in Chapter 5) or by highlighting a particular category. By using a color to highlight a particular aspect of the chart (as in Figure 3-20), you can focus the reader's attention where you want it to be. This is a really useful technique for communicating with data.

Even though bar charts use the most powerful pre-attentive attributes, you'll need to use their elements carefully to communicate as clearly as possible.

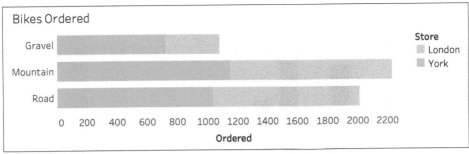

Figure 3-20. Using color to highlight important parts of a bar chart

Some bar charts are particularly effective at communicating certain kinds of data. Let's consider three: the histogram, the percentage-of-total chart, and the waterfall chart.

Histogram

Histograms are a form of bar chart that is great for looking at the distribution of data points. A histogram is a chart plotting two numerical axes. On one axis, you are counting the number of occurrences of a certain value. The other axis is used to group values into *bins*.

The histogram in Figure 3-21 shows the age distribution of the first 1,000 customers of Allchains. The store has captured its customers' ages as integers and then split them into groups according to age: 25 to 29, 30 to 34, 35 to 39, and so on. The bar labeled 25 on the horizontal axis represents all customers who are 25 to 29 years old.

What do you notice when you look at this histogram? You might notice the following:

- The majority of customers are between 25 and 50 years old.
- Very few customers are older than 60.
- The store has many more customers aged 25 and older than under 25. This might be an issue for the future of the company.

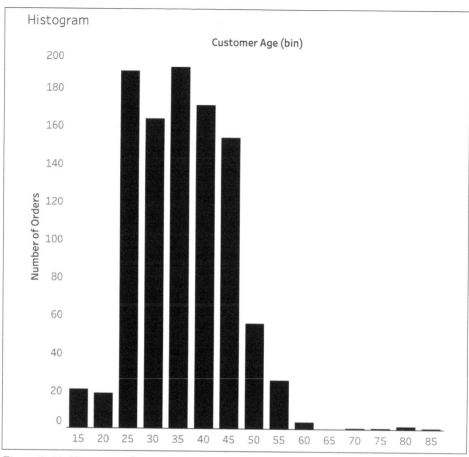

Figure 3-21. Histogram showing customer age distribution

Percentage-of-total charts

Bar charts can also show percentages effectively. Sometimes you want to show how one member of a category contributes to a measure. Maybe it is a particular product or salesperson in the bike store. While you can show this in a bar, it's often clearer when shown in a percentage-of-total bar chart.

Let's revisit the chart we used in Figure 3-20, showing the breakdown of our orders into bike type by store. Figure 3-22 does the same but converts the values to percentages of the bikes ordered by each store.

If I am trying to understand ordering patterns of each bike type, this chart communicates the answer much more clearly than the original chart in Figure 3-20. You can see that the York store orders slightly more road and mountain bikes than London but significantly more gravel bikes. The percentage-of-total bar chart is a simple way to communicate this split, with the color highlighting that particular message in the data.

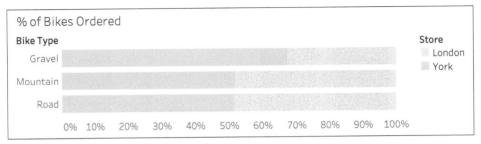

Figure 3-22. Percentage-of-total bar chart

Waterfall charts

What do you get if you combine a bar chart with a Gantt chart? A *waterfall chart*.

The waterfall chart is frequently used in financial analysis, because it shows both inflows and outflows. But it can just as easily show customers joining or leaving a company, customers changing their product purchases, or students choosing different courses.

The waterfall chart shows the first value as in a standard bar chart. What makes a waterfall chart different is the next categorical value, often a different measure, which uses its starting point as the end of the previous bar. Figure 3-23 shows an income statement, and Figure 3-24 visualizes that data as a waterfall chart.

	2021	2020
	£ '000s	£ '000s
Turnover	4,592	3,402
Cost of Sales	(2,301)	(1,927)
Gross Profit	2,291	1,475
Administrative Expenses	(421)	(123)
Operating Profit	2,712	1,598
Tax on Profit	(325)	(192)
Profit for the Financial Period	**2,387**	**1,406**

Figure 3-23. Income statement

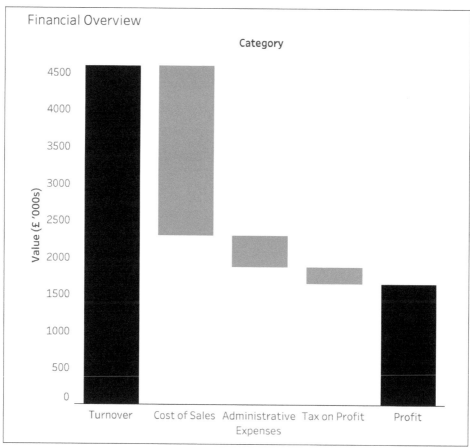

Figure 3-24. Waterfall chart

Here I've used the traditional color vocabulary of finance: being "in the black" means you are profitable (so positive values are black), whereas being "in the red" means a loss. *Turnover* is the value generated from sales and services through the year, so it is a positive value. The Cost of Sales Gantt bar begins at the top of the Turnover bar and falls. As the red indicates, Cost of Sales is a negative financial movement.

One great thing about waterfall charts is that you can read across to the axis from the endpoint of any bar to see a running total. The order of the measures is important to make that read-across meaningful. Notice that I have followed the same order as the income statement, but I've removed the total lines: the waterfall chart shows them, so I don't have to state them explicitly. The final bar shows the final position—in our example, the organization's profit.

Waterfall charts are fundamentally more challenging for first-time users to read than are most bar charts. Despite the learning curve, though, they can be much clearer than a table at providing an overall picture. A waterfall chart can allow you to see which type of gains or costs are proportionally higher than you'd expect, which can trigger a need to investigate further.

When You Might Not Want to Use Bar Charts

As I noted earlier, there aren't many situations in which a bar chart *won't* show your data clearly. They're the best choice in many situations, but not all. Even a bar chart can become overly complex if you put too much information in it.

You've just seen how color can reduce clarity in stacked bar charts. But bar charts become *really* difficult to understand when you have more than two categories that don't have a natural hierarchy. Figure 3-25 has simply too much information in one single chart.

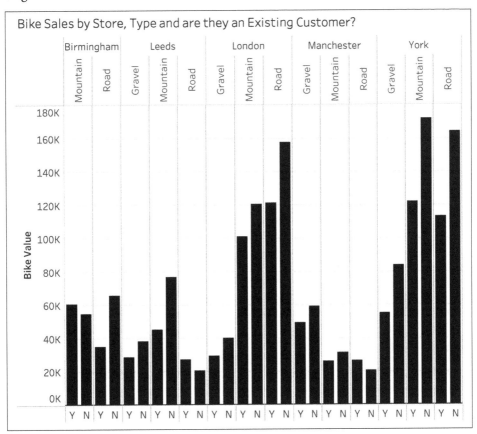

Figure 3-25. A bar chart with too many categories

Is it possible to find the information you want in there? Sure—but it's going to take some thought to extract, and you'll need to check for any unexpected patterns. I've seen too many charts like this and created a few myself. The answer is perfectly clear to the chart's author, since they've been analyzing the data set in several ways to reach this point. In Chapter 6, I'll show you how breaking this single view into multiple charts will reduce its cognitive load.

The rest of this chapter covers many more instances where bar charts aren't the optimal choice. You will see that connected data points in line charts or area charts can help show trends. You'll move beyond bar charts as you explore other ways to communicate data, but you'll still work with them constantly, and they'll still form the basis for a lot of your analysis and communication, so it's important to get comfortable with them.

Bar Charts Summary Card

✔ Uses strong pre-attentive attributes effectively.

✔ Familiar chart style to many.

✘ Take care when stacking three or more categories within a bar, as it becomes harder to analyze.

✘ Difficult to use too many categories in a single view.

Line Charts

Line charts will quickly become another staple of your chart choices. They're fantastic for showing trends. Any data that has a logical order to it—like dates, ages, or year groups in schools—can be effectively plotted on a line chart.

Line charts need *ordinal* data, or data that goes in an easily understood order, with one data point following another in a logical progression. Some examples of ordinal data are military ranks, levels of education, and job grades in organizations.

How to Read Line Charts

Line charts, like bar charts, have at least one axis to indicate the value of data points. The measure axis should be the vertical axis, since in Western cultures we expect to read the ordinal points from left to right (Figure 3-26). This rule has a few exceptions, but if you use them, expect your audience to spend a lot more time trying to understand how to read your line chart.

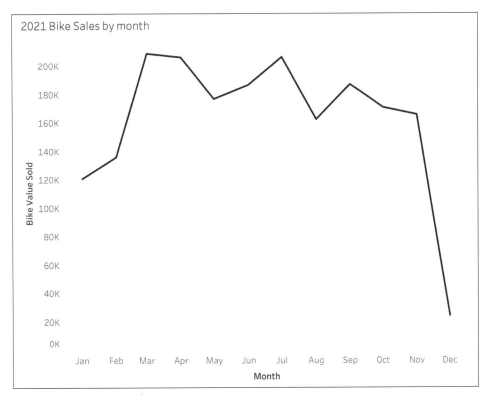

Figure 3-26. Basic line chart

The horizontal axis of a line chart can be made up of categorical members forming ordinal headers or an axis.

Mistakes can be made when dates are sorted in a nonordinal way. This may seem like something that would never happen, but I have heard too many stories of incorrect conclusions being drawn because the date parts were sorted based on the measure—and as the months were relatively in order, a quick glance at the horizontal axis didn't spot the issue. If you use dates ordered in the normal early-to-late manner, you will avoid potentially sorting the members of the category in an incorrect order.

Line charts are particularly effective because they use 2D position as a pre-attentive attribute, and the line itself guides the user through data points. The line offers your audience a view of whether the measure is increasing rapidly or slowly or is decreasing. Figure 3-27 is the chart from Figure 3-26 with the line removed. Even though you have just seen the trend in the data, removing the line makes it slightly harder to see the overall trend.

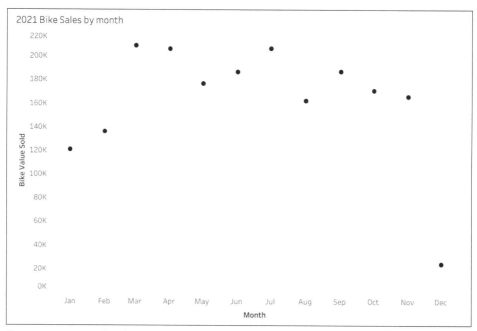

Figure 3-27. Dot plot demonstrating the importance of the linking line

If a single line is in place, it is easy to reference the point's location relative to the axis and the ordinal data point (Figure 3-28).

If you need to use categories in your analysis, you can use color much as you would in a bar chart. In "Bar Charts" on page 79, you saw how stacked bar charts can be difficult to read, like Figure 3-17. In Figure 3-29, I've split the sales based on whether the buyer is a new or existing customer of the store. This category has only two members (No and Yes), so the lines are easy to compare as one line is not stacked on top of the other.

Notice that sales to new customers have two peaks, which fall shortly before those of the existing customers. This information about buying patterns can help our marketing team tailor their message at different points in the year.

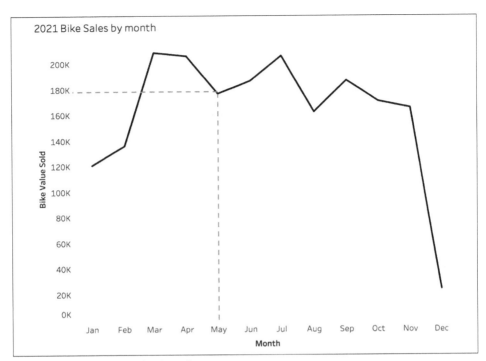

Figure 3-28. How to read a line chart

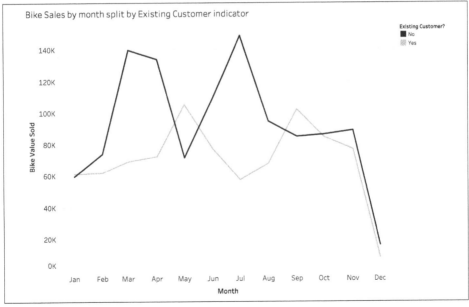

Figure 3-29. Line chart split by categories

Line charts are another chart type that can quickly overwhelm the user by using too many categories. In Figure 3-30, I have added Bike Type to the Existing Customer field, making the chart much harder to assess. If you need to assess how sales of the various bike types have changed over time and whether sales are affected by the customer being an existing buyer or not, this chart will do the job.

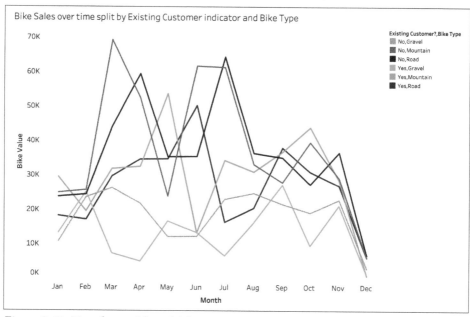

Figure 3-30. Line chart with multiple categories

Simple line charts showing basic views over time are not your only option. Adding color to other categories can help add more detail to your analysis.

How to Optimize Line Charts

Line charts use a strong pre-attentive attribute and are often familiar to audiences. They are thus a constant go-to for many data communication needs. Some variations of the line chart can highlight certain parts of the data more clearly than just a simple single line on a chart can.

Cycle plots

The parts of a date can be useful categories to compare when analyzing data. When I worked as a data analyst for a bank, I looked at when customers were coming into physical branches as well as when they used the mobile banking application. Splitting dates in different ways made this analysis much richer. Showing the patterns I found on line charts made the messages clear.

Normally, line charts have a single timeline that goes from left to right in Western cultures. In a *cycle plot*, the line still reads from left to right but is broken up by a higher-level element of the date. For example, in Figure 3-31, we have weekdays. But we don't get Monday to Sunday across the whole chart. Instead, each day is broken down by quarter: we see how Mondays in Q1 differed from Mondays in Q2, Q3, and Q4.

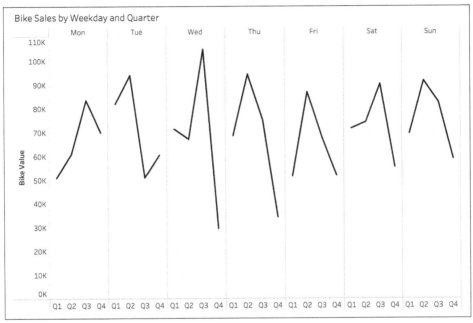

Figure 3-31. Cycle plot of bike sales each weekday

By understanding these trends, you can determine when you need to have stock in your stores and staff there to sell it. For example, would you have noticed that during the spring and summer, midweek sales are higher than on the weekends? These midweek sales fall during the winter quarter. Weekend sales appear more consistent all year round. These charts are fantastic for finding patterns in data that you would never find in a standard line chart.

Slope charts

In Figure 3-30, you saw how adding just a few categorical variables can increase the difficulty of reading a line chart. But what if you just want to know about change across a certain time period? Let me introduce you to the *slope chart*.

If you don't need to see the trend at a more precise point, just overall, the slope chart does this effectively. By removing the intermediary data points, the gradient of the chart makes it much easier to assess the change from the first date to the last.

In Figure 3-32, you can see the impact of December's sales slump, as we did in Figure 3-30. Yet, in the slope chart, it's much easier to see that what was originally the top-selling bike type, mountain bikes, is now on the bottom.

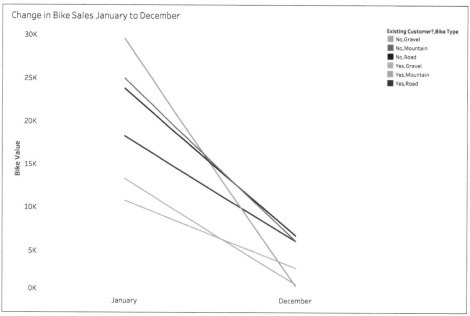

Figure 3-32. Slope chart

I certainly didn't see this in the original line chart: I was focused on the summer peak sales. Slope charts can oversimplify the representation of the data and miss seasonal trends where data points are removed. Slope charts are best used when the two points on each line are both key periods for your organization.

Sparklines

A *sparkline* is a line chart that takes little room but can make a big impact. This mini-version of a line chart is used to show the trend but is not designed for finding precise values. The original concept was coined by Edward Tufte. Sparklines can have multiple uses in communicating data, from providing additional context to prominent numbers to showing trends of individual categorical variables. You will notice in Figure 3-33 that this chart has no horizontal or vertical axis labels for the consumer of the information to reference specific values against.

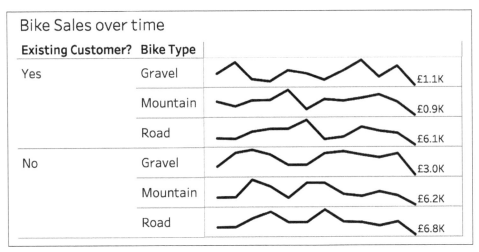

Bike Sales over time		
Existing Customer?	**Bike Type**	
Yes	Gravel	£1.1K
	Mountain	£0.9K
	Road	£6.1K
No	Gravel	£3.0K
	Mountain	£6.2K
	Road	£6.8K

Figure 3-33. Sparklines

The aim of a sparkline is to demonstrate trends. It's small (like a spark), so multiple categories can fit into a small space. The best format for sparklines is a hotly debated topic. I will let you make up your own mind, but here are four ways to create sparkline charts:

Remove the y-axis.
    The y-axis is the name for the vertical axis. If you kept this axis, it would be very small. Would it be useful anyway?

Remove the x-axis.
    The x-axis is the name for the horizontal axis. When sparklines are used individually, this axis is often removed.

Include some labels.
    If you remove the y-axis, including at least a line-ending label helps quantify the values shown in the sparkline. Occasionally, a start point is labeled. Sometimes the minimum and maximum values are labeled to show the range of values (but this often requires taller sparklines).

Use an independent y-axis range.
    Allowing each sparkline to spread across the whole y-axis space you have given it makes the trend clearer. This is controversial (although I did it in Figure 3-33), since you lose the relative relationships between each categorical variable.

Sparklines make more appearances later in the book. They are one way to add a lot of context to single numbers and indicators, especially in printed work. By showing the trend to your audience, they will be able to understand whether those end points are improvements or reductions compared to many previous data points. This will make the sparkline able to answer more of your audience questions than just that single data point at the end of each line.

Area charts

Line charts are just a single line on the page. When you want the trend to have a stronger impact, area charts can be the answer. Area charts have the additional bene-fit of utilizing the pre-attentive attribute of height. An *area chart* is simply a line chart that uses the length of the shaded part of the chart against the axis to represent the data. This means you can deploy intense color and big, bold shapes to grab the audi-ence's attention (as I've done in Figure 3-34). Even if you were just casually browsing a company report, could you ignore this chart?

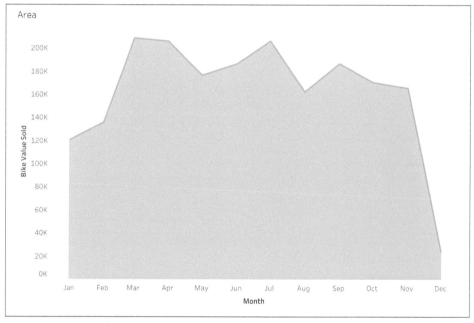

Figure 3-34. Area chart

Compared to Figure 3-26, which uses the same data in a line chart, Figure 3-34 makes it easier to quantify the value shown, as height is being used. The benefit of assessing the intensity of change over time isn't lost, though, as the top of the area chart acts like a line chart. This is harder to assess with bar charts.

 Area charts use the length of the shaded part of the chart against the axis to represent the data. Removing the zero line could easily mislead the audience. If you want to remove the zero line because the values are high and differ minimally, a line chart is likely to be a better choice.

When You Might Not Use Line Charts

Anytime ordinal data is being analyzed, a line chart is a good starting point—as long as you don't need to show too many categorical variables. Line charts are highly effective, but they can still be used poorly. Here are some situations when you might not want to use a line chart:

Your data is not ordinal.
 As you've seen, one reason line charts are so effective is that they leverage one of the strong pre-attentive attributes, 2D position. Line charts make it so easy to see a trend in the data that you need to be careful not to indicate a trend where there is none. The easiest way to do this is to *avoid using lines on nonordinal data*. For example, the bike types sold do not have a natural order, so the line should not link the three sales values together (Figure 3-35).

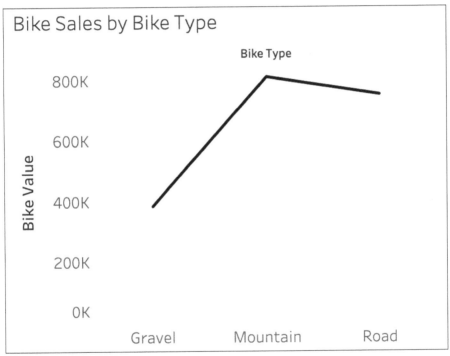

Figure 3-35. Poor use of a line chart

You're stacking too many categories.
 You've seen that too many lines on the same line chart can make the trend much harder to see. This can also happen with area charts. The members of a category are often shown as different-colored sections stacked on top of each other, known as a *stacked area chart* (Figure 3-36).

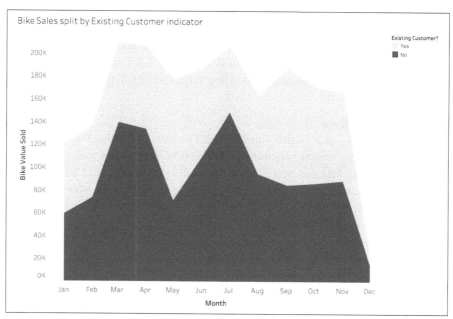

Figure 3-36. Stacked area chart

Like a stacked bar chart, the category that runs along the zero point of the axis can still be read clearly, with peaks and troughs quantified. But what about the area for existing customers? Can you see the change in sales to existing customers (the light-gray area)? I've been using area charts for many years, and I still can't.

To determine significant change among the categorical values, you often need to be able to see the areas change their trends: for example, one falls, and the other rises. In Figure 3-36, can you find the two months in which the divergence between the categorical values is the strongest? Come up with your own answer, and then look at Figure 3-37.

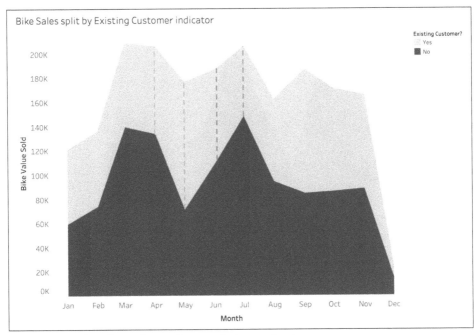

Figure 3-37. Identifying change in a stacked area chart

In this stacked area chart, the two months with the most significant divergence are June and July (red lines). If you didn't get this right, you're not alone. The red lines highlight an interesting trend that is tough for the audience to spot. Despite the overall height of the chart increasing, the level of bike value sold has fallen for existing customers. This is part of the challenge with using this chart type when looking for trends in the data.

I've also shown the opposite happening with blue dashed lines: existing customers' sales are increasing, but because of the steeper decline in new customers' sales, the light-gray area seems to fall. You can see differences, but it is challenging.

Should you ever use a stacked area chart? They are useful to show the contributions of various category members to the overall measure. When the different categorical variables results diverge, a stacked area chart can prove challenging for spotting those results. One option you might want to use is to unstack the areas so they both sit on the zero-baseline (Figure 3-38).

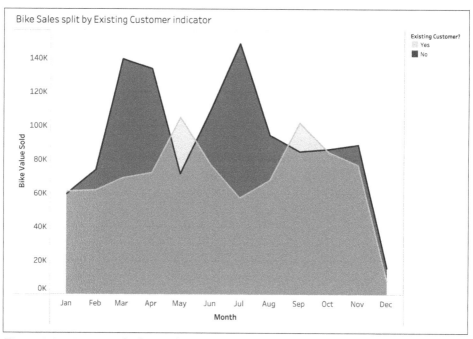

Figure 3-38. An unstacked area chart

Although the cumulative effect of a stacked area chart is lost through this technique, assessing the individual categories is easier. These charts can pose a challenge to design in a way that shows whether the areas are stacked or not. Also, as soon as multiple areas are stacked on top of each other, it can be difficult to differentiate one area from another as well as to follow the trend. Even with just two areas, following the trend of the area representing existing customers is tough.

As with any data visualization, the question is what message your audience will receive and how easily they'll be able to take it from the work. Area charts, when stacked, show the cumulative contribution of each category. Spotting the relative trends for each category can be a challenge with an area chart. If your question requires assessing those relative trends, using a line chart is probably the best approach.

Line Charts Summary Card

✔ Shows trends.

✔ Familiar chart to many.

✘ Using many categories over time can create complexity in the view, as lines cross each other.

✘ Stacked area charts can hide trends in the data, although they look effective at first glance.

Summary

Congratulations on becoming familiar with these fundamental methods of communicating with data. As you get used to creating effective tables and charts and supporting your points through other forms of communication, your audiences will find it much easier to interpret your messages.

Even though bar and line charts seem basic, your options are nearly infinite, as they can be designed in many ways. As they utilize the strongest of the pre-attentive attributes, you will likely use them frequently when communicating data. In the next chapter, we'll cover more chart types that enable you to communicate more clearly in various situations.

CHAPTER 4

Visualizing Data Differently

If you choose to just use tables, bar charts, and line charts, you will be able to fulfill most data communication needs. However, by using only these basic forms of communicating with data, you may restrict your analysis and risk boring your audience.

Using alternate chart types can help you find different messages in the data. Using two measures on a chart instead of one can show relationships you would not see otherwise. Comparing one metric directly to another means that you don't have to look at two separate charts and form the analysis in your head. And showing the individual data points, instead of aggregating values to show a summary metric, can uncover new trends in the data.

This chapter looks at some alternate charts and ways to use them.

Chart Types: Scatterplots

I'm going to have to mention this at the outset: I love scatterplots. There, I've said it. Of course, I'll give you an unbiased opinion, but I will also share why I think they are so powerful.

I love scatterplots because of their flexibility; they can cover several use cases. Many people also find them easy to interpret. The combination of multiple metrics is useful for analysis. Finally, scatterplots allow you to combine hundreds, if not thousands, of data points on a single chart, which can uncover stories in the data that might be lost if you filtered the data to fit on a single page. (Color can help here, highlighting the key data points.)

With so many options, let's ensure that you understand the fundamental building blocks of scatterplots.

How to Read Scatterplots

You can add a lot of detail to a scatterplot, but that doesn't mean you should. Too much detail can make the chart difficult to read.

We'll begin by looking at a simple scatterplot from our bike shop, Allchains. This scatterplot compares the sales value to profit for each of our bike types (Figure 4-1).

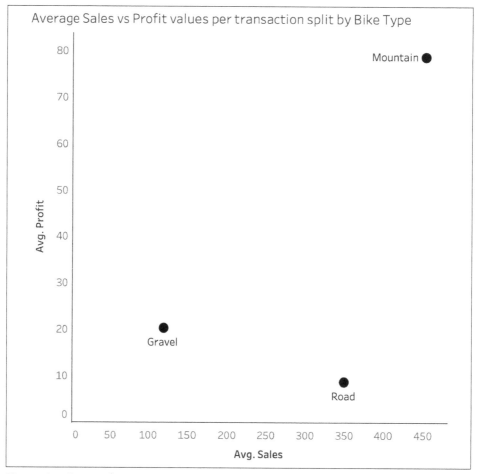

Figure 4-1. Scatterplot

Let's explore the elements of a scatterplot: multiple axes, plots, color, and shapes. We have lots of choices to make within each one.

Multiple axes

Scatterplots have two axes, rather than the singular axis we have seen on charts thus far (Figure 4-2). This is useful when you want to directly compare two metrics.

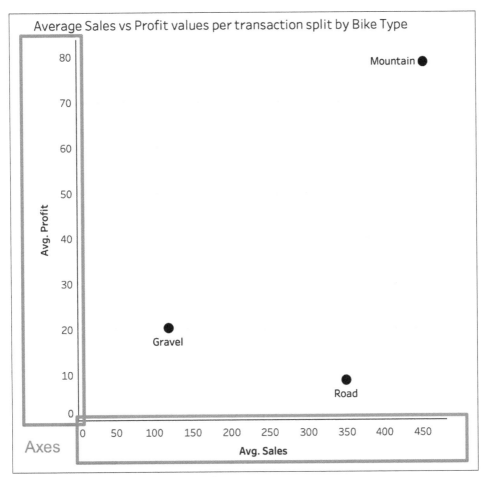

Figure 4-2. Multiple axes in a scatterplot

The axes create a 2D position against which you can compare the data point. By plotting multiple points, you will be able to find and analyze patterns among them. Also, the measure forming the x-axis should be the *independent variable*: the measure that is not reliant or driven by the y-axis. The y-axis's measure is therefore described as the *dependent variable*. In Figure 4-2, the sales value is plotted on the x-axis, since without any sales, no profit could be generated: profit is dependent on sales.

The patterns created by these plots are classified as *correlation patterns* (Figure 4-3). You may have heard of the false cause fallacy (*https://oreil.ly/quwEH*), or "correlation doesn't equal causation." It means that just because you find a strong correlation between two factors in your data, you can't assume that one factor is causing the other.

In this example, Allchains sells more bike helmets on sunny days. Can we assume that sunny days cause more sales of bike gear? Not necessarily. Personally, I ride my bike a lot more on sunnier days than on rainy ones—and most of those sunny days occur in summer. If more helmets are sold on sunny days, it's probably due to the overall warmer seasonal weather of summer, not the sunshine itself. After all, winter days can be sunny and icy at the same time, but I'm not going riding on those days!

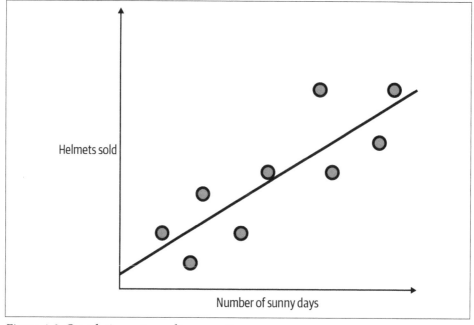

Figure 4-3. Correlation not equaling causation

Correlations can be grouped into numerous types; the main terms you will come across are positive and negative correlations and strong and weak correlations. In a *positive correlation*, as the measure forming the x-axis increases, so will the measure on the y-axis (Figure 4-4). We can demonstrate these with a *trend line* on our scatter-plot. In Figure 4-4, I've used orange to make the trend line really pop.

If the dependent variable reduces as the independent variable increases, you have a *negative correlation* (Figure 4-5). For example, if X is the number of times Allchains provides maintenance services to bikes, Y shows a reduction in the number of mechanical breakdowns for our customers in the following year.

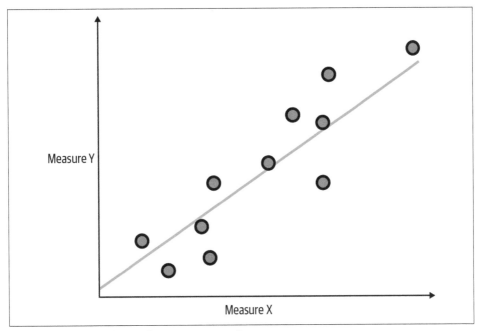

Figure 4-4. Scatterplot with a positive correlation

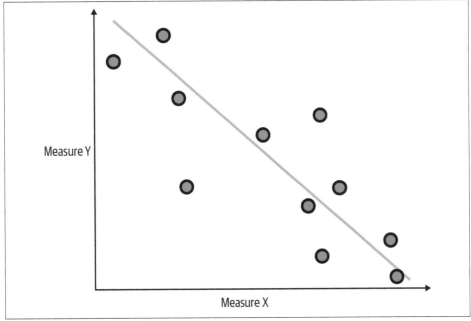

Figure 4-5. Scatterplot with a negative correlation

However, just being aware of the direction of the correlation isn't enough. How much attention you should pay to the relationship you have found depends on the strength of the relationship between the variables. A *strong correlation* means the data points are tightly packed around the trend line (Figure 4-6). The less distance between the data points and the line, the stronger the relationship is.

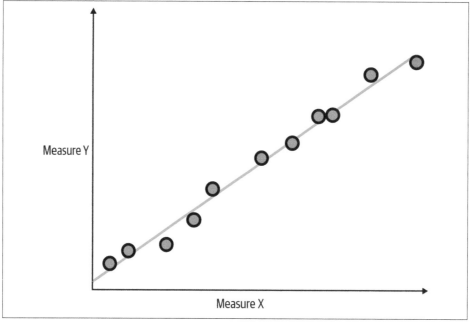

Figure 4-6. Scatterplot with a strong correlation

The farther the data points are from the trend line, the weaker the relationship is (Figure 4-7).

Not every scatterplot will show a correlation. If no relationship exists between the measure on the x-axis and the measure on the y-axis, the scatterplot has *no correlation*. That might look something like Figure 4-8.

Whether you draw the trend line or not, showing the patterns in scatterplots can be easier than explaining the relationship through words or other chart choices. Once you see the pattern in the data, it also becomes easier to spot the *outliers*, the data points that don't fit the pattern you've established. Investigating outliers can reveal issues in your organization that wouldn't be apparent otherwise.

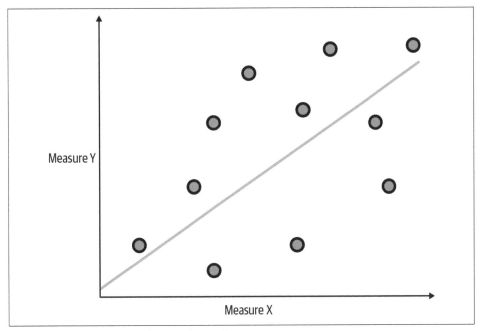

Figure 4-7. Scatterplot with a weak correlation

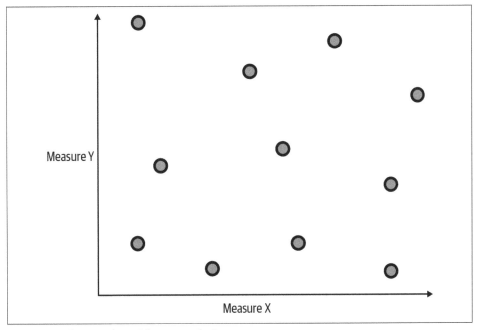

Figure 4-8. Scatterplot with no correlation

Plots

The superstars of the scatterplot are the actual data points. A *plot*, or a point on the scatterplot, represents two data points, one from the measure forming the x-axis and one from the y-axis (x, y).

When you have too few data points, as in Figure 4-1, drawing anything useful from the chart can be hard. The converse is *overplotting*: having so many data points makes it difficult to see what the chart is showing. Figure 4-9 is an example: it shows sales value and profit data from about 800 bike sales.

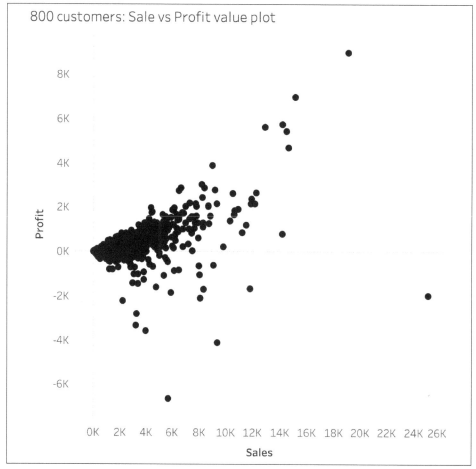

Figure 4-9. An example of overplotting on a scatterplot

Can you identify 800 distinct plots here? I can't. Many of the plots are right on top of each other. This technique helps when only a few plots are overlapping each other. In

Figure 4-9, though, the darkly shaded area is an amorphous mass of indistinguishable plots. This chart is not completely useless, however, since it shows the outliers.

If the question you are trying to answer requires individual data points, like analyzing all students in a school, you can adjust the chart style to help. By increasing the transparency of the plots, you can see where the overlapping points exist more clearly. In Figure 4-10, I've reduced the same plots to 30% of their original opacity.

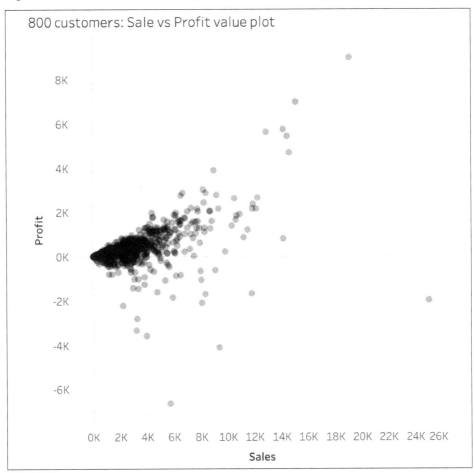

Figure 4-10. Increasing the transparency of the plots

Another technique to break up the amorphous blob is to add borders to the plots, to show the number of data points at least on the surface. In Figure 4-11, I have used a light-gray border to make the individual points "pop" off the page when they overlap.

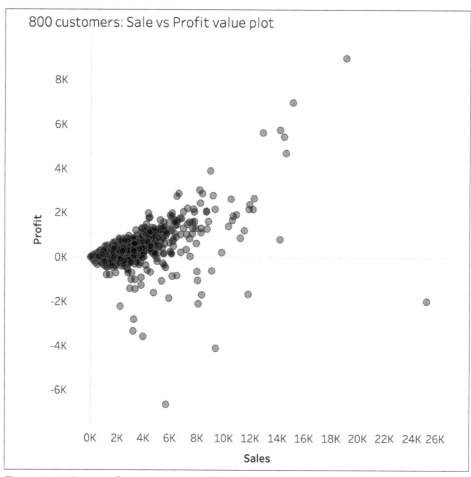

Figure 4-11. Increased transparency with borders

Sometimes it's difficult to get everything you need into a single, static chart. We'll explore this in Chapter 7 when we look at using multiple charts to show various aspects of the data rather than trying to squeeze all of them onto just one.

Color

One thing you may have noticed about our scatterplots so far is that it is difficult to see which point relates to what categorical value. The plots are often categorical values, like the headers on bar charts. Figure 4-12 adds color and a *color legend* (the small reference on the side of the chart that explains what each color represents).

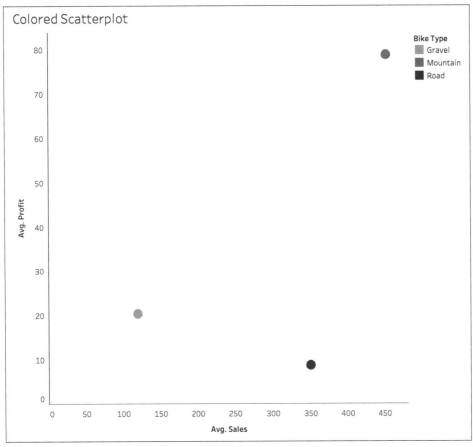

Figure 4-12. Colored scatterplot

Be careful not to overuse color on scatterplots: your audience probably won't remember what each of 20 colors represents, and forcing them to look back and forth to the legend too much adds more cognitive effort to understand your communication. As discussed in Chapter 1, one of our focuses is to *reduce* the cognitive effort required to understand the message you are sharing.

Most cultures already associate many meanings with colors, and you can use this to your advantage. If you use colors in ways that are already linked to familiar concepts, the audience will need to refer to the legend a lot less. If, for example, you are visualizing the sales of fruits and vegetables for a grocery store, using the hues related to the foods—such as red for strawberries and yellow for bananas—will make it easier to read. Using red for bananas and yellow for strawberries, on the other hand, would add to the cognitive load. Similarly, you might use black and red to indicate profit and loss, since "in the red" is a common idiom for loss-making companies, and "in the black" describes profitable ones. Wherever you can use the consumer's awareness of such factors, do so: it reduces the cognitive load. The term for this is using your audience's *psychological schema.*[1]

In Figure 4-12, I've intentionally used colors that look like mud for mountain bikes, stone for gravel bikes, and gray for road bikes. Using individual colors like this to represent categories is known as a *categorical* color palette.

If your plots represent an ordinal data field, you may wish to use a *sequential color palette.* This uses grades of shading of a single color, from light to dark, to represent a sequence of values (such as low to high or early to late). With 16 data points in Figure 4-13, it would be difficult to see whether later quarters have had higher sales and profits than earlier quarters. With a sequential color palette to indicate when in the year the sale occurred, it is at least possible to draw some conclusions from this chart. In this case, plots of higher sales and profits are all darker blues, showing they happened more recently.

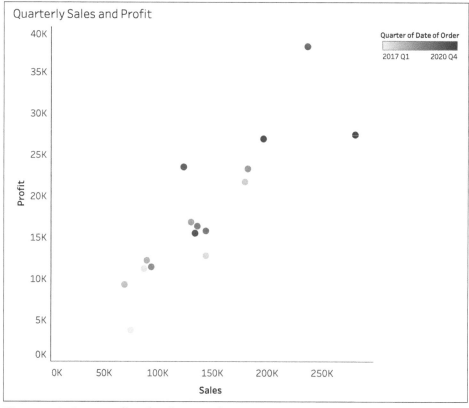

Figure 4-13. Sequentially colored scatterplot

---

1 Ryan Sleeper, *Practical Tableau* (Sebastopol, CA: O'Reilly, 2018), 495.

Another palette type you can use is a *diverging* color palette, which uses two colors to represent values that cross above or below a certain threshold, such as zero or a target. One color could represent underperformance, and another color could represent overperformance.

Finally, you can use color to make certain points stand out among all the others. In Figure 4-14, I have highlighted my own purchases at Allchains amid those of hundreds of other customers.

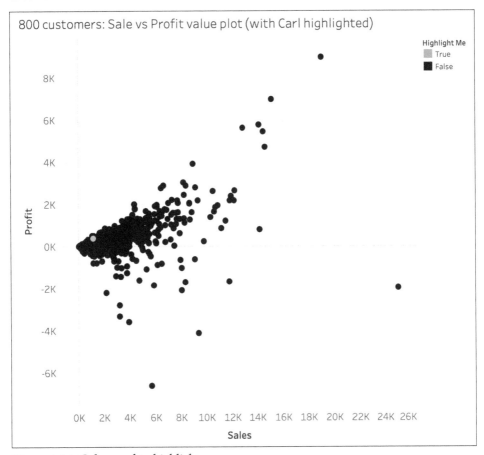

Figure 4-14. Color used to highlight

This is a simple technique that shares the message without losing the context of all other customers' behavior. Chapter 7 covers more about color.

Shapes

The plots on your scatterplot don't have to be circles. You can use shapes to represent categories, as shown in Figure 4-15.

Shape scatterplots are particularly useful for ensuring accessibility. You don't always know if all of your consumers can easily distinguish colors. What's commonly called *color blindness* is an inability to differentiate part of the color spectrum, and it can manifest differently in many visual disabilities.

Trade-offs exist here: shape is a pre-attentive attribute, just as color is, but color triggers pre-attentive responses more strongly. Interpreting shapes takes more cognitive work. To make this easier, you might use representative shapes where possible, or pair shapes with color. Chapter 5 discusses shapes further.

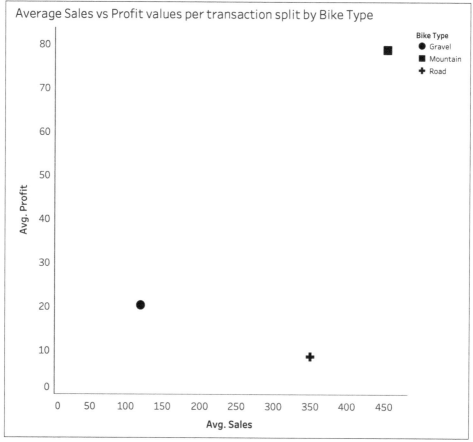

Figure 4-15. Shape scatterplot

How to Optimize Scatterplots

Scatterplots are a good chart option whenever you are comparing two measures, especially when one measure has (or might have) an impact on the other. Think of the sales and profit measures used throughout this chapter. As sales increase, you'd expect profits to increase, right? But that might not be the case! What if sales increase as our company lowers prices to undercut the competition? Or the cost of each sale might rise, forcing the company to spend more than usual to keep up with production volumes through extra sales.

The scatterplot may not always be able to tell you *why* something is happening, but it will nudge you in the right direction and make you ask the right questions. A few variants of scatterplots, discussed next, can prove useful in certain situations.

Small multiple scatterplots

As seen in "Multiple axes" on page 110, using trend lines in scatterplots can be a strong technique to communicate the relationship between two metrics. However, too many plots on a single scatterplot can hide significant or changing trends. One workaround is to break the single scatterplot into many scatterplots. You can shrink the charts and change the formatting to convey the message on a single page or screen.

The term *small multiples* refers to the trellis-like pattern of charts that is created when each chart is subdivided into categories. Small multiples can be formed from most forms of charts, but I find scatterplots particularly effective. In Figure 4-16, I have broken up a scatterplot by year (vertically) and quarter (horizontally) to compare quarterly trends clearly against each other. I also made formatting alterations to make the trend the clearest part of the chart. Highlighting the trend in color against a strong x- and y-axis makes the trends quickly comparable. The plots have had their transparency increased to still be visible but fade into the background.

In Figure 4-16, you can quickly see the negative correlation between sales and profit in Q1 2017: it is the only trend line that tracks downward as sales increase. The trend lines demonstrate that the most profit for sales occurred in Q1 2020, and this message is clearly shown by the small multiple scatterplot.

This technique is particularly useful when sharing static versions of the chart. However, even if you make an interactive version of your scatterplot that includes filtering to create each individual small multiple in turn, you may still want to consider using the small multiple option. The trellis shape of small multiples allow you to compare trends horizontally—in this case, quarter-on-quarter, and the same quarter in a different year.

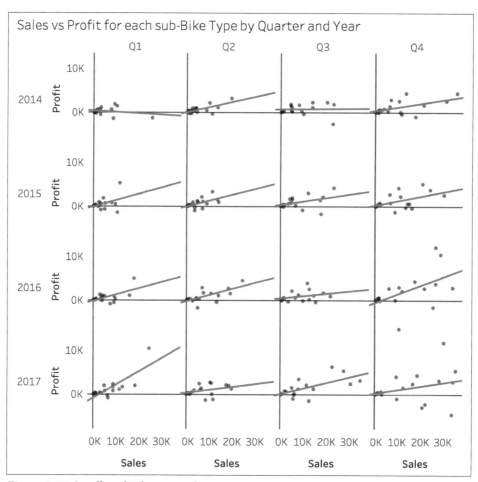

Figure 4-16. Small multiple scatterplots

Quadrant charts

Just like the small multiple scatterplot makes trends more apparent, a quadrant chart also simplifies the interpretation of the data in the scatterplot. *Quadrant charts* effectively dissect the scatterplot with reference lines linked to the axes. This clarity makes it much easier to determine next steps.

Take the scatterplot in Figure 4-17: with a weak correlation, how do you interpret the message in this chart? The x-axis shows sales, the y-axis represents profit, and each plot is a different category of each bike type.

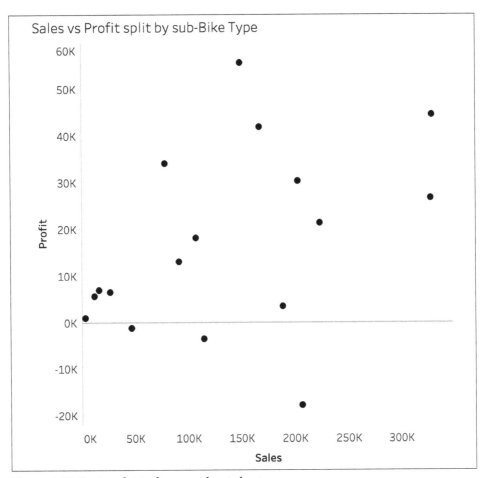

Figure 4-17. Scatterplot to form quadrant chart

It's difficult to see much in this scatterplot, as the data has very little grouping. *Grouping* is another pre-attentive attribute that helps your audience understand the messages in scatterplots.

You can add an average line of the mean for each metric for easier analysis. Figure 4-18 shows how using two average lines can divide the plots, creating a quadrant chart.

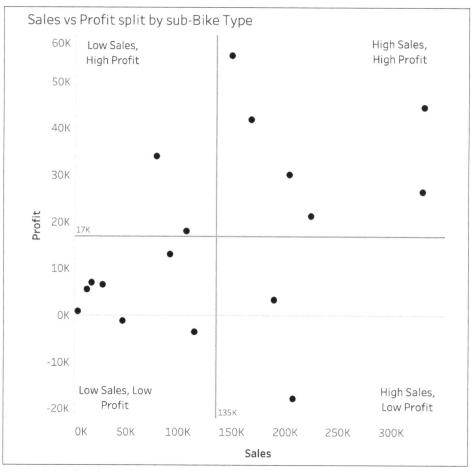

Figure 4-18. Quadrant chart

The quadrant chart's sections can now be easily described, allowing the reader to see which decisions might be made about each point. For example, the plots in the High Sales, High Profit section are very important for the store: they are generating high cash flow while still making money for the stores.

The Low Sales, High Profit section represents an opportunity for the business, by allowing us to understand why we've been able to generate such high value from such a meager amount of sales. If the company was able to sell more, would the profit increase in equal proportion, or would the sale price have to fall, eating into those profit margins, to sell more?

The High Sales, Low Profit section poses an interesting challenge: these bike types are selling well, yet the company can't seem to generate profit from them. This is a drain on resources. Should Allchains stop selling bikes in these categories and focus on other types?

The Low Sales, Low Profit section should be monitored to determine whether there is any chance for growth or whether it's time to stop selling these items.

Quadrant charts are useful for showing the data points clearly while also simplifying the analysis. They are particularly useful for audiences that are not used to using scatterplots to interpret data.

When to Avoid Scatterplots

Sometimes scatterplots make the message harder to understand. You might see these used often, but I recommend staying away if too many colors would be required or if you need to add a third measure. Let me show you why.

Too many colors

In the words of my colleague Luke Stoughton, using too many colors on a scatterplot can look like you've "squashed a unicorn." It's hard to disagree with him when I've seen too many charts that look like Figure 4-19.

A potential alternative is *interactive* charting. With interactive charting, the user can instead hover over each plot to see what it represents—so you don't need the splatter of unicorn colors. (The challenges of interactivity are discussed more deeply in Chapter 8.) To mitigate this issue, it is much easier to highlight just a single plot, or at worst a few key points to highlight, as shown previously in Figure 4-14.

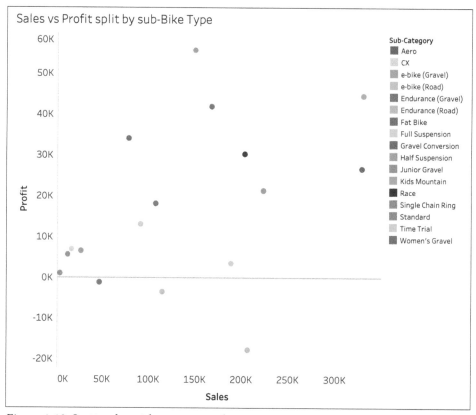

Figure 4-19. Scatterplot with too many colors

Nondifferentiable color palettes

Scatterplots are so effective at showing two measures that you might be tempted to add a third, to demonstrate an additional relationship in the data. Figure 4-20 adds a new dimension, average discount, to the plots used as the base for the quadrant chart in Figure 4-17.

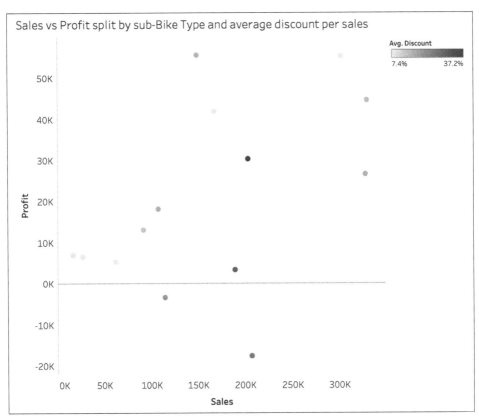

Figure 4-20. Scatterplot with sequential color palette

No, it's not your eyes—it's just tough to distinguish the average discounts shown by the blue gradient in the sequential color palette. You can probably spot the highest average discount, but trying to separate the lower third of the points is difficult. This chart would be much better if Discount was added as a set of bands, to allow the user to draw clearer distinctions among the levels of discount (Figure 4-21).

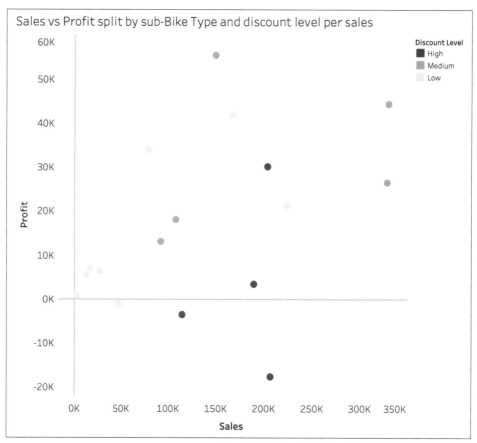

Figure 4-21. Scatterplot with banded color

When users have to pick out only a few shades of the same color, it is much easier for them to form a relationship between color and meaning. In addition, to clarify the relationship between the two metrics shown as the axes of the scatterplot, each axis should be the same length. Any distortion of their length can change how the relationships and correlations are perceived.

Again, don't try to squeeze too much into a single chart. If you find yourself struggling to see the colors clearly, try creating a separate chart instead, or consider using interactive charting.

Chart Types: Maps

Maps grab readers' attention. Children are taught how to read maps from an early age, so they're usually a familiar form of data communication, which can make absorbing the message much simpler. This section presents a few key aspects of visualizing data with maps, including how to determine whether a map is your best option.

How to Read Maps

If you really think about it, maps are a form of scatterplot. Think of longitude and latitude as the x-axis and y-axis of a map, respectively.

Understanding this allows us to take advantage of a pre-attentive attribute we looked at Chapter 1: grouping. A cluster of points on a map, such as incidences of natural events like meteor strikes, can show areas of activity; the absence of points then shows a lack of the same activity.

If your data shows human activity, though, you will frequently find data points clustering in population-dense areas, like major cities, as Figure 4-22 shows. In these cases, clustering can obscure the stories in your data.

Figure 4-22 is a *symbol map*: a symbol (in this case, a circle) is placed on the map to represent the data point for that location.

Figure 4-22. Symbol map showing sales by city from our bike stores across the United States

Size and shape

Data is visualized in a symbol map by sizing the shape to represent the values of the measure; the larger the shape, the higher the value. This makes it easy to see the largest values, but the lowest values, being small, often fade into the background. If you need to identify low values (such as markets with underperforming sales), this can be a problem. Symbol maps are great when you need to show the reader the range of values quickly, but since readers can't measure the precise size of the shape, these maps aren't good for showing exact differences.

Here's another potential problem with symbol maps. The clusters in the top-right corner of the map in Figure 4-22 make it look like sales are especially high in the Northeastern US. In reality, many major cities are much closer together in that area than in other parts of the US, skewing the display.

Symbol maps can use any shape to represent the data point. With circles, the center of the shape often represents the location of the data point. However, Google's inverted drip shape (discussed more in Chapter 5 with Figure 5-21) uses the point at the bottom of the shape to indicate a precise location. Make sure the shape you choose clearly demonstrates the location.

Choropleth maps and color

You can also use color on a symbol map, but I recommend giving it a different meaning from the shape. Using two forms of pre-attentive attributes for the same information, such as both color and size for the same aggregation of the same measure, is called *double encoding*. It can hide other stories within the data by overexaggerating the main message and is best avoided.

Sequential or diverging palettes are frequently used with maps to show how a range of values corresponds with the shape of a geographical element. These maps are called *choropleth maps*. Figure 4-23 uses data that's similar to the data in Figure 4-22, this time at the state level rather than city level, but the resulting effect is very different. Here, greater values are shown as more intensely colored. However, as with the symbol map, trying to distinguish between anything but the highest and lowest values in a choropleth map is challenging.

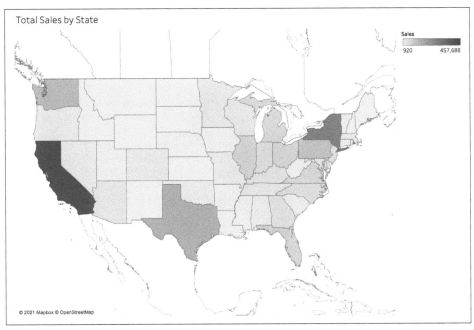

Figure 4-23. Choropleth map

How to Optimize Maps

You might have noticed that the maps I have used so far all have a minimal background. Removing as much unnecessary detail as possible allows the data to stand out. Remember, your data visualization is the primary purpose of the map. Think carefully about adding and removing roads, rivers, or borders, based on the purpose of the visualization. If you strike the correct balance between background and data, your audience will get a clear view of the data points as well as of their geographical context.

As you saw with shapes, with choropleth maps, variation in the size of the mark can affect how your message is perceived. Small locations, like the states in Figure 4-23, are hard to see; large areas are likely to draw your audience's attention even if they are not the intended focus. Take Figure 4-24, which shows bike saddle sales for each state east of the Mississippi.

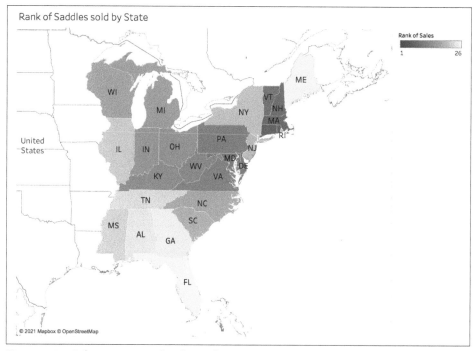

Figure 4-24. Bike accessory sales shown by a choropleth map

Quick, which state sells the most saddles?

Could you tell that it's Rhode Island (RI)? What, you mean you can't? You're not alone. I think most people would struggle to draw that conclusion from this map, since Rhode Island is so small. Your eyes are likely drawn to the larger states, since they are bigger blocks of the same color.

How can we fix this? Visualizing the same data as a symbol map instead makes even the smallest state stand out (Figure 4-25). The symbols in Figure 4-25 have to remain rather small so they don't overlap each other and hide any smaller symbols behind. Tile maps might be a better approach in this situation.

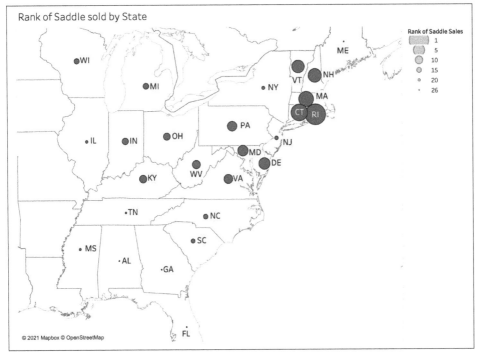

Figure 4-25. Better symbol map

Tile maps

Tile maps offer equal space for each entity (in this case, each state) but in a layout similar to a regular map: for example, Maine is still at the top near Vermont and New Hampshire. Figure 4-26 shows the profit for Allchains bike stores in each state.

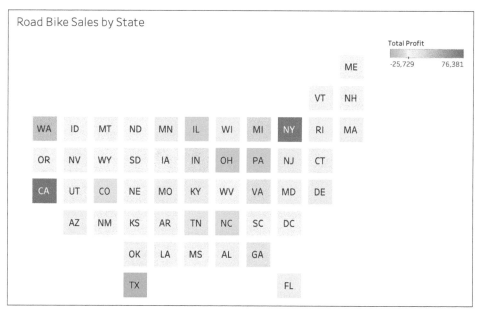

Figure 4-26. Tile map of profit by state

Data thresholds

Choropleth maps can be more useful than symbol maps when you want to visualize data that crosses a threshold, like zero or a target. Being able to see what falls above and below the threshold is likely to be the key aspect of the visualization. The shapes of a symbol map are sized on a linear scale. When data goes past the threshold tipping point, like zero, it becomes difficult to make that linear scale make sense.

Take, for example, profit and loss for Allchains stores in each state. We have three ways to visualize profit and loss by using the size of symbols (Figure 4-27):

- Small symbols represent the most negative values; large symbols represent the most positive values.

- Large symbols represent the most negative values; small symbols represent the most positive values.

- Large symbols represent the most negative values, tapering to small as the values cross the zero point; the symbols then become larger along with the positive values.

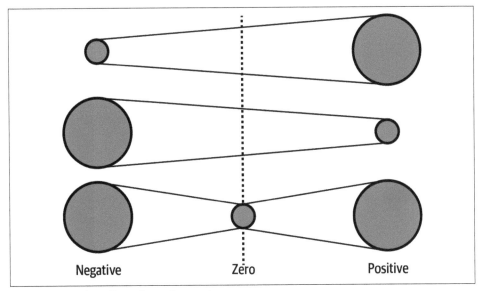

Figure 4-27. The effect of a scale crossing zero

None of these three options is very effective.

Option 1 in Figure 4-27 could hide the largest negative values. The most profitable items would dominate the map, but the items making the largest loss wouldn't be visible. This might a great choice if you wanted to put a positive spin on the numbers, but it wouldn't be a clear representation of the data.

If you reverse the sizing from largest to smallest as the values go from the largest negative number to the largest positive, as in option 2, you give the opposite impression. Neither helps the audience identify the biggest winners *and* losers to make a balanced judgment.

Option 3 creates that balance, but it's completely confusing: here, size does not tell the reader whether a number is positive or negative. You *could* add color to show whether the value is positive or negative, but that would be double encoding.

A choropleth chart would be much more effective at highlighting the largest positive and negative values. Figure 4-28 uses a diverging color palette to differentiate negative and positive values.

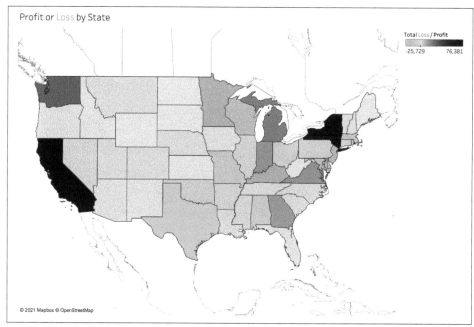

Figure 4-28. Choropleth map using a diverging color scale to represent state profit

The darker or more intense the color of each state, the more significant the profit or loss. In Figure 4-28, your eyes can easily find the highest profits (in black) or the largest losses (in red, to use the audience's psychological schema for accounting colors), on the same chart. You can see that no states have losses to the same extent as others have profits.

Density and hex bin maps

As internet-connected devices and trackers create ever-larger geographical data sets, a common mapping challenge is to visualize many thousands of data points on the same map. This brings us back to the problem of overplotting, as discussed in "How to Read Scatterplots" on page 110.

Let's look at taxi-journey data from New York City. If we were trying to work out where to open an Allchains store, we might look for places where we know lots of people are starting journeys and offer an alternative transportation option. But in Manhattan, taxis are so common that there are nearly 800,000 data points. On the map in Figure 4-29, even if each data point is shrunk to a dot, they cluster into a mass the shape of Manhattan.

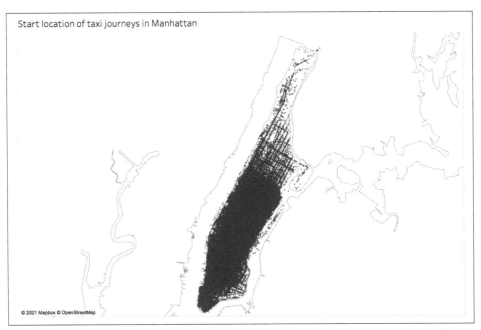

Start location of taxi journeys in Manhattan

© 2021 Mapbox © OpenStreetMap

Figure 4-29. Map of hundreds of thousands of taxi-journey starting points in Manhattan

Two alternative map types can assist us in solving the dilemma of overplotting. The first is a *density map*, which accounts for plots that are close to or on top of each other. Density maps use a sequential color palette: the higher the number of plots, the lighter and brighter the color.

In Figure 4-30, the density map shows a higher level of activity in midtown Manhattan. Lower-value plots are blurred out almost entirely, as on the northern tip of the island. This data story was also present in Figure 4-29, but the style of map made it impossible to see.

Another alternative is a *hex bin map*. The same Manhattan taxi-journey data is shown as a hex bin map in Figure 4-31. This style of map counts the number of points found in a certain area. Those areas are often shown as hexagons that tessellate closely together, like a honeycomb. A sequential color palette shows the range of values captured in each area, with darker colors representing the highest values.

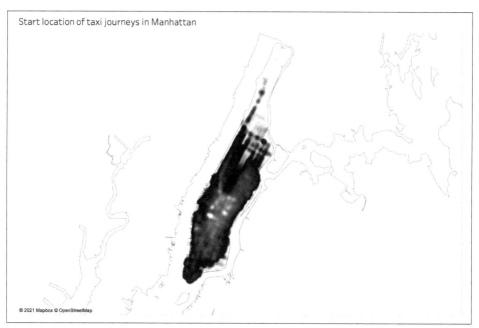

Figure 4-30. Density map using the same data as in Figure 4-29

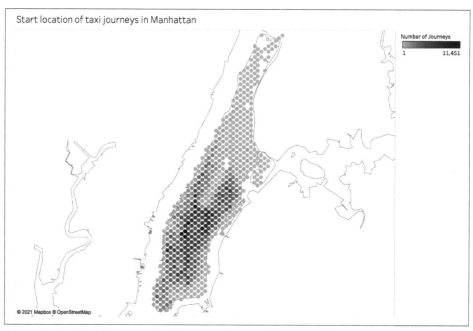

Figure 4-31. Hex bin map using the same data as in Figure 4-29

The density map and the hex bin map tell a similar story: they both suggest locating the store in Midtown, somewhere between 30th and 54th Streets. With the hex bin map, though, it's a little easier to identify more precisely where the bike store location should be.

Lots of map styles are available to choose from, but depending on the message you are conveying, the amount of data you have, and the scale of the geographical areas, some styles are more useful than others.

When to Avoid Maps

Sometimes you should shy away from certain styles of maps, but other times maps just aren't the answer. Let's look at a few such situations.

If you are analyzing data that contains geographic fields, don't assume that you necessarily need a map. Let's go back to the Allchains accessories sales shown in Figure 4-25. What if the data is converted to a rank, with 1 indicating the highest sales. How would multiple ranks for different products be shown? The original data set has three values for each state, showing how each ranks in terms of three products.

Would three maps be the best way to show this data? Certainly not: that would take up a lot of space, unless you want to make each state tiny. This option would also require the audience to remember the rank of each state to compare the variances.

Instead, you could use a *parallel coordinates plot* to show the change in rank among the various measures (Figure 4-32).

In a *parallel coordinates chart*, the rank of a categorical member (in this case, state) determines where the mark is made against a vertical axis. The left-to-right flow of the chart in Figure 4-32 shows changes in rank for various products. (If the change is shown over time, the chart is called a *bump chart*.) In this example, I've added a highlight to show that Rhode Island is ranked first in two categories of accessories but not for pedals. The lines connecting the circles representing each state can show changes among the categories. A steep rise or fall is a strong indication of change in the rank, drawing your attention more than a change in color saturation on a map ever would.

When you have multiple measures or categories, it's tempting to try to squeeze too much onto a single map. Figure 4-33 demonstrates how confusing multiple measures can be on a map.

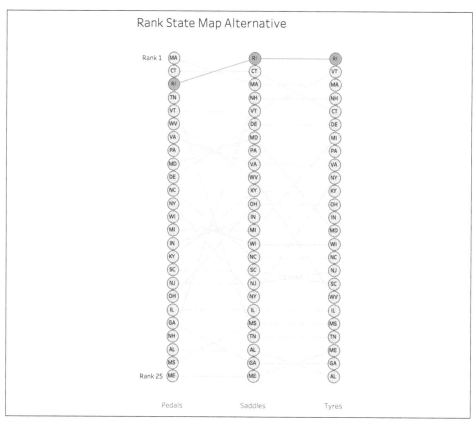

Figure 4-32. A parallel coordinates chart as an alternative to a map

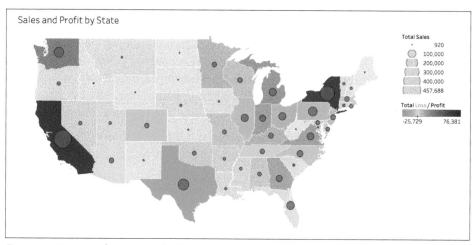

Figure 4-33. Map showing multiple measures

This map isn't impossible to read, but it isn't easy. Including two metrics forces us to use two mark types: profit as the choropleth and total sales as sized shapes. The message in Figure 4-33 is not clear. As an alternative, a scatterplot is a great method to communicate two measures split up by a category (Figure 4-34).

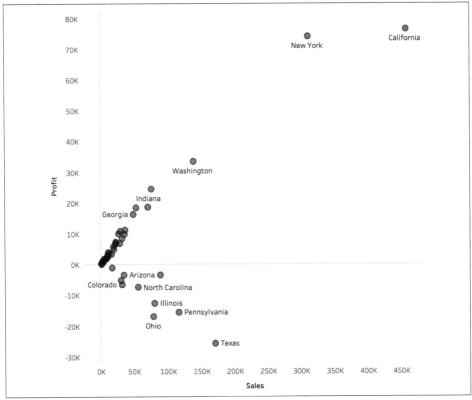

Figure 4-34. Scatterplot showing sales compared to profit for each state

Occasionally, you might need to use multiple categories as well as multiple measures. I've seen too many maps like Figure 4-35, with multiple chart types layered on top of the base map. This might seem extreme since the chart types used together are so different, but this kind of juxtaposition is common. Resist the temptation!

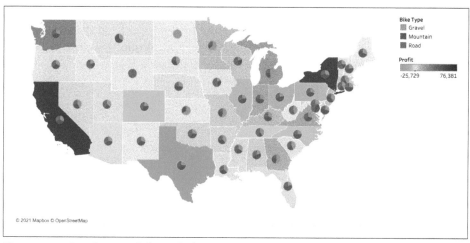

Figure 4-35. Pie chart and choropleth map

In Chapter 7, I will demonstrate why it is much easier to create multiple charts than to encode too much information into one chart.

Maps Summary Card

✔ Leverages the consumer's general knowledge about locations.

✔ Draws the attention of readers.

✘ Can be easily overloaded with too much detail.

✘ Lots of detail in the background map can obscure the data points.

✘ Not a good method for visualizing measure for comparison.

Chart Types: Part-to-Whole

Anytime you visualize a total value, people will ask you how that value breaks down: what are its constituent parts? The breakdown of the value will be a categorical data field, which can be a challenge to visualize, especially in a static form. We have multiple part-to-whole chart types to choose from (including bar charts), but this section looks at two of the most common: pie charts and treemaps.

How to Read Part-to-Whole Charts

Like maps, pie charts are covered early in most schoolchildren's education and are common in news media, so audiences find them familiar.

Sections

The circle, or *pie*, represents the total of the measure being analyzed. A category's individual contribution to the overall measure is demonstrated by the colored-in section of the circle. In Figure 4-36, wheel sales at Allchains, represented by purple, makes up a quarter of the overall amount, so a quarter of the circle is colored purple. All of the other categories have been combined to form the Everything Else group.

If you have more than two sections, the largest section should start at the top of the circle unless the other section is the grouping of all other categorical variables. Assume that the reader's eye will rotate clockwise.

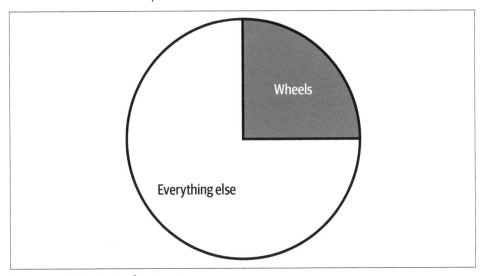

Figure 4-36. Basic pie chart sections

Additional categories follow clockwise from the end of the initial section. In Figure 4-37, brake sales make up an eighth of the overall total, so the colored-in section covers 12.5% of the circle. The highlighted categories should be shown in order from highest to lowest value, for easier interpretation.

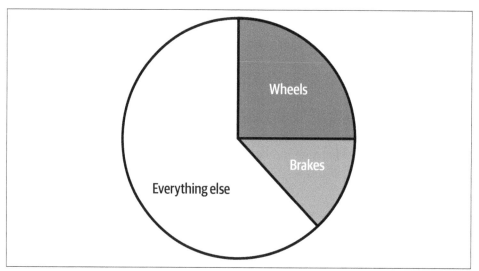

Figure 4-37. Basic pie chart with additional category

Angles

Pie charts are all about angles—and you'll notice angles don't appear in the list of pre-attentive attributes. Size does appear in that list, however, and that is what we are comparing when we look at various sections of the pie chart. Humans aren't great at assessing angles precisely, but that doesn't make pie charts impossible to read. Learning to read analog clock faces from an early age helps. I've found people can visually determine a quarter, half, or three-quarters of a circle. Starting that section at the top point of the circle makes it easier still to recognize, as in Figure 4-38.

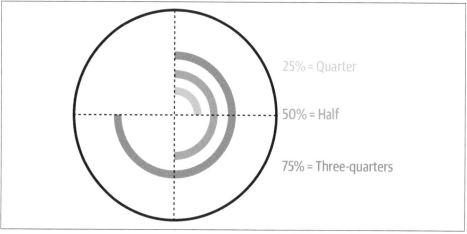

Figure 4-38. Reading pie chart angles

When those sections don't start at the top of the circle and are offset by another category, they become much harder to interpret. For example, in Figure 4-39, wheel sales is the same size as in Figures 4-36 and 4-37 but in a different position. If I hadn't told you it was the same size, would you have been sure?

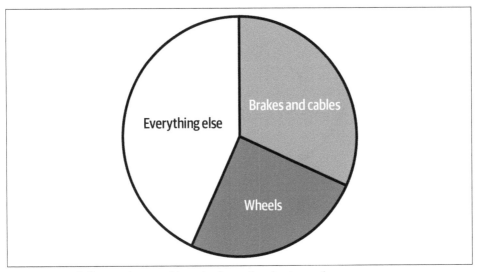

Figure 4-39. Offset sections making pie charts harder to read

Labels

One element that is more frequently shown on a pie chart than others we have featured so far is labels. The *labels* can show the name of the category, the value, and/or the percentage of the total represented by the section (Figure 4-40).

Labels can help the user more precisely interpret the values being shown. However, take care to avoid having your audience see the chart as secondary to the label.

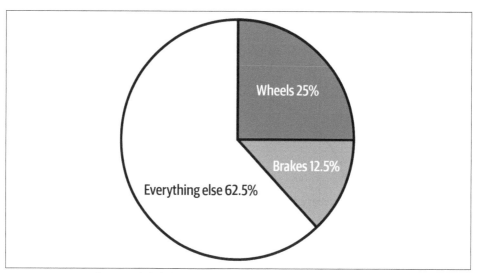

Figure 4-40. Pie chart with labels

Donut charts

Another variant of the pie chart, often seen in news media, is called a *donut chart*—named for the hole in the middle (Figure 4-41).

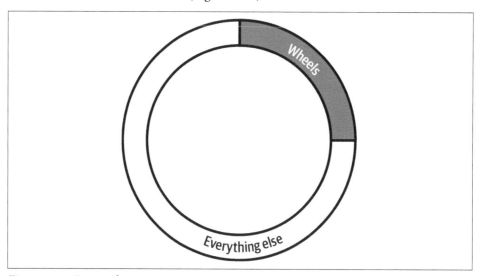

Figure 4-41. Donut chart

Donut charts offer more whitespace, which you know is important when designing communications. However, the missing middle section can make it slightly harder to determine the angle of the data section, and therefore the value it represents.

Treemaps

Instead of using angles to represent values, *treemaps* use area, shown as a rectangle. The treemap in Figure 4-42 shows the same values as the first pie chart in this section (Figure 4-36).

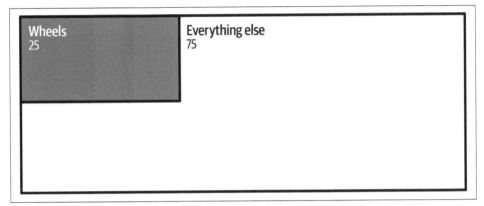

Figure 4-42. Basic treemap

Researchers debate (*https://oreil.ly/zt2tm*) what is easier to interpret, but personally I find it easier to interpret an area with squares or rectangles than with the angles or circular sections of pie charts.

Labels are helpful for donut charts, especially if one section is being highlighted. You can get creative with the blank middle of the donut. You might use it to show the value of the highlighted section and any other information you'd like to share about it (Figure 4-43). You could add small percentage change indicators or even sparklines (covered in Chapter 3) to give additional context.

In a treemap, you can place labels on top of the sections representing each categorical member (Figure 4-44). If the area of the treemap section is too small for a label, that section probably doesn't warrant the attention the label would draw.

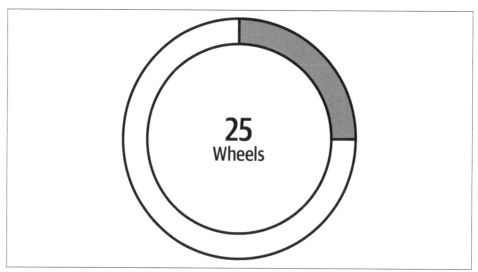

Figure 4-43. Donut chart with labels

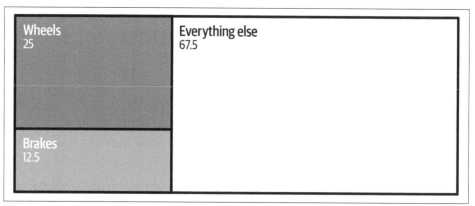

Figure 4-44. Treemap with multiple sections and labels

When to Use Part-to-Whole Charts

Pie charts work well only when you have few categorical variables. Two variables are ideal. When visualizing the sales of the road bike type, for example, I've chosen to group the other bike types' sales to simplify the view for the reader (Figure 4-45).

The message is much clearer than it would be if I showed every bike type, even with labels (Figure 4-46). The other sections detract focus from the message, which is about the percentage of road bike sales.

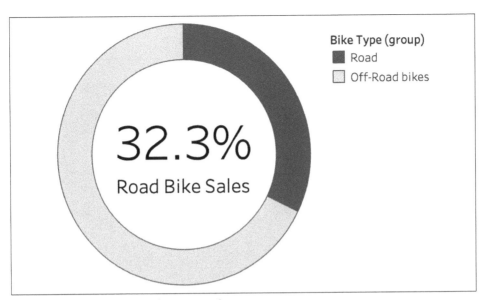

Figure 4-45. Simple donut chart example

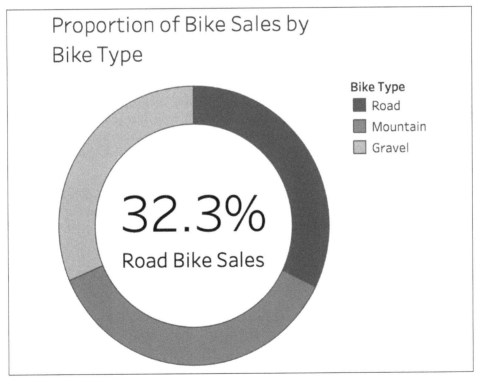

Figure 4-46. Donut chart with multiple segments

When using multiple segments, treemaps offer more space for labels and make it easier to compare sections with similar values (Figure 4-47).

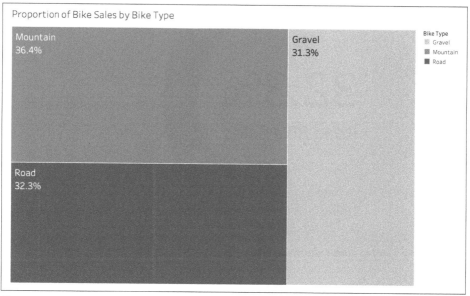

Figure 4-47. Basic treemap with multiple segments

I've also found treemaps particularly useful when showing *long-tailed distributions of data*, in which each category has lots of small contributions. For example, if you sell a large range of products, it can be useful to compare the value of sales from each of the products. In Figure 4-48, I've broken down each bike type by manufacturers, showing all of the brands sold through the bike store over time. This creates a lot of subdivisions, but you can still draw conclusions: for example, the top five manufacturers of gravel bikes make up about half the sales of that bike type.

Most business intelligence tools used to build treemaps will automatically present the largest value at the top left, so it is easier to rank the sales visually and see how many values it takes to make up significant proportions of the overall or segment value.

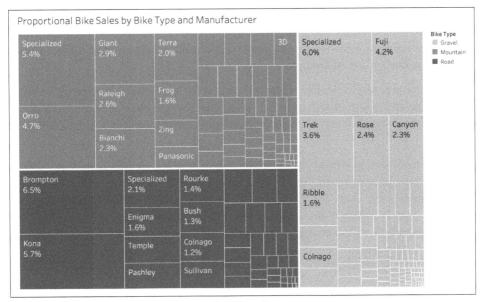

Figure 4-48. Treemap showing long-tailed distribution

When to Avoid Part-to-Whole Charts

To use part-to-whole charts, you need a whole. If the chart doesn't visualize the total amount of the value, this is not the right chart type to use. In Figure 4-49, the gravel bike type has been removed. Depending on the title, this chart might lead you to believe that the stores sell only two bike types.

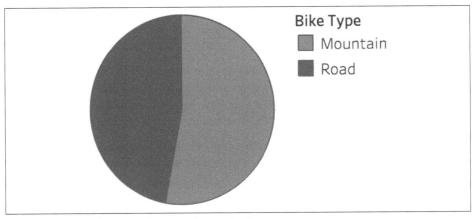

Figure 4-49. Pie chart not showing the total sales

Survey results are often displayed in pie charts, but this can get complicated. If the survey allows respondents to give multiple answers, for example, the relationship is not one of separate, nonoverlapping parts to a whole, and doesn't add up to 100%. A pie chart is likely to be misleading.

In addition, you can't visualize the total amount in a pie chart or treemap—even if you include all the potential categories—if any members of the category have negative values. There is no clear way to visualize a negative contribution as a proportion of an area.

Finally, avoid part-to-whole charts when demonstrating change over time. If you want to show how proportions of bike sales change by type over time, and you've already made a pie chart for a single year, you might be tempted to replicate a pie chart per year. In Figure 4-50, because of the changing proportions of each bike type, it is challenging to see the change in proportion of sales over time.

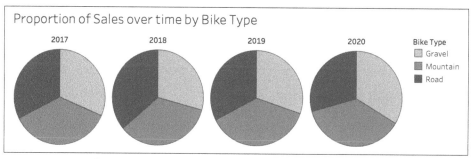

Figure 4-50. Pie charts demonstrating change over time

Using pie charts to show change over time can also hide the *absolute* change in the overall amount the pie chart represents. It takes a lot of labeling to make pie charts communicate this information clearly.

A line chart would be a much clearer way to communicate the change in percentage of total sales each bike type achieved each year. Figure 4-51 shows exactly this relationship, but it's much easier to see the changing patterns across the years. In the pie charts, the mountain bike type angle didn't have a consistent starting point.

Too many categorical variables will make any pie chart difficult to read. The same detail that works well in the treemap in Figure 4-48 becomes unreadable in pie chart form, as seen in Figure 4-52.

Finally, you should not use part-to-whole charts to show any measure that may go beyond 100%, like progress toward (and hopefully beyond) a sales target.

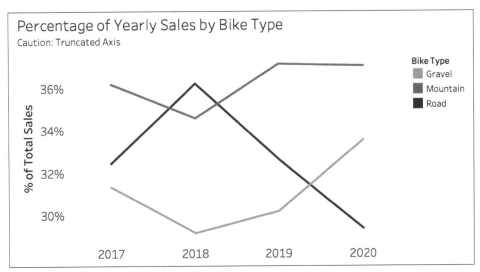

Figure 4-51. Percentage of yearly sales line chart

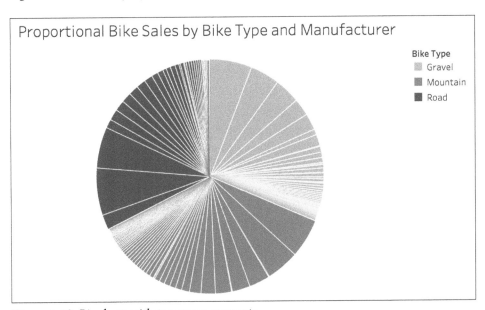

Figure 4-52. Pie chart with too many segments

Part-to-Whole Charts Summary Card

✔ Highlights a single category contribution to the overall.

✔ Use treemaps to visualize higher numbers of categorical variables.

✘ Avoid pie charts when analyzing change over time.

✘ You can't use negative values in a part-to-whole chart.

Summary

In language, the more words you know, the more options you have when making your point. In data visualization, chart types are your vocabulary.

While less-common charts do gain the attention of the audience because of their unique aesthetics, they are also more challenging to interpret, since they're less familiar and don't always use pre-attentive attributes as effectively.

This chapter has covered just a small portion of the alternate chart types available. Once you've grasped the basics, you can explore even more. The primary reason to use alternate chart types is that they're eye-catching. You've seen throughout this book that a big part of the battle is making your data visualizations stand out to audiences' eyes and in their memories.

Figure 4-53 shows a visualization inspired by my colleague Joe Kernaghan that offers an alternate way to show a company's income statement. This chart, called a Sankey chart, shows the various profit types included in Tesla's 2020 financial statements.

The chart doesn't offer precise information but does show how the various amounts fit together. It also educates readers about how these amounts form the company's gross and operating profit. Its unusual shape also grabs people's attention, so it works well as a chart.

When you go beyond basic bar charts and start exploring the wide variety of chart types, you'll make active choices about how you communicate different types of information. The more experience you gain in making those choices, the better your visualizations will be.

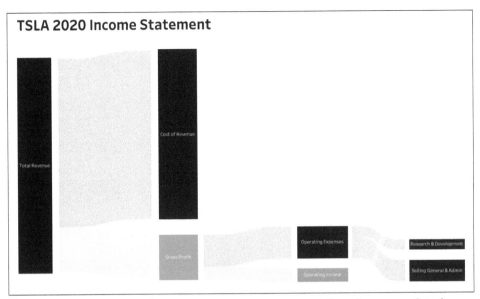

Figure 4-53. Sankey chart for TSLA 2020 income statement (based on a template from the Flerlage Twins (https://oreil.ly/0VRll))

CHAPTER 5

Visual Elements

In the previous two chapters, we focused on understanding charts. Charts are ultimately the main focus of any communication with data. However, if you concentrate only on deciding the type of chart you want to use, you'll miss the opportunity to communicate your point to your audience even more clearly through the use of visual elements. *Visual elements*—such as color, size, and shape—make a massive difference to your audience's ability to interpret your charts, which I focus on more deeply here.

As mentioned in previous chapters, color, size, and shape are three pre-attentive attributes. Knowing how to use each of these aspects of your data visualizations will improve the overall aesthetic of your work as well as clarify your communication's message.

Aside from pre-attentive attributes, this chapter also looks at the use of multiple axes when deciding on efficient visual elements. When looking at visualizing multiple measures on the same chart, the only communication style we've shown thus far is the scatterplot. In this chapter, we'll look at another option, *dual-axis charts*, which make you think about the type of mark you are using as well as the range of values each axis covers.

Any element that can help focus the audience's attention, or highlight a key set of data points, will help dramatically to communicate your message. Reference lines and reference bands are a key element that can amplify your message, but their use goes beyond just a simple line or band. We'll also take a look at box-and-whisker plots, a more advanced use of reference lines and bands that can quickly show complex trends in your data.

The final element we'll look at is totals. Adding a total to your chart may be an easy step to take when working with any data tool, but totals pose challenges when using color or length to visualize their value compared to their constituent parts. In this section, you will gain a better understanding of your options.

By the end of this chapter, you will be comfortable with making great charts that communicate your message clearly and even allow your message to jump off the page.

Color

I've mentioned color several times in the previous chapters. Both hue and intensity are pre-attentive attributes that have shown up in our examples so far. As a reminder, *hue* refers to the type of color, and *intensity* refers to the color's level of purity.

Types of Color Palettes

You will frequently encounter three types of color palettes as you view data communications or create your own: hue, sequential, and diverging. The pre-attentive attribute of intensity is covered by sequential and diverging color.

This section will help you pick the right colors to communicate your data to your audience. The number of colors you are planning to use changes how you might use them:

Three or more colors
> You will be selecting a palette of different hues.

Two colors
> You might still be creating a color palette of two hues or can use a diverging color palette to show progression from one color to the other.

One color
> You can use a single hue on its own, but you may want to show different levels of intensity of that color by using a sequential color palette.

Let's look at each of these color options in turn to see how you might best utilize them when communicating with data.

Hue

Each color you see is a different *hue*. Color is determined by the wavelength that light possesses as it is reflected off an object. The primary use of hue in data visualization is to show different values in a categorical data field. Depending on the chart type and the medium the chart is used in (for example, print or digital), hue is either an essential addition or a factor adding confusion.

For example, when using a scatterplot to show various categorical variables, hue is a clear way to show which plot refers to which variable. Using the soap retailer Chin &

Beards Suds Co. as our example, Figure 5-1 shows how a separate color can be used to easily identify each store on the chart. Figure 5-1 shows the stores from the Southern region.

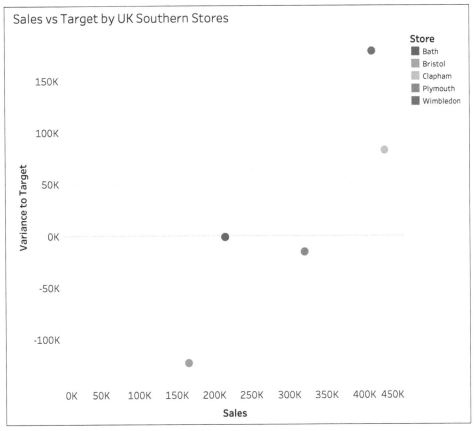

Figure 5-1. Hue per categorical variable

However, as soon as you approach 10 or more colors, recognizing which plot is which becomes much harder. Adding in sales for the rest of the UK's stores and France's stores makes assessing the scatterplot much harder (Figure 5-2). Using so many hues enables you to see which store performs the best against their target while also comparing their sales to other stores. However, the cognitive effort required to compare store locations to each other is significant.

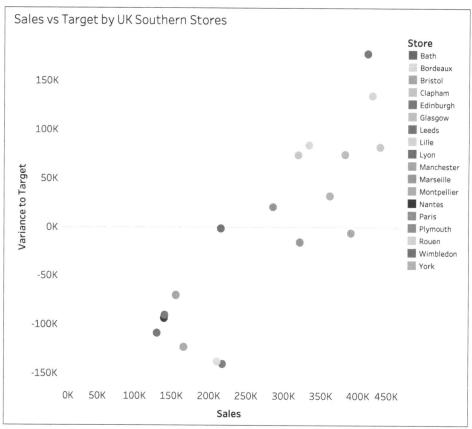

Figure 5-2. Too many colors makes analysis harder

If I asked whether France or the UK's stores did better against their targets, would you know the answer? Possibly not. This is where the use of hue depends on the question you're asking. To answer this question, let's instead use one hue per country, with different levels of intensity for each color to represent the different stores (Figure 5-3). This makes the data much easier to interpret as to the balance between the French and UK stores meeting their targets.

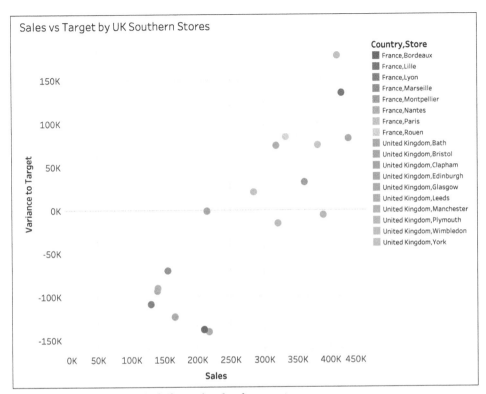

Figure 5-3. Two hues with differing levels of saturation

While it isn't easy to differentiate the store locations, it is easy to pick apart the stores from the two countries. The UK has more stores in the top-right corner of the scatterplot, as we see more orange plots.

Using hue to show differences isn't always required, though. If charts segment variables by category, you don't need different hues, because they add to cognitive load rather than reduce it. Figure 5-4 shows exactly that effect: the colors distract from the consumer's ability to compare the length of the bars, rather than improving it.

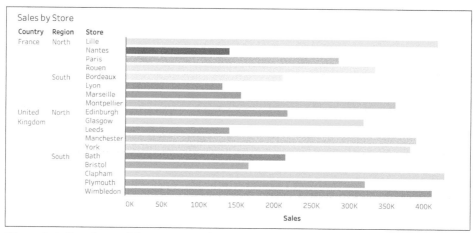

Figure 5-4. Bar chart with too many colors

Removing the colors makes the chart much easier to read and consume (Figure 5-5), as the colors are no longer distracting the audience's attention.

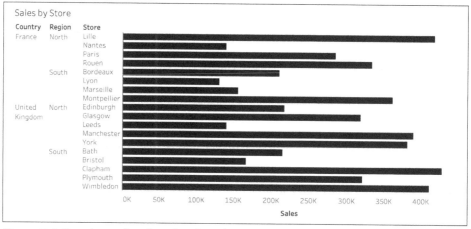

Figure 5-5. Bar chart after the colors have been removed

If you wanted to highlight a specific store, you could, by coloring just one bar and not the others. You saw this approach in Figure 4-14.

Intensity: Sequential color palettes

The other pre-attentive attribute that utilizes color is intensity. *Intensity* is shown through two methods: sequential and diverging color sets. These two techniques differ in the number of hues involved.

A *sequential* color scheme involves only one color, and the data points are shown based on the level of lightness. The lower the value, the more transparent the plot will be. Darker, more intense colors represent plots with higher values (Figure 5-6).

0   100

Figure 5-6. A sequential color palette

Sequential colors allow the audience to quickly determine at a glance whether values are high or low without even needing to check the position of a mark against the axis. A sequential color palette allows an additional measure to be shown on a chart that wouldn't be possible otherwise.

Figure 5-7 shows an example from an airline: not only is the total sales value shown on the x-axis, but quantity is shown using sequential color. This helps you see that as the number of tickets sold increases, so does the overall sales for each of the ticket classes per quarter. Without the use of the sequential color palette, an additional chart would need to be used to show this behavior.

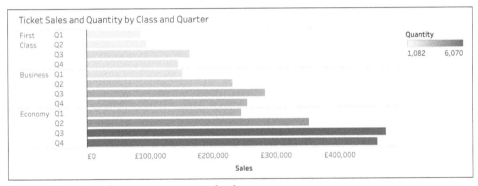

Figure 5-7. A bar chart using sequential colors

Intensity: Diverging color palettes

A *diverging* color scheme uses two colors that go from one to the other. The lowest values in the data set represent one color on the far left, and the color on the far right represents the highest values. As the values near the crossover point to the other color, they normally fade to a white or light gray (Figure 5-8).

-100   0   100

Figure 5-8. A diverging color palette

As you can see in Figure 5-8, diverging palettes pop off the page more than sequential palettes, since you are using two bold colors. However, it's important that you choose which palette type to use based on the data being visualized.

For example, a diverging color palette is likely the best option when a measure crosses either the zero point or a target, as a different color represents values either above or below that level. This color change allows the audience to clearly see when the threshold has been crossed. As the value diverges further from the threshold, the audience will be able to use the color as an indicator for the level of progression beyond that point.

Being able to quickly determine whether something is above or below a target allows you to focus on what actions you might want to occur to ensure that the target can be met. Using a sequential palette to show a range of values that cross zero isn't effective, because it does not have a clear visual indicator to demonstrate whether the value is above or below that key point (as Figure 5-9 demonstrates).

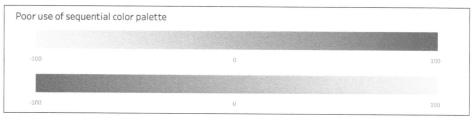

Figure 5-9. Poor use of sequential color palettes

Choosing the "Right" Color

By picking the right type of color palette for the communication, your audience will be able to effectively decode your message. To help them decode it faster, you can choose colors that are related to the subject of the communication.

Theme

You can use the theme of the data to help highlight the key messages and focus the audience's attention. Let's go through some examples to highlight which colors could be used to highlight your data:

Black/Red
> Financial terminology refers to "in the black" for being profitable and "in the red" for a loss. Red and black can also be used to represent deaths. The context of the communication provides a lot of information about whether the color scheme represents deaths or company profits.

Green

Can highlight ecological benefits or, in the US, can represent money because of the color of the currency.

Red/Blue

Can represent heat and cold, respectively. This color range isn't just about visualizing temperatures. "Hot" can represent growth or intensity, and "cool" can represent cooling off or falling values.

Yellow

Can represent daytime or hours of sunlight.

Green/Yellow/Red

Can represent colors of a traffic light meaning go, caution, and stop. Most organizations have adopted this color scheme to represent good, OK, and bad.

Your audience is likely to have a thematic color palette in mind when they access your work, based on the reasons they are accessing the work in the first place.

Let's consider the color red in a cultural context. The difference between Eastern and Western cultures is significant when it comes to the color red. As I've mentioned, red is used in many organizations to signal *stop*. This is not the case in Eastern cultures, where red is used to signal luck, happiness, and joy. The stark difference between the two interpretations means you need to consider your audience and its likely association with the color before making your choice.

Limitations to the effectiveness of color

Although society has common associations to certain colors, those colors are not always perceived by all members of that society in the same way. *Color blindness* is the common name for the condition in which cones at the back of the eye don't respond to certain colors. The condition is normally genetic but affects enough people that you should consider your design choices when communicating with data via color. About 1 in 12 men and 1 in 200 women have one form or another of color blindness (*https://oreil.ly/SIZco*).

You should be aware of the various types of color blindness so you can test that your communications are making the right impact:

Deuteranomaly

Reduced sensitivity to green light

Protanomaly

Reduced sensitivity to red light

Tritanomaly

Reduced sensitivity to blue light

Deuteranomaly is the most common form of color blindness, while tritanomaly is the rarest. Protanomaly and deuteranomaly often combine to form red-green color blindness, which presents as the inability to distinguish between colors that have red or green shades, like oranges and browns as well as red and green.

Many websites will let you upload an image to show how your visualization might affect those with color blindness. Even in a visualization intentionally using contrasting colors suitable for color-blind users, major differences remain in what you'd see if you had color blindness or not (Figure 5-10). Running tests against the most common forms of color blindness is a must if you are sharing your work with the public.

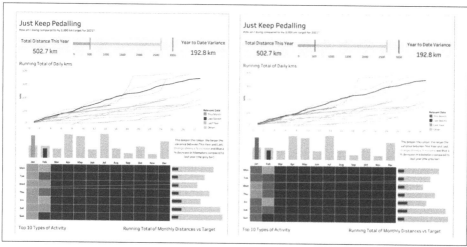

Figure 5-10. Using a protanopia test (https://oreil.ly/xYLv2) on a visualization (left) to see the effects (right) for a reduction in perception of red light

Avoiding Unnecessary Use of Color: Double Encoding

Though color can greatly benefit a visualization, you've already seen examples in this book where the overuse of color can weaken your communication and make the audience have to think hard about what each color represents. Figures 5-2 and 5-4 are common examples you will likely come across as you help others start to make clearer communications with data. But beyond simple overuse of color, what other unnecessary use of color will you commonly encounter?

Double encoding is the use of two attributes (such as color and size) to indicate the same metric, or category, on a chart. Why would you want to do this, you may ask? Well, there are a few reasons, but none of them justify the use of the technique.

One place you might consider double encoding is to make your communications more accessible to people with color blindness. Ideally, though, you should be selecting a color palette that removes the risk that someone who is color blind might not see the message in the data clearly.

First, double encoding is used to make a chart look more interesting than just another chart of that type. Using Chin & Beard Suds Co. international sales data, a simple sales bar chart can be given extra flair by adding color to the sales metric too (Figure 5-11).

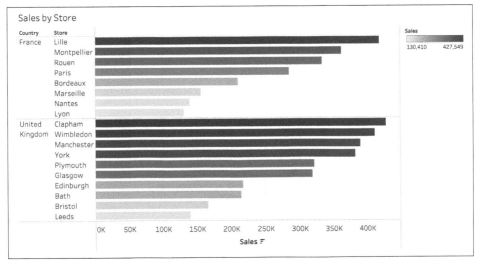

Figure 5-11. Double-encoded bar chart

If this chart wasn't ordered, the message would not be as clear. When you first look at Figure 5-12, you notice it uses the same data and color as Figure 5-11 but is much harder to read. When I first look at the image, I still take a moment to try to determine that the color of the bars is actually a second representation of sales.

I see examples of the two previous charts frequently, from both less-experienced and more-experienced data workers. Forcing your audience to ask the question of what the color represents is wasted cognitive effort. Yes, you could use a color legend on the chart, but just removing the use of color makes the chart much easier to read, as Figure 5-13 shows.

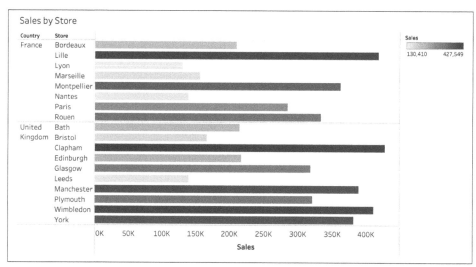

Figure 5-12. Unsorted double-encoded bar chart

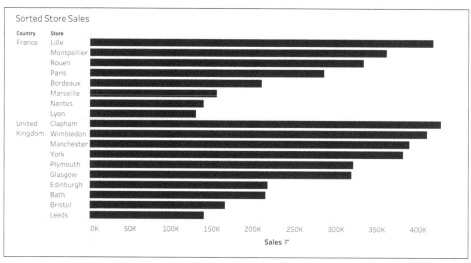

Figure 5-13. Figure 5-11 without double encoding

Another reason to avoid using double encoding is that it overexemplifies the message within the data. Let's use the same sales data as the previous bar charts but show the data on a symbol map instead (Figure 5-14). Not only does the darker color pop off the map, but the size of the circles also indicates the sales values.

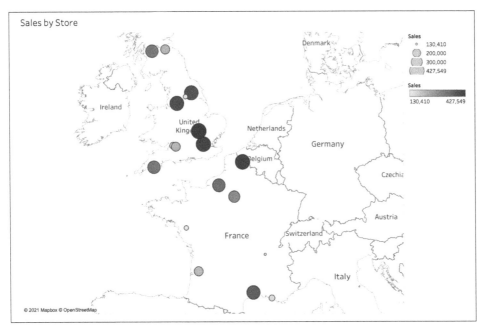

Figure 5-14. Example of double encoding overexaggerating the message

You have already seen how dark, bold colors attract the audience's attention, so by coupling that factor with a larger circle, you are overexaggerating the message within the data. Our role as communicator of data is to display the message clearly but not be overtly biased in what we are sharing based on the techniques we use.

Creating unbiased data visualizations is a widely covered subject that's difficult to achieve because every choice you are making when communicating with data can introduce bias into your work. Potential biasing decisions include where to source data from, what data points to include, how to represent the data, and how to title the work. By removing a clear bias like double encoding, you are giving the audience a fairer representation of the data.

Color Summary Card

✔ People see color differently, so test with different audiences to avoid accessibility issues.

✖ Less is more when using color.

✖ Avoid double encoding.

Size and Shape

Size and shape are inadvertently linked because whenever you use one, you need to think about the other too. Both are pre-attentive attributes that can have a significant impact on the way your audience will view the message you are communicating, especially when you use them in tandem.

Both attributes require careful use to avoid confusing the audience or adding heavy amounts of cognitive effort to interpret what you are presenting to them. As we've seen in "Chart Types: Maps" on page 131, it isn't easy to decode the difference in size of two marks into a value. In Chapter 4, I showed the impact of crossing a target or the zero point of an axis if a measure might return either positive or negative values. Let's take this idea further and see whether you can determine the values of each of the following circles representing store sales (Figure 5-15). Can you tell me how much the sales were in Leeds compared to Lille? What about Paris compared to Plymouth?

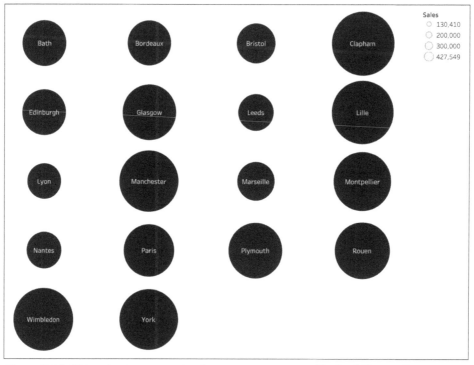

Figure 5-15. Using size to represent values — can you quantify the difference?

Don't worry; it's not your analytical skills that are weak. It's the chart choice that is causing the issues here. If you want to check your answer, feel free to use Figure 5-5, which is much easier to interpret. I have used Tableau to build this chart, so it's a standard way to represent size before anyone gets out any rulers and starts to measure the specific circles and work on some trigonometric calculations.

The Leeds store's sales were 140,157, while the Lille store's sales were 417,544, making a difference of 277,387. The difference is nearly double the Leeds store's sales, but did you get that from this chart? I didn't. The difference between Plymouth and Paris is much less but still difficult to determine exactly how much. Plymouth had sales of 320,850, and Paris had 284,686, making a difference of 36,164, or just over 10% of Plymouth's sales. Again, this is difficult to calculate just by looking at the chart.

This isn't to say size is not a suitable charting technique to show the story in your data. You can use the technique to draw the audience's attention to either end of the size spectrum but not much else. It's important to allow the audience to focus on what they want to understand most about the data being presented, and this chart doesn't allow for the range of investigation we've seen from a bar chart or scatterplot.

Figure 5-15 can be adapted to fit many other questions if the values are added to the image too (Figure 5-16). But because the chart doesn't utilize strong pre-attentive attributes, it's quite limited even with the labels.

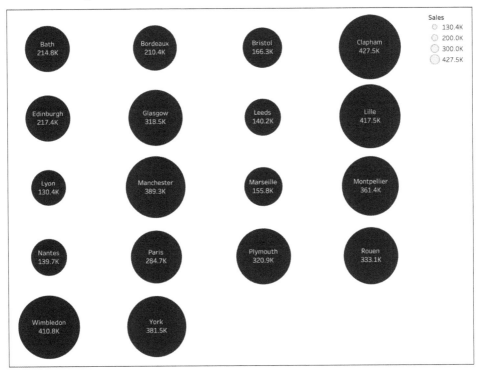

Figure 5-16. Size with added labels to assist interpretation

Themed Charts

Using shapes in your data communications is another way to help set a theme for the audience. If you are sharing data about countries, using a flag will set the theme. For sports teams, team logos allow the audience to know which data point represents their favorite team and how they compare to their competitors. When using shapes to visualize data, you suddenly have almost infinite options for the charts you can create and the themes you can use.

Scatterplots

In Chapter 4, we explored the challenge of referencing individual plots back to the categorical variables they represent. If you use a different color or arbitrary shape for each variable, it puts a significant burden on the audience to look up each in turn, to understand what each plot represents. You can use shapes to simplify this lookup process by using icons that represent each variable.

In Figure 5-17, I used the bike store accessories to show the sales performance against a target. Each item is easily identifiable, but a legend is included if the image isn't telltale enough.

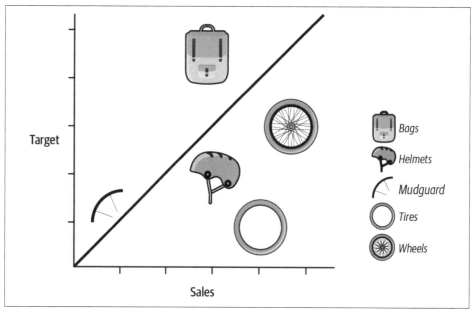

Figure 5-17. Shapes used to represent categorical variables

As in other scatterplots, relating each shape to the variable it represents can be challenging if too many shapes are present on just one chart or if the plots are densely clustered. Yet, reducing the cognitive effort is a useful step to take while also giving the work a different look and feel compared to a standard scatterplot. Using shapes in a scatterplot leads to some challenges, but I'll get to those shortly.

Unit charts

Shapes can be used to show a measure in the form of a unit chart. *Unit charts* can use a single shape to represent a set value. In Figure 5-18, the bicycle shape represents 100 bikes being sold. Unit charts work in a similar way to a bar chart, as we notice the length of the shapes end to end first to make comparison easier among the categorical variables.

To ensure that the images are clear, you need to either round the values to the unit size of the shape or use partial shapes. To infer the actual value, your audience will need to count the number of shapes they see.

Figure 5-18. Unit chart showing bike sales

By forcing the consumer to count, you are not creating a visual representation that is very quick to find values in, but it does direct your audience to an answer. Tooltips, discussed further in Chapter 6, can provide clarity on providing your audience with exact answers when using an interactive format.

Size and Shape Challenges

Using shapes and their sizes is not always an easy option for communicating with data. Let's go through some of the common challenges you will come across so you can avoid making mistakes.

Scaling

As we've seen in Figure 5-15, size is a difficult metric to use to interpret the amount represented in a visualization. It is also difficult to articulate to your audience what you are actually showing with the data point via height, width, or area. Figure 5-19 shows the effect of scaling if the value 1 increases to 2. If you are not clear to your audience about what the size represents, they won't know whether the shape on the right of the figure represents 2 or 4.

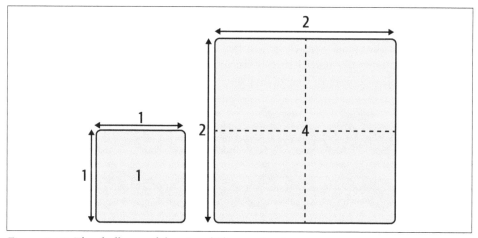

Figure 5-19. The challenge of showing difference by size

It's important to ensure that the audience clearly understands how you are scaling the shapes. A legend is a common way to guide them.

Different devices

With modern technology, audiences are consuming data-based communications on a range of devices. The varying sizes of screens and methods to interact with those devices can pose a challenge when communicating with shapes. Chapter 6 covers how we interact with charts and how the device type dictates the types of interactions to offer the audience.

When viewing shapes, the size of the screen is the most significant factor. Being able to differentiate each shape can be a lot harder on smaller screens. The range of sizes will also be much harder to determine when the overall scale of the image is much smaller on a mobile screen compared to a desktop's screen.

Unsquare shapes

You can also change the size of the shapes to represent a third measure that isn't shown by either axes. This choice can pose an additional challenge to interpret beyond what is covered in Figure 5-15. The size of customized icons can be complex to calculate, as the shape isn't always square. You must take care as to how the data visualization tool will determine what size to make the shape compared to how your audience might read it.

Figure 5-20 shows an example: even if you make each icon consistently 30 pixels × 30 pixels, the blank space around the sides of the backpack logo won't be factored into the sizing as seen by the audience. Imagine that the square border isn't present in this image; you would be left guessing whether the area of the shape being used to represent the measure was square or not. This is where a size legend becomes important, and I cover those in Chapter 6.

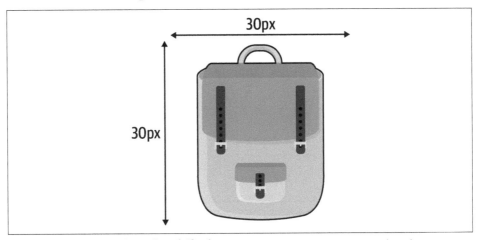

Figure 5-20. Custom shape but difficult to use to represent a measure using size

The same sizing issue is true for a common shape that is used to demonstrate location. The inverted droplet shape can be a challenge to use, as many mapping tools will plot the middle of the icon over the top of the exact point, rather than the tip of the droplet. Figure 5-21 demonstrates this issue.

Depending on the data visualization software you use, you may need to alter where the point of the droplet sits within the image. To fix this effect, you need to change the middle of the shape to be the bottom of the droplet. To do this, you can pad the same length of the shape onto the bottom of the image, as illustrated in Figure 5-22.

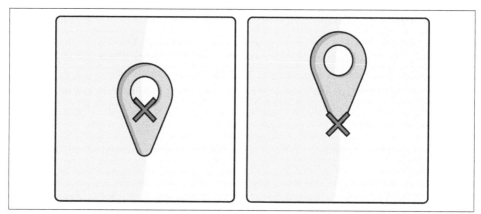

Figure 5-21. The incorrect use of the droplet icon (left) and the correct use (right)

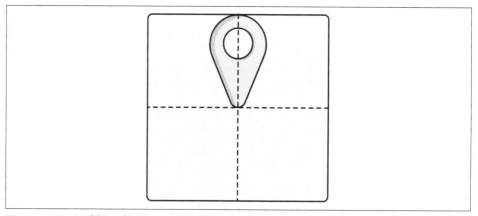

Figure 5-22. Padding the shape so it will be positioned correctly

Limitation of uses

You should use shape and size to represent only certain data types. For example, categorical variables should be differentiated by only shape but not size. There is no series of shapes that would clearly show different values of a measure. As seen in this section already, size can represent differing values of a measure, but the shape would have to remain consistent throughout.

Likewise, size would be a poor representation of different categorical variables. You could scale a shape to represent ordinal data, with the earliest mark being the smallest and the latest mark being the largest. Whether the audience would find this method of communication intuitive is a significant question that would require testing.

In summary, there are some intuitive use cases for using shapes to represent the variables themselves, to save the audience from having to look up which variable is represented by each shape. However, limitations do exist when comparing a measure based on size of differing shapes. Size can be useful to direct the user to find the data points of interest but is difficult to compare accurately. Used carefully, size and shape can be an effective communication method, but you must use caution and consideration to achieve the desired effect. You are likely to use color rather than size or shape much more frequently when communicating with data or receiving communications from others.

Size and Shape Summary Card

✔ Great for setting a theme.

✔ Unit charts are a nice change from a bar chart but are limited.

✖ Tough to accurately compare differences in size of shapes.

Multiple Axes

When I think about *multiple-axis charts*, I instantly think of scatterplots, closely followed by maps. Another common feature of charts that we'll explore is the use of multiple axes for the same axis orientation (for example, two y-axes). These charts are commonly called *dual-axis* charts.

You might question why I'm recommending using multiple axes on the same chart when I've been preaching simplification whenever possible. The reason I find dual-axis charts useful is the ability to overlay two layers of data on top of one another for direct comparison.

Let's take a common example of a dual-axis chart that compares one metric against the other by using two mark types to show the data on the page. Figure 5-23 shows the direct comparison between the profit generated by the sales in each month. In this example, sales is represented by an area chart to act as background information for the profit value that is shown as a line chart. As profit is the focus of the chart, I've made it a more intense color.

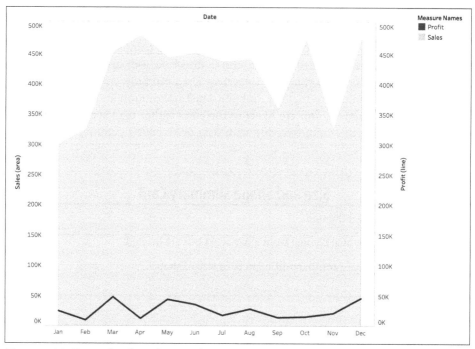

Figure 5-23. Example of synchronized axes

You've already seen a couple of ways this chart could be visualized differently, but let's quickly assess why this method is a useful way to communicate the data. The first option is to use two separate charts—one to show sales, the other to show profit. Although you'd see the overall pattern between the two charts, the cognitive effort to spot divergence of the trends is quite significant when they are displayed separately. By relying on your audience to spot this trend on their own, you are risking them not seeing this clearly and missing the message entirely.

The second option is to use the two measures as a scatterplot. The challenge with this approach is how to show the trend between the months and not just the overall distribution of the plots. To show the trend, we could link up the plots sequentially with a *connected scatterplot*, as shown in Figure 5-24. The line linking up all the plots can be a tangled mess, so this technique doesn't work for every data set. I'd always recommend you try to follow the path created by the line to see how much cognitive effort you have to expend in interpreting the chart. If you struggle to follow the path yourself, it is unlikely your audience will be able to, and therefore, you should use a different technique to visualize the data.

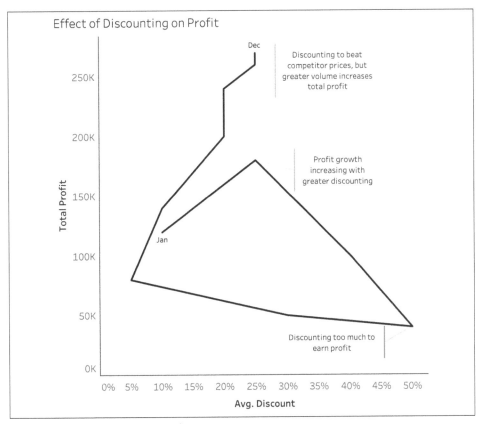

Figure 5-24. Connected scatterplot

One choice you need to make when using two measures in a dual-axis chart is whether to synchronize the axes together or leave them to be independent of one another. *Synchronizing axes* means making sure the scales on the axes are identical to one another. When deciding which approach to take, I look to the question I am trying to answer to decide which is the best approach:

Choose to synchronize

> If you are answering a question about what proportion of one metric is driven by another, you will need to synchronize the axes (Figure 5-23). For example, student attendance to a lecture should always be a proportion of the number of people taking that course. This ensures that the visual represents the direct comparison of the two on the same scale.

Leave the metrics independent

> If you want to find any common trends between the metrics, you could leave the axes unsynchronized. The metrics will overlap more, but you won't be able to tell the proportion that one metric makes up of the other (Figure 5-25).

The best practice approach is to synchronize axes to ensure that your audience is clear on what proportion of sales forms the profits made. However, a data-literate audience will carefully check the axes, and any titles shown can use the unsynchronized axes to form different views of the data.

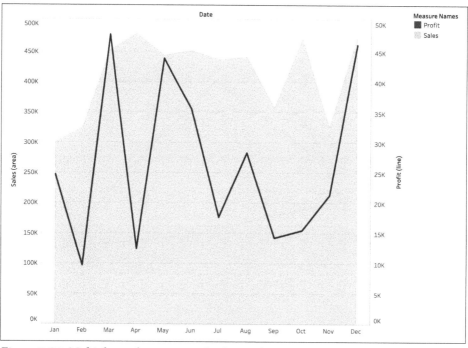

Figure 5-25. Multiple mark types on a dual-axis chart

The most common use of dual-axis charts I make is to compare performance from one time period with the same time period last year. In a bar-in-bar chart like Figure 5-26, I use the same mark type, but formatted differently to show the story in the data. The bars are sized and colored differently to help the audience understand what the chart is showing.

The main metric in Figure 5-26 is the profits earned in 2021, which is represented by a thinner bar that sits in front of the comparison metric. The 2021 profits have been colored based on whether they exceed the 2020 profits. Those that exceed last year's total are colored in orange, while those that don't are dark gray.

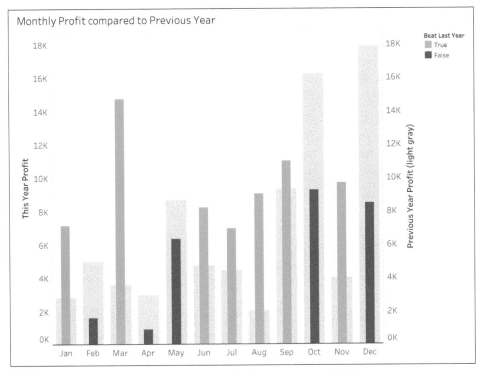

Figure 5-26. Bar-in-bar chart showing profit for 2021 versus 2020

Bar-in-bar charts are very effective as a communication tool because they utilize length but have much more detail built within them than just a simple bar chart. The ability to include additional context of the comparison period is useful while also comparing the trends of last year versus this year.

Multiple Axes Summary Card

✔ Useful to compare multiple measures on a single chart to find trends and correlations.

✔ Scatterplots make complex comparisons easier to understand.

✘ Take care to not add too much detail to a single chart.

Reference Lines/Bands

In this chapter so far, I have shown you how to use various techniques to alter the marks showing the main data points of your chart. The next two sections dig into additional chart features, starting with reference lines and bands.

Reference Lines

I've already shown how to highlight marks against another data point as used in the bar-in-bar chart. However, reference lines allow much more flexibility in many situations. A *reference line* can show a constant value, be calculated based on the data points, or be driven by a measure in your data set. Let's have a look at each situation in turn.

Using the profit values of our bike store in 2021, let's apply a target of $20,000 per month and show how that appears on the chart (Figure 5-27). You can still use the technique of coloring based on whether the target is met or not.

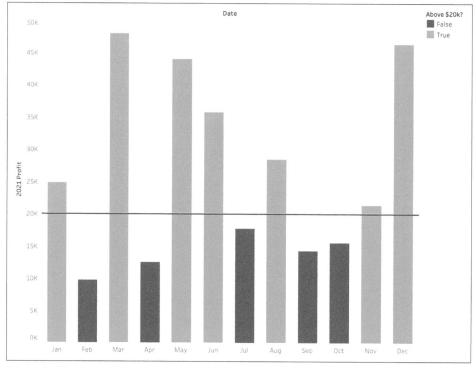

Figure 5-27. Constant reference line

Reference lines don't have to be used for just targets. You can use a reference line to help the audience interpret the chart too. If we took two years of profit data from our bike store, it might be challenging to piece together the stories within the data. Breaking the 24 months into 8 quarterly periods can make the chart easier to interpret (Figure 5-28).

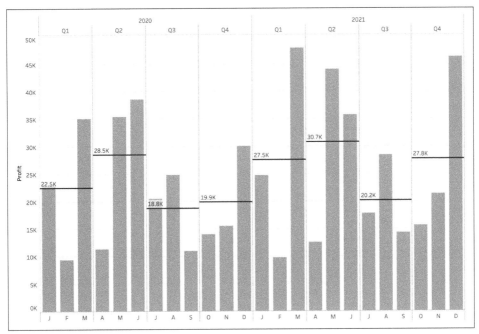

Figure 5-28. Quarterly average reference lines

To make the chart easier to understand, I've increased the transparency of the marks to allow the reference line to be the dominant mark on the chart rather than the bars. The benefit of using averages is that if the data updates, the reference lines should also update to continue to show the latest message in the data.

You can also use the reference line as the main feature of the chart by exchanging the bars for circles instead to stack the data points per quarter, as seen in Figure 5-29.

The reference lines themselves can also be their own data field rather than being based on existing data points in the chart. In Figure 5-30, the targets have been set by a separate data field rather than the reference lines we've used previously that have been set based on the data points shown in the visualization. When working with real-world data sets, data often comes from separate sources when adding targets to an existing view. The granularity at which targets are set is often a less-detailed level than the main data set, which can cause a challenge with data preparation.

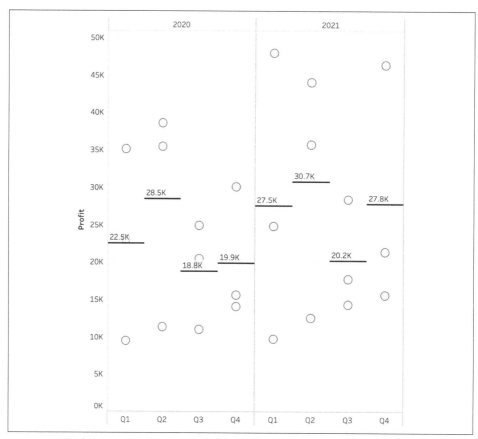

Figure 5-29. Showing distributions and stories by using reference lines

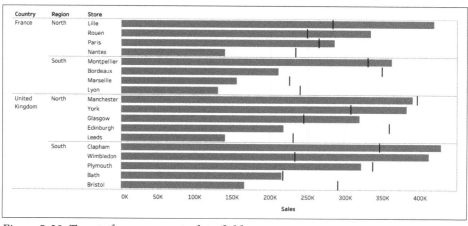

Figure 5-30. Targets from a separate data field

Reference Bands

Reference lines are not the only formatting option you have when adding visual elements to a chart to help guide the audience's interpretation. Using *reference bands*, which highlight a range of points, is another option that you can use. Using reference bands is a good way to simplify reading distributions of data. A *distribution* is a summary of all the varying data points in a data set for a particular measure. Understanding how your data is distributed is an important part of analyzing a data set.

Reference bands can be used to highlight the range between any of the following:

- Minimum/maximum
- Quartiles (for example, between 25% and 75% of the data)
- Standard deviation on either side of the median

The most common form of reference bands you are likely to come across is used in a *control chart* (Figure 5-31). A control chart is often used in operational situations, from call centers to manufacturing, to understand levels of demand placed on a system. In a call center, for example, the demand would be the number of calls a team might receive each day. By understanding the typical levels of demand, the right number of call handlers can be on the lines, ready to answer the callers' needs. Too many call handlers could result in a team that is likely to be bored as well as the excessive cost of employing that many people to be in the office. In Figure 5-31, the chart is split into two sections, with the mean and control limits recalculated because of a change being made to the process being measured. This is a common requirement when measuring effectiveness.

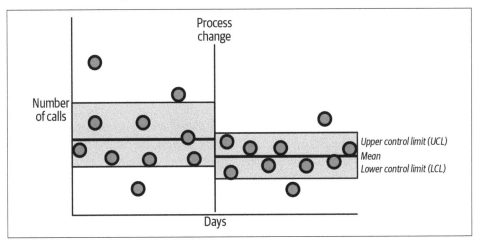

Figure 5-31. How to read a control chart

A control chart can be complex to read at first glance. But these incredibly useful visualizations allow the audience to use the key data points to make decisions and to avoid being misled by more extreme data points. A standard deviation on either side of the mean in a normal distribution focuses on roughly two-thirds of the data points in the data set. Two standard deviations capture 95%, and three standard deviations capture 99%. Any outliers are the more extreme data points. In the real world when you are measuring varying levels of demand, you want to build your operational system to meet the most common needs and not design to meet just the extremes, unless you absolutely have to.

The control chart shows several key metrics all in the same chart. First, the *mean* is calculated by adding up all the plots and dividing by the total. The *upper control limit* is determined by adding three standard deviations to the mean in the traditional Six Sigma view, but other numbers of standard deviations are used in alternative versions. The *standard deviation* is calculated by taking the square root of the collective variance of each value from the mean. The *lower control limit* is calculated by taking the same number of standard deviations away from the mean. The band between the upper and lower control limits demonstrates what plots are within control and should be designed into the operational systems. Any point that falls above the upper control limit or below the lower control limit should be ignored. This is because designing a system to fit every eventuality would lead to a poorly optimized system. The system would be expensive to operate and increase the charges made to customers. Data points that fit outside the control bands are rare instances and therefore shouldn't be factored into the design of the system. Control charts might show changes in the reference bands at certain points where the demand is known to have changed.

Ideally, you want the reference band to be as thin as possible, as this means the measure has little variation, which in turn means the operational systems can be developed to meet this need. Where the reference bands are wide, the levels of demand will vary, and therefore it will be harder to design a system to meet that demand.

Figure 5-32 shows what the number of calls looks like for our bike store. If you had to determine how many people we'd need to answer the calls, it would be difficult to say even if you knew each person could handle 20 calls a day. By showing the data points on a control chart, you can begin to see how the volume of calls is becoming more consistent until the final quarter. Greater consistency is useful to ensure that you are able to meet the needs of your customers.

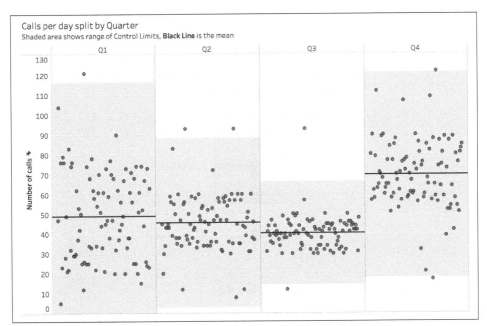

Figure 5-32. A control chart of number of calls received by the bike store

Another chart type that uses reference bands is called a *box-and-whisker plot*. It uses a reference band to show distributions of data, like the control chart but in a different way (Figure 5-33). The chart gets its name from the reference band that is used to show the difference between the first quartile and the third quartile. *Quartiles* are a distribution of data that orders each data point from smallest to largest and then splits them into quarters.

A line is drawn out from either side of the box, also known as the *whiskers* because of their appearance, to show the full range of the data points. The whiskers can be used to show one and a half times the interquartile range or the full range of the data. The *interquartile range* is the difference between the first and third quartiles, times 1.5. The middle line of the box is the *median*—the midpoint if all points were ordered from smallest to largest.

You can show multiple box-and-whisker plots on the same chart to show how the distributions change over time. When building your own box-and-whisker plots, you have the choice of shrinking, or not making the plots visible, to allow the box plot to stand out rather than the data points themselves to simplify the message for the reader.

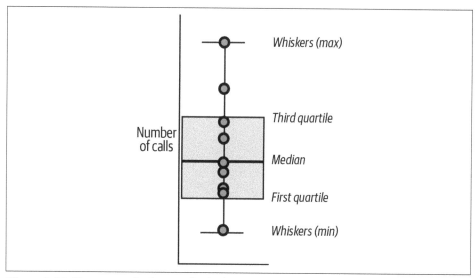

Figure 5-33. How to read a box-and-whisker plot

Measuring the change in the length of the box and the whiskers will demonstrate how the distribution of your data changes over time. As discussed with control charts, smaller ranges of data mean the elements you are measuring have greater consistency. In most businesses, having better consistency means processes are easier to plan for and optimize, so visually showing improvements is a key message to communicate.

Reference Lines/Bands Summary Card

✔ Simplifies the message in the chart

✔ Lots of ways to summarize key data points on the chart

Totals/Summaries

Another common addition to a chart is a total. A *total* often represents the sum of all the data points shown in a table or chart but can show different aggregations instead if required. Adding a total to a table is often easy to complete in any tool that you are using to form your analysis. The same can't be said when using totals in data visualizations, but I will cover that after describing the basics.

Totals in Tables

You've likely read a table that contains a set of totals. Let's explore the choices you have when using totals within a table.

Column totals

Column totals are formed by adding up each of the measures in a single column. Remember, to form the rows within the table, categorical data fields set the granularity of each row. Therefore, each row is a breakdown of the total for the metric being totaled. Frequently, the column total is shown at the bottom of the table (Figure 5-34), but it can be moved to the top of the table if required.

Category	Measure
A	1
B	2
C	3
D	4
Total	10

Figure 5-34. Column totals

Row totals

Row totals are created by adding up each value found within a single row of a table. Row totals are more frequently used within pivot tables, as a measure is spread across multiple columns rather than down a single column. The columns are likely to have headings that are different variables of the same category or part of a date (Figure 5-35). Row totals are likely to appear on the right side of the metrics they relate to but can be moved to the left if required.

Category	2019	2020	2021	Total
A	1	2	3	6
B	4	5	6	15

Figure 5-35. Row totals

Subtotals

An additional feature can be added to tables to show an intermediate total when tables are broken up by multiple categorical fields. Choosing which category forms the subtotal is driven by the questions the table is answering. In Figure 5-36, the category is broken into subcategories, so a subtotal gives the value for each category within the table.

Category	Sub cat.	Measure
A	AA	1
A	AB	2
Subtotal		3
B	BA	3
B	BB	4
Subtotal		7
Total	Total	10

Figure 5-36. Subtotals in a table

While totals in tables are the sums of each column, *summaries* describe other aggregation methods. Any aggregation can be used, as long as the user is clear on what is being shown. Averages, minimums, or maximums are different aggregations that can be used where you'd typically expect to find the summed amount. This is frequently the case when highlight tables (first covered in Chapter 3) are used because, otherwise, the total value will sway the color palette too much.

In Figure 5-37, we include the totals in the same sequential color palette as the values in the table. The overarching effect is that the color differentiation is reduced, as the scale of the color covers a wider range than would be the case without the totals.

	France	United Kingdom	Grand Total	Sales
North	1,175,011	1,446,833	**2,621,844**	858,030 5,020,063
South	858,030	1,540,189	**2,398,219**	
Grand Total	**2,033,041**	2,987,022	5,020,063	

Figure 5-37. Highlight table with summed totals

To ensure that the color scale is still useful within the chart, a summary can be shown as the average across all the values in that column or row (Figure 5-38)—but clearly this shows a different piece of information than the total. If you need to have totals in the view, clearly an average isn't useful, and therefore an alternate chart might be more effective.

	Country			Sales	
Region	France	United Kingdom	Average	858,030	2M
North	1,175,011	1,446,833	1,310,922		
South	858,030	1,540,189	1,199,110		
Average	1,016,521	1,493,511	1,255,016		

Figure 5-38. Highlight table with average totals

Totals in Charts

You may need to add totals to charts as well. The total in your chart can have a similar effect as what we saw when looking at the highlight table, but instead it would affect the length of the bar rather than the range of the color.

A poor use of totals in a chart would be to include a summed total at the bottom of a standard bar chart (Figure 5-39). The length of the total bar makes analysis of the other bars much harder, because differentiating the lengths becomes more difficult. This example uses the same data as Figure 5-13 but adds the total.

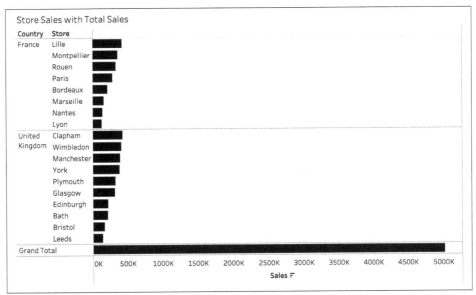

Figure 5-39. Bar chart with summed total

It would be easier to *not* visualize the total but instead to share it elsewhere. Chapter 6 covers some of the options.

Totals are often required when charts don't otherwise provide a clear view of the total. When bar or area charts use stacked sections, a total can allow the reader to view a total accurately (Figure 5-40).

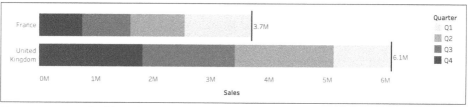

Figure 5-40. Stacked bar chart with total

Totals can help your audience find some key values to support their analysis. However, you need to use totals carefully to ensure that they don't actually hinder your audience's analysis.

Totals and Summaries Summary Card

✔ Can clearly summarize points in a table.

✔ Doesn't have to be a summary; can be many different aggregations.

✘ Use with care in bar charts or highlight tables as they can reduce the impact of the pre-attentive attributes.

Summary

A range of visual elements play an important role in enhancing the message of your data visualizations. Using color, size, and shape to alter the marks on the view can help reduce the cognitive effort the audience must use to decode the message you are sharing.

Dual-axis charts can be used to provide additional context to standard charts. Deciding when to synchronize the axes (or not) will depend on the question your visualization is answering. Additional elements can be added to charts to add extra detail or to help the audience interpret them. Totals can be used in either tables or charts, but take care not to let them detract from the original chart.

You make many visual choices when forming charts. The next chapter covers the elements that surround a chart to help you communicate with data clearly.

CHAPTER 6

Visual Context

Context is key. A well-constructed chart can convey a lot of information, but all the other elements on the page can change how the audience interprets that information. This chapter focuses on the page/screen elements that form the context for your data visualization, from title to background color. *Context* is the circumstances in which your analysis happens, the baseline it's based on, and the influencing factors that surround it. Context *positions* the points you are communicating in the audience's minds.

The cumulative effect of your visualization and its context can determine whether your audience notices, reads, or remembers your work. The key messages should jump off the page.

Creating memorable but clear data communications is a balancing act between focus and context. Some of the contextual elements this chapter covers include the following:

- Titles
- Text and annotations
- Contextual numbers
- Legends
- Iconography and visual cues
- Background and positioning

I'll finish the chapter with a look at interactive elements that can help users dive deeper into your analysis.

Titles

Titles set out what the audience should see. A clear title will direct the reader to refer to the right pieces of content, while poorly conceived titles can frustrate or confuse them.

Main Title

Titles can describe many things about the content of a work, such as its subject, the question the work poses, or the key finding from the data. What you choose guides the user's expectations. Let's look at the impact of each of these choices in turn, using a view that you will see more in the next chapter. The focus of this analysis is the revenue Prep Air has earned in the first quarter of the year. Here are your choices for the main title:

The subject of the work
> You might think this is obvious, but the title should convey the subject your work covers, especially if the audience is browsing rather than specifically looking for your work, such as while skimming through email, scrolling through a web page, or flicking through a document. Figure 6-1 shows an example.

Figure 6-1. Subject-based title

Question being posed
> Including the question the work is answering can really focus the audience's attention (Figure 6-2). For example, I love watching basketball games, but that doesn't mean I am going to look at every piece of analysis produced in depth. I don't have the time, and neither does anyone else these days. My favorite team is the San Antonio Spurs, so if the title is "Are the Spurs Assisting on More Baskets Than the Duncan Era?" you are likely to get my attention. If you tell your potential audience what you're asking, they can decide whether they want to dig in.

Figure 6-2. Question-based title

The key finding

You can also use your title to share your most important finding (Figure 6-3). Sharing the finding in the title might seem like a spoiler: if you've answered the question, will anyone look further? In reality, if the audience knows your position on a subject, they are likely to read your analysis to see why and how you arrived at your conclusion. If your finding is controversial, however, leading with your finding may turn away potential audience members—especially if your results are unexpected.

Figure 6-3. Finding-based title

Your main title will likely contain only a few words, so choosing clear words that convey a lot of information can be a challenge. Remember, too, that the more words you use, the more space your title will take up—space you could otherwise use for your data visualizations.

The main title of the communication is possibly the first thing your audience will read. You'd probably expect me to write that it will *always* be the first thing, but that's not always the case. Color and positioning can draw the audience's attention to a chart before the title.

If your audience is looking for the title of your work, they are likely to look in the top-left corner (Figure 6-4).

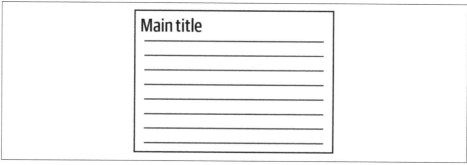

Figure 6-4. Traditional placement of the main title

However, breaking the audience's expectations can attract their attention. For example, placing the title halfway down the page (or anywhere except the top left) is unique and memorable (Figure 6-5). Just ensure that it's visible; without a title, your intended audience might not know the work is aimed at them and skip it altogether. Use an alternate location for the title only when you know your target audience is already likely to pay attention.

The key challenge with a nontraditional location is that you risk the audience not giving their attention to the work in the first place. If your audience is just flicking through pages not looking for anything specific, and the title is not in a logical place, they might just skip past your work.

When deciding which type of title to use, my preference is using a question when you are less sure of the expertise your audience will have about a subject. By using a question, you will clearly demonstrate the situation you are assessing. If you know your audience understands why they are receiving the work, leading with the key finding means they can then use your communication to learn why you have made that finding.

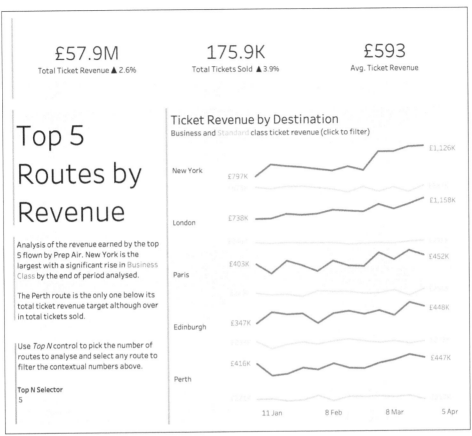

£57.9M
Total Ticket Revenue ▲ 2.6%

175.9K
Total Tickets Sold ▲ 3.9%

£593
Avg. Ticket Revenue

Top 5 Routes by Revenue

Analysis of the revenue earned by the top 5 flown by Prep Air. New York is the largest with a significant rise in Business Class by the end of period analysed.

The Perth route is the only one below its total ticket revenue target although over in total tickets sold.

Use *Top N* control to pick the number of routes to analyse and select any route to filter the contextual numbers above.

Top N Selector
5

Ticket Revenue by Destination
Business and Standard class ticket revenue (click to filter)

New York — £797K ... £1,126K

London — £738K ... £1,158K

Paris — £403K ... £452K

Edinburgh — £347K ... £448K

Perth — £416K ... £447K

11 Jan   8 Feb   8 Mar   5 Apr

Figure 6-5. Alternate positioning

Subtitles, Standfirsts, and Chart Titles

Each section or chart within your work may also have its own title. These can take the same forms as the main title, introducing the subject, question, or key finding.

Subtitles help your audience understand what each section is about—that's what told you that this section is about subtitles and chart titles, right? Subsections let you walk your audience through various aspects of a subject, breaking it into easier-to-consume chunks.

This is also true for question-based subtitles. You can use subtitles to pose additional questions that explore the initial question more deeply. This technique can also help you take your audience along the same path that you took, to show the reader how you arrived at your analysis. Alternately, you can use subquestions to explore the initial question from different angles and perspectives.

Choose your approach based on how much your audience knows about the subject of the visualization. If they understand it well, contrarian subquestions can allow the work to explore new topics. Expert readers can navigate to the areas that interest them more, to validate their own opinions or understanding. For less-familiar subjects, questions are a great way to show the direction of your analysis.

Finally, you can also use subtitles to convey your findings from each subsection. This technique is my favorite because it allows you to show your audience each factor that contributes to your overall finding. These subtitles can become lengthy, but occasionally you might want to consider using a standfirst instead.

A *standfirst* comes from British written journalism: directly after a title, this short paragraph introduces the rest of the work to the audience (this is called a *lede* in US journalism). With people in your organization having significant time pressures, the standfirst can be used to really sell the audience on why they should consume the communication. An example of a standfirst can be found in Figure 6-6. Standfirsts can not only help with the hook but also ensure that your audience takes the correct message from your work.

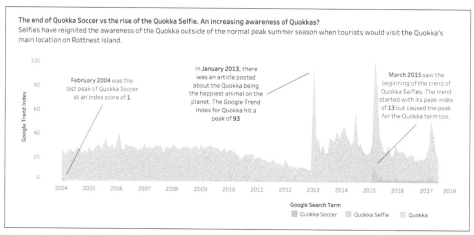

Figure 6-6. Standfast and annotations on an area chart

While the main title of the work hooks the audience's attention, the subtitles help you retain it. You can locate subtitles in your chart headings as well as independently from the charts. When subtitles are used as chart titles, you need to remember to explain not just the section you are subtitling but what the chart presents too.

Text and Annotations

Titles aren't the only text you'll use in your data communications. Small amounts of *text* can help clarify or highlight points to your audience. The challenge with text is to avoid relying too much on it. It feels ironic to write that sentence in a book! But while books are usually composed mostly of text punctuated by occasional images, data communications should reverse the proportions. They should be mostly visuals with occasional text, to let the audience see the data before the words.

While your charts should clearly communicate your message within the data, adding some clarification can help a lot, especially for readers with lower levels of data literacy. Let's look at two forms text can take within your work: annotations on charts and text boxes.

Annotations

Chart *annotations* are a powerful tool. These should be short snippets of text that highlight key data points or areas of the chart. In Figure 6-6, I have highlighted three points in a long area chart. The analysis is about the quokka, an Australian marsupial illustrated on the cover of my first book. In popular media, quokkas often appear in two themes: soccer and the quokka selfie. The data set I had access to caught only the tail end of the quokka soccer theme, so without wanting that to become lost on the chart, I used an annotation to highlight to my audience that it was even there. Quokka soccer was a brutal fad in which quokkas were used as soccer balls for fun, often killing them. Thankfully, a quokka selfie is a much nicer trend that celebrates the cute animals and doesn't hurt them.

Keeping annotations short and pertinent is important. If your annotations take up a lot of space, you may risk text sitting over data points, which makes it hard to take in either one.

Annotations are much like the data points on a chart, in that you should minimize the amount of time it takes the audience to consume the information within them. Notice in Figure 6-6 that I've highlighted the key points of the annotation with bold text. I wanted to highlight the key dates I found in the analysis of the last mention of quokka soccer and the peak interest in quokkas and quokka selfies. Even if the audience doesn't commit the cognitive effort of reading the whole annotation, they will still see the points I am trying to convey.

When positioning your annotation, ensure that you are placing it in a space that will remain blank when data is updated or filtered. This can be hard to predict, but certain chart types like maps will retain blank spaces in the same location as the data points are likely to be measured in similar locations. Whitespace around your charts is covered later in this chapter and might be able to be used to host annotations if your charts lack whitespace around the data points.

When your data will update, place your annotations carefully. In Figure 6-7, the measure shown is a cumulative total. That means the values will always increase over time, so I can safely position an annotation to the left of the line chart.

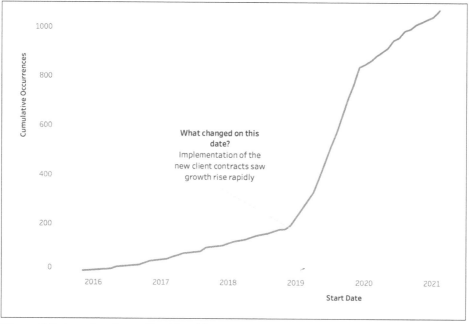

Figure 6-7. Annotate in predictable whitespace

Text Boxes

Text boxes are blocks of text that can be used to give context, describe the charts, or tell the story that ties your analysis together. Without text, it's difficult to tie your work together and ensure that your audience interprets it the way that you intend it to. In Chapters 3 and 4, you learned the importance of making your message jump cleanly off the page. But when a data set contains multiple stories, it can be difficult to highlight them all by using only visualization techniques.

After the main title, it's common to include a block of text describing and contextualizing the work (Figure 6-8). Since it generally comes at the top, the audience will likely read this text before the charts, unless the charts are really eye-catching.

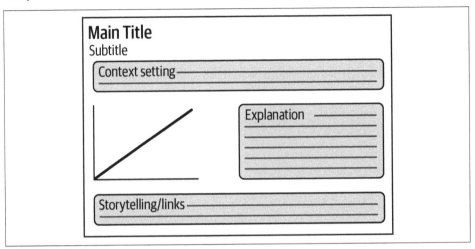

Figure 6-8. Position of text boxes

You can also use text boxes to describe findings. Telling your audience how to interpret the chart allows you to avoid any misunderstanding and reach people with different levels of data literacy.

The final main use of text boxes is to tie the sections of your work together into a coherent statement. Trying to do this by just using charts can be quite challenging. Adding text to link charts together can make it easier to guide your audience through the work.

Since you've purposefully designed your charts to make the key messages jump out, be careful to not become overly reliant on words. If you bury your findings in text, you lose the benefits of data visualization (and you might lose your audience too). Keeping text to a minimum ensures that the data is the primary method of communication. Journalists who use charts to validate their points and add to their story would rely much more heavily on more words but in a work context. Your audience's time pressures should be considered and wording kept to a minimum unless you know your audience would consider reading through a more word-focused communication.

Text Formatting

The primary formatting consideration for text is font choice. Like any visual choice, having too many styles and sizes will make finding the information you need harder rather than easier.

Text font

Most organizations have a *corporate style guide* that dictates font choice, color palettes, and imagery. If your visualization has to conform to your organization's style guide, just use what it prescribes.

If you do get to choose your font, fitting the font to your theme can add to the overall impact of the work. Take care not to lower the readability of the text. In Figure 6-9, I've used a different font choice to show that the work, which is about honey production in the US, is a little more lighthearted and different from my usual analysis.

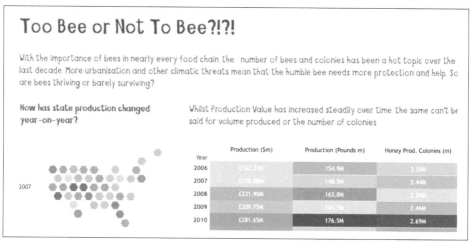

Figure 6-9. Fitting the font to the theme

Matching the fonts to the theme can create a more memorable piece of work. However, I find the font harder to read than the majority of font types I choose to read. Font is one element that can be tested with a small subset of your audience before publishing. Ensuring that the text is accessible for all of your audience, including those who use screen readers, is important.

Text size

With titles and subtitles likely using two text sizes, you need to be careful not to add many more. Using a consistent pattern of text sizes can ensure that the audience can identify and differentiate the title and descriptive text. In descriptive text, you can still highlight points by using **bold** or *italic*. Use these techniques sparingly, or your points will get lost! It's also important to use them for the same purpose consistently: if you use bold for emphasis, use italics to highlight key terms.

Text color is another important factor in readability. Creating text that is easy to read for everyone is the aim, and that means thinking about making sure your design is accessible for people with visual and cognitive disabilities, such as color blindness (see "Color" on page 160 for more detail) and dyslexia. Both color choice and contrast can create challenges.

Text and Annotations Summary Card

✔ Annotations can provide clarity where complexity exists.

✔ Just because data visualizations are so powerful, don't ignore the importance of text.

✘ Keep the number of font sizes and types to a minimum.

Contextual Numbers

What are the key measures your audience needs to focus on? Let's imagine you've found out your sales are 100. Is that good? Terrible? Is that performance better than last year? Your audience needs context to interpret what you're telling them.

Let me introduce you to what I call *contextual numbers*: prominent, standalone figures that draw attention and are often read first. They help the reader understand what to expect.

Figure 6-10 shows a contextual number: the number of participants in a weekly data preparation challenge I run called Preppin' Data. The number shows how many people have recorded their solutions to the week's challenge in a Google Form. Showcasing the popularity of the challenges can encourage more people to participate.

380
Total Participants

Figure 6-10. Contextual number of Preppin' Data participants

Using multiple contextual numbers can also deepen audience awareness. In the Participation Tracker for Preppin' Data, I also share the number of solutions submitted (Figure 6-11). This helps the audience understand that participants can undertake multiple challenges.

Figure 6-11. Multiple contextual numbers

The contextual numbers let the audience answer some key questions before digging into the details:

- How many people have taken part in the Preppin' Data challenges?
- How many submissions have been completed?
- How many submissions does the average participant make?

The charts are then positioned below the contextual numbers (Figure 6-12).

Understanding your audience's level of awareness of a subject can be difficult, especially if you don't have direct contact with them. In the Preppin' Data initiative, I don't know many of the participants. If they want to monitor their own progress with the challenges, I have to assume what their questions might be. You will also need to make assumptions as to your audience's awareness of the subject. You can make your work more suitable for a wider audience if you can provide a solid context.

You can add detail to your contextual numbers to improve the depth of context your audience has before they start trying to understand your work. Adding change indicators, colors, or simple charts can all help to add depth to the context you are providing. These additions are discussed in "Improving the Visualization Mix" on page 257.

Contextual Numbers Summary Card

✔ Simple contextual numbers are key in providing a great baseline for your analysis.

✔ Not a visual element but powerful in communicating effectively.

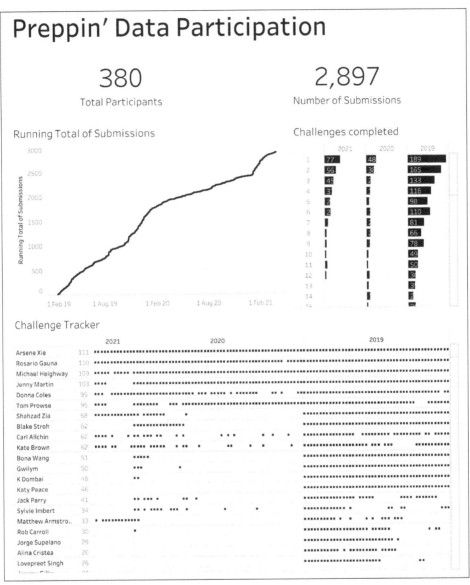

Figure 6-12. Preppin' Data participation tracker

Legends

Legends, or *keys*, are the guides that help the audience understand how your work uses shapes, colors, size, or other encoding. It's easy to forget about legends, but they are an important part of your data communication.

The legend often sits next to or beneath the chart it decodes. It should be easy for your audience to see and reference. Make sure the legend clearly shows every variation you use: for example, every color should have an attached meaning (Figure 6-13). If you have followed my advice in the other chapters, you've kept it simple, limiting the colors and shapes you use, so your legend should be simple too.

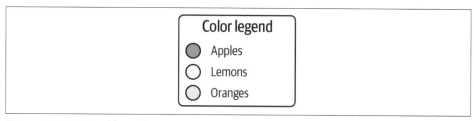

Figure 6-13. Typical legend

Each element in your chart should be listed in the legend. You can sort them alphabetically or based on a measure in your chart (such a color scale or size order).

Without a legend, your audience will likely struggle to interpret the chart unless the meanings of the shapes, colors, or sizes have an obvious logical link to the attribute they represent. Even then, however, the link might not be as obvious as you think.

Let's say you're measuring the sales of fruits. You might be tempted to apply a logical color to each, as in Figure 6-13: making lemons yellow, oranges orange, and so forth. But unless you list all of these items out, it still might not be clear which color refers to which fruit: red could be raspberries or strawberries; yellow could represent pineapples or bananas as easily as lemons.

This is where the legend comes in. It clarifies the link between the visual technique and the data points and makes the meanings explicit. In the next few sections, we'll look at some more visual techniques and the legends that should accompany them.

Shape Legends

You learned in Chapter 4 about using shapes in charts, such as scatterplots and maps. Different shapes can represent different variables from a categorical data field. If you're using only one shape to represent all data, there is no need to add a legend. When you use multiple shapes, however, you need a way to differentiate what each shape represents.

In a scatterplot, you have a choice about whether the shapes you use illustrate the variables, but they don't *have* to. I recommend using illustrative shapes (as in Figure 6-14) whenever possible so that the audience won't have to rely on the legend to understand what each represents. Notice my choice of words here: your audience might not rely on the legend to interpret all of the shapes, but some people are unlikely to recognize all of the shapes. Therefore, illustrative shapes can help reduce the number of times the legend has to be referenced.

If illustrative shapes are generally familiar to the audience, they are easier to interpret. These might include product images or silhouettes or the logos of various companies.

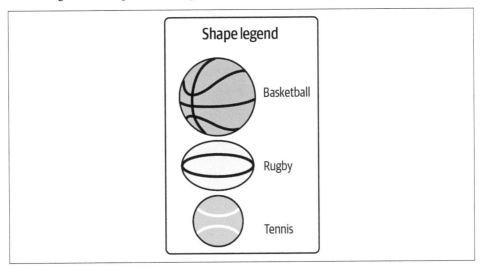

Figure 6-14. Shape legend

Not all data corresponds to an easily recognizable shape like a baseball or a logo, though. What shape should represent a sales region, salesperson, or software product? In such cases, you might use nonillustrative shapes. This might mean assigning something more abstract to each variable, like a square or a triangle. Just make sure the shapes you choose are different enough for the audience to tell them apart easily.

Shapes can also represent measurements. A common example is indicating relative performance by using up and down arrows. In Figure 6-15, the arrows represent whether each store's sales this quarter were above or below sales from the previous quarter. Shapes become challenging to use in this context, however, when an up arrow actually demonstrates a worsening condition. For example, a rise in complaints is a bad thing, and therefore you can still use an up arrow to demonstrate the increase, but you will need to change the color to show it's not a positive movement for your organization.

Store	This quarter complaints		Last quarter complaints
London	358	▲	2,700
Manchester	557	▼	5,700
York	564	▲	2,100

Legend

▼ Better performance

▲ Worse performance

Figure 6-15. Nonillustrative shapes: using up and down arrows to show relative performance

Remember, too, that shapes and colors can carry emotional messages. Pay attention to how your audience will feel about the news you are delivering. Similarly, choosing a color with positive or negative associations (such as black for profit and red for loss) will help the audience decode whether the increase is something to be celebrated or not. Let's look more closely at color now.

Color Legends

As with shapes, when you can use colors that illustrate the variables you are analyzing, you can make your audience's decoding task easier. The challenge with color legends is that your communications might use color in many ways, and each will need its own legend.

As you learned in Chapter 5, color palettes come in three types: hue, sequential (intensity), and diverging. Let's look at each in turn.

Hue

Hue palettes use a different color for each variable. The colors you pick for different categorical variables should be easy to differentiate. You might choose illustrative colors, like brand colors or the color of your product, to help audiences spot the link (Figure 6-16).

Prep Air Loyalty Level

● Platinum

○ Gold

○ Silver

Figure 6-16. Hue color legend example

Sequential (intensity)

A sequential color palette uses different levels of lightness of a single color to represent different values of a single measure. The legend will need to show the range of color values used and the minimum and maximum values (Figure 6-17).

Choose your base color carefully, with emotional associations in mind. For a value representing a good outcome, you might use the company's dominant brand color. Reds and oranges are often used to represent bad outcomes. If your brand color is a red or orange, the use of it in your communications will likely mean that the negative coloring needs to be gray instead.

Figure 6-17. Sequential color legend

If your work is interactive and allows the audience to filter their view, you will need to decide whether the color legend should respond by reducing the range of values it shows: if they zoom in on, say, the 10 to 50 range, will your legend show only the colors for 10 to 50? Showing the lowest range of values possible makes the color differentiation clearer, but your audience might lose the context of the previous range of data. I'd always keep the scale as your audience would see with the unfiltered data set, to avoid miscommunication occurring if screenshots are passed on to others.

Diverging

A diverging color palette uses two colors to show a binary measure that falls on either side of a center point with a defined value, like a target or zero point. This legend will need to show the minimum and maximum values covered by the data but also the midpoint where one color turns into the other (Figure 6-18). As with any other color choice, consider what specific colors mean to your audience.

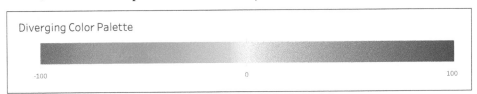

Figure 6-18. Diverging color legend

No legend

Legends are not the only place you can tell your audience what each color represents. You can use color in the chart's title or subtitle (Figure 6-19) or add labels to the data points instead. Leaving out the legend saves space in your work, allowing you to make other design choices.

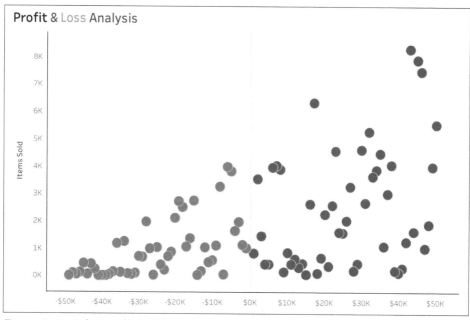

Figure 6-19. Color used in a title

To reduce accessibility issues, you can also name the color next to the object. For example, Profit (black) ensures that the correct colors are associated with the correct elements.

Size Legends

Size legends involve fewer choices: size is used to show a measure, with larger values represented by larger shapes. The scale should be in the legend and the chart. Size is difficult for audiences to assess precisely, so the legend just needs to demonstrate the range, as shown in Figure 6-20.

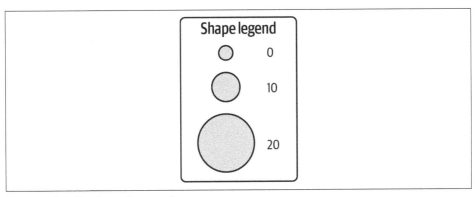

Figure 6-20. Size legend example

Legends Summary Card

✔ Should follow best-practice advice on shape, color, and size.

✘ Too many items will add significant cognitive effort to your audience.

Iconography and Visual Cues

Communicating clearly includes ensuring that your audience retains your message. The overall look and feel you create can make the work more memorable. Iconography and imagery play a large role in setting a theme. *Theme* can be defined as the overall look and feel of the piece.

Thematic Iconography

Setting a theme can grab attention and provide additional context before the audience even starts to read a chart. You'll need to strike a balance between the imagery and the chart itself. Your visual imagery can allude heavily to the key message.

Take Figure 6-21, my visualization of data about London air pollution. The car image at the top of the view sets a theme *and* conveys the message. It doesn't show blue skies or small circles: I intentionally chose gray to mimic the pollution and show that it remains a problem, as well as an image of a fossil fuel–powered vehicle.

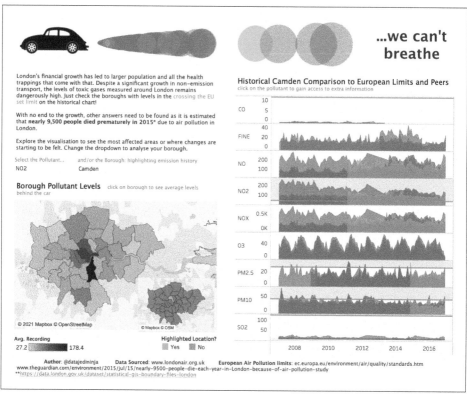

Figure 6-21. Air pollution visualization header

Ensure that your iconography doesn't distract from the message of your data. The audience needs to understand that your analysis is based on a data source, not just your opinion.

Audience Guidance

Your audience might not be as familiar with data-based communications as you are, so think carefully about their ability to confidently understand and interact with your work. The goal is to support less data-literate audiences without patronizing those who have more experience. Let's look at elements you can use to support and guide all users.

To provide more information on your content and the data source, you can provide an *information* or *help button*. Space is always limited, so holding things elsewhere can be useful. Your audience is likely used to using information buttons on websites. A familiar-looking icon, such as a small "i" in a circle, will require less explanation.

Information buttons (ⓘ) typically either display a pop-up text box or link to a different page. The button should contain information like this:

- Source of the data
- Any data that has been filtered out
- The range of dates the data covers
- Explanation of terms in the data or visualization
- Background detail the audience might need
- Instructions for the user (see the next section)

The amount of content to include is another fine balance: you don't want to overload your core page with information, yet you want the audience to read the additional details. As your audience becomes more accustomed to working with data communications, especially from the same data source, you can reduce the amount of background information on the page and add it to the information button instead.

Information and help buttons can also contain brief text instructions to help the audience interact with the work (Figure 6-22).

You can also use icons and a legend to represent actions your audience can take, such as hovering, filtering, or selecting. As with any details that are not held on the main page, such instructions can easily be missed by a casual reader.

Iconography and Visual Clues Summary Card

✔ Can set a theme, making the communication more memorable

✔ Use to guide your audience through the communication

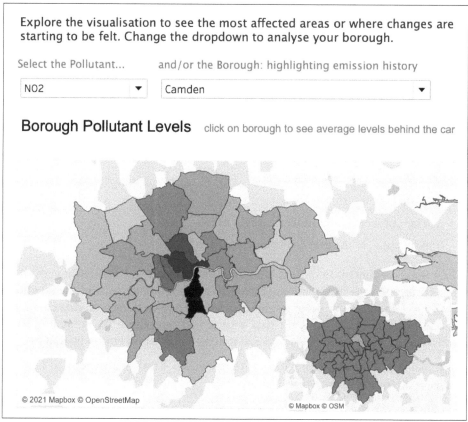

Figure 6-22. User instructions in the London air pollution analysis

Background and Positioning

The way you position the charts within your work determines in what order the audience will consume them. That makes a significant difference to how they are understood, as will the background that surrounds them. I explain layout principles more thoroughly in Chapter 7.

The order of the charts, titles, legends, and other elements is vitally important to the story you tell—just as in a book, where positioning can be the difference between an incomprehensible story and a bestseller. Let's look at two key principles that help you structure your communications clearly: the Z pattern and whitespace.

The Z Pattern

If you grew up speaking English or other Western languages, you have been taught to read from left to right, from the top of a page to the bottom. If you drew a line on the page that followed the eye movement of the reader, it would form a zigzag pattern that would repeat down the page (Figure 6-23). While speakers of many other languages read in different patterns, the general principle usually translates well: try to understand in what order your audience is likely to view the content on the page, and then ensure that you are positioning the content in the order you want the audience to read it.

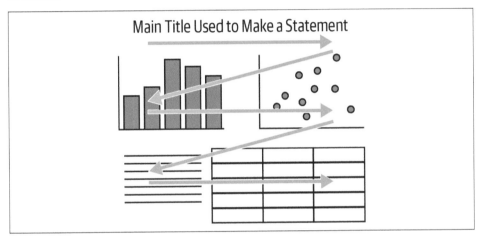

Figure 6-23. The Z reading pattern

So what should that order be? We'll start with titles:

Titles

> Titles set the subject and hook the audience's attention. Your audience will usually expect the title to be at the top of the page. You *could* put the title elsewhere, but that might lead your audience to start looking at whatever is at the top of the page. If main titles are used in the middle of the page, you will often find much larger fonts to draw attention.

Key charts

> If you are sharing multiple charts, be aware that the chart at the top-left corner of the page will likely be seen first. You can either use this position to deliver your key message or set the scene for the charts to follow, which you can then position in the Z pattern to encourage reading in the correct order.

Contextual numbers

Positioning contextual numbers at the top of the page, before any charts, will make them more likely to be read first. The idea of contextual numbers is to set the scene for the rest of the communication to build upon. If they aren't seen first, it can be difficult to know what background information your audience might have about the subject.

Legends and text boxes

Legends and text boxes can be positioned to the right of or below their corresponding charts, to be seen after the chart itself.

Planning out the view by using this basic principle will help your audience consume the work in the way you intend.

Whitespace

Whitespace refers to the gaps on the page between pieces of content in your layout. It gives your content room to breathe. Whitespace can also be used to break your view into easier-to-consume chunks.

This technique is called the *Gestalt principle*. *Gestalt* is a German word meaning "unified whole," as humans perceive groups and patterns in images that group elements together. This principle, when applied to data visualization, can be useful when breaking up complex dashboards.

Whitespace plays a big part in this. In Figure 6-24, I have used whitespace as well as background color to group the contextual numbers, marginal histograms, and the tickets that are still open.

Spacing out your charts can help your audience see what legend or text box relates to each one, as in Figure 6-24. This can be quite subtle.

If you want to be less subtle, you can use colorful backgrounds to show the sections of your work. You've seen that using color sparingly makes its impact greater. Faded or pastel background colors are less likely to distract. You can place a continuous block of color behind content you want your audience to consume together (Figure 6-25).

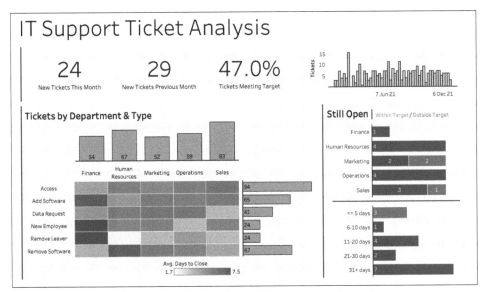

Figure 6-24. Using whitespace to show relationships between elements

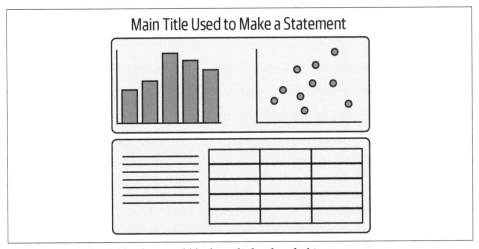

Figure 6-25. Colorful background blocks to link related objects

Another option is to use thin lines to divide your work into separate sections (Figure 6-26). This technique works just as well as using color but doesn't distract as much. If you keep the lines quite thin (just one or two pixels wide), the effect can subtly guide the reader. This technique can also help to break up the Z pattern if you want the audience to read the charts in a different order.

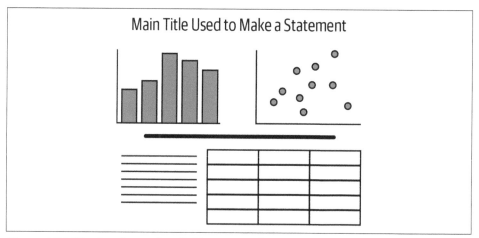

Figure 6-26. Line breaks used to divide your work into sections

Interactivity

When you ask your audience to interact with your work, you are asking them to invest cognitive effort. It can be challenging to convey the depth of your message without asking too much of them. Too much detail—for example, too many reference lines, marks, and colors—can make a chart difficult to interpret. The next chapter dives into the benefits of interactivity, but here, let's focus on how nonchart elements can aid understanding.

In the decades since the general public began using the web, people have become accustomed to interacting with hypertext, such as linked text and images. Audiences thus often expect to be able to interact with the work as they would with a website.

Tooltips

The most common but frequently overlooked interactive element in data visualization is the *tooltip*. This small information box pops up on the screen when a user hovers the cursor over or clicks a data point. This is particularly useful when marks are close together or overlap. Annotations are useful to highlight particular points but can take up considerable space. By contrast, tooltips appear only when the user interacts with that mark.

Most data visualization software shows tooltips by default. The basic tooltip will contain the variables and values the mark represents (Figure 6-27). Whereas a data point represents only a few categories or measures, the basic tooltip format will still be clear. As soon as you start adding more data fields, it can become more challenging for your audience to pick out the most pertinent ones. Remove anything unnecessary from the tooltip to make it easier to interpret.

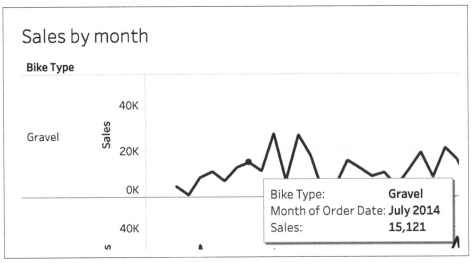

Figure 6-27. Basic tooltip

You can customize tooltips in most data visualization software. You might add descriptions, extra data points, or even another chart.

Descriptions

Tooltips can help guide users on what to take from that data point or how it fits in the overall message. To make it more readable, you can turn the data points into a sentence describing the mark in the chart (Figure 6-28). The downside of the sentence structure is that the data points are then harder to find among the rest of the text in the sentence.

Figure 6-28. Descriptions in tooltips

Extra data points

At times, you may want to add additional data points that appear *only* in the tooltip. This provides access to extra information, without making the chart more complex (Figure 6-29). Additional data points can contextualize the marks in the view—for example, indicating whether they are ranks or percentiles.

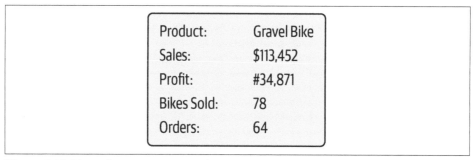

Figure 6-29. Extra data points in a tooltip

Charts

Adding charts to your tooltip can reinforce your message without taking up valuable space in the main work (Figure 6-30). Not every software and coding language allows for this option. Use it with caution. Remember that not all of your audience will see the tooltip charts. Use them for supplemental information, not for crucial information that might alter the users' decisions.

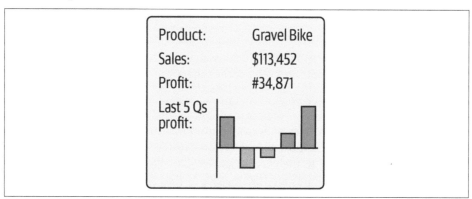

Figure 6-30. Chart in tooltip

However, it's not always easy to tell which information is supplementary and which is crucial. If the chart in the tooltip is *static*—that is, it doesn't update when you hover over various marks—readers are less likely to miss key insights, as you know exactly what the chart will look like wherever the audience views it.

It can be challenging to find the balance between what you share on the main page and what you share within the tooltip, but clear instructions to your audience will help.

Interactions

Tooltips are not the only way to save space in your work. If you find yourself repeating the same charts again and again with slightly different data sets, consider introducing highlighting and filtering. These interactions will allow your audience to find something more specific to them.

Highlighting

When your audience or your data sets begin to grow larger, it can be difficult to focus everyone's attention on the parts that are important to them. You might be tempted to create multiple versions of the same piece of work, with different underlying data sets. However, this quickly becomes difficult to administer, since even a single change has to be reflected in every version. Having all of the data sets feed into a single version will mean less work for you.

For audiences with varied interests or from varied teams, *highlighting* can be a good way to ensure that everyone can find the marks most relevant to them. Users can select their team from a list, which will then show either all other teams faded out or colored differently, easily distinguished but still providing context (Figure 6-31). This is particularly useful when your chart is a scatterplot with a lot of detail (see Chapter 4 for more detail on scatterplots).

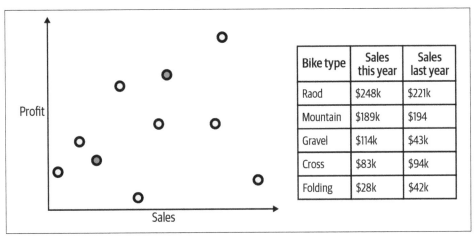

Bike type	Sales this year	Sales last year
Raod	$248k	$221k
Mountain	$189k	$194
Gravel	$114k	$43k
Cross	$83k	$94k
Folding	$28k	$42k

Figure 6-31. Highlighted marks in a scatterplot

You can also use a highlighting technique called *proportional brushing* instead: the original mark that summarizes all of a metric is retained, but color is applied to show what proportion of it is made up by the selected mark (Figure 6-32).

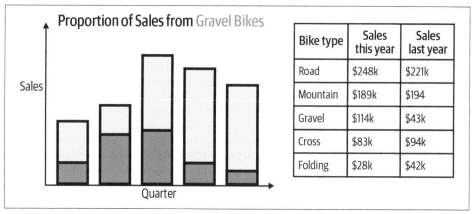

Bike type	Sales this year	Sales last year
Road	$248k	$221k
Mountain	$189k	$194
Gravel	$114k	$43k
Cross	$83k	$94k
Folding	$28k	$42k

Figure 6-32. Proportional brushing

Filtering

Sometimes users need to *filter out* irrelevant data to reduce the range of results. This makes the remaining data points much easier to read, especially if the axis of the chart scales to match the range of filtered values (Figure 6-33). For example, if you wanted to look at the sales of just gravel bikes, filtering out road and mountain bikes makes it easier to see the trends in the resulting chart.

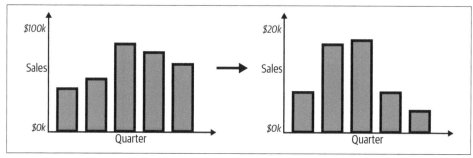

Figure 6-33. Two charts, pre and post filter, showing reduced axis

You can give your audience the option to filter by selecting from a list, or set it so that selecting something in one chart updates another. We'll explore the possibilities of interactivity more deeply in the next chapter, where you will learn how to bring multiple charts together for different forms of analysis.

> # Interactivity Summary Card
>
> ✔ Allows your work to reveal extra details only when the audience is ready
>
> ✔ Allows your audience to customize the analysis to their own interests

Summary

Every object you use on the page should clarify your message, help your audience interpret the information, or guide users toward the key points.

Titles establish your subject but can also highlight your key findings and convince your audience to spend time reading your work. Text boxes and annotations can be helpful, but make sure they don't smother the data points or make your audience think they are going to have to read lots of text to understand your points.

Providing contextual numbers early in the work can help establish a baseline for understanding everything that follows. They can also provide quick answers, allowing your audience the option to dig further in if they need more information.

Legends, iconography, and visual cues will help your audience quickly understand what the marks you are using represent. These visual cues also allow you to guide your audience on how to interact with your work. This is especially important when you want your audience to use tooltips, filters, and other interactive features. Careful use of whitespace around your charts can help shape the storyline.

This chapter also showed you how to work with the positions of the objects on your page. Understanding the order in which your audience is likely to take in your work enables you to control the narrative.

This might seem like a lot of elements to control, but you'll find that it quickly becomes second nature. In the next chapter, we will explore the overall composition of a single piece of work and analyze its form to discuss what you should include and how you can represent the data.

CHAPTER 7

The Medium for the Message: Complex and Interactive Data Communication

So far, you've learned how to use charts effectively one at a time. But single charts aren't always the answer. When your findings are complex, trying to squeeze everything into one chart can make things confusing, convolute the key points, and confuse the message. This is even more true when you are not personally present to guide your audience through interpreting the data.

The solution to this problem is to use multiple charts that each tell an individual part of the story you've found within the data. This allows the reader to absorb your message in chunks. You can use each chart to build your story as well as provide context.

This chapter begins by looking at two communication styles: explanatory and exploratory. The style you choose will determine many of your design decisions.

The second part of this chapter examines how the medium of your data communication affects your work and your audience's understanding, especially when it involves multiple charts. We'll spend particular time on dashboards. The term *dashboard* is ubiquitous, but just because your stakeholder asks for a dashboard, it isn't necessarily what they need or want. Your communications can take many forms, including infographics, presentations, and emails.

Explanatory Communications

Explanatory communication clearly articulates your findings to your audience. This book has so far focused on explanatory data visualization techniques.

Why focus on explanatory communication now? Because explanatory communication is especially important when you're asking your audience to interact with your work, such as through filters and highlighting. They'll need your guidance to use the work as you intend them to.

Figure 7-1 has been designed to guide the audience through its analysis into the revenue being produced by each of Prep Air's routes.

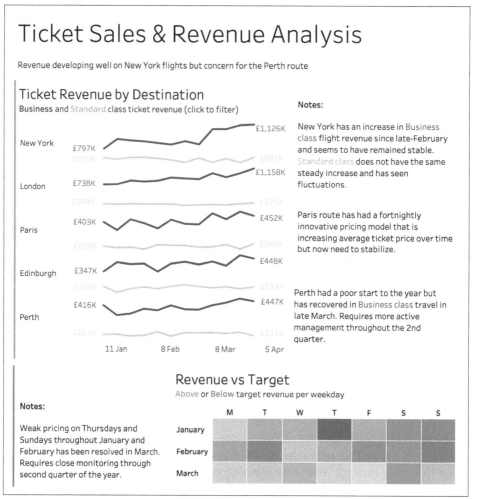

Figure 7-1. Explanatory analysis of Prep Air's revenue by route

Gathering Requirements

Building a clear explanatory communication takes a lot of careful planning and requirement gathering. To guide your audience, you need to ensure that you are absolutely clear on what they need from your work. In Chapter 2, you learned that what a stakeholder requests first is often not exactly what they need. Following up with additional clarifying questions will help you understand what they really need. With explanatory work, focus on that need closely.

You won't often have space in your final communication for every single chart you have built. You will have to make tough choices about what to include, always keeping the audience's goals in mind.

Updating Data in Explanatory Views

What happens when you need to update an explanatory communication with new data? And what if the new data points don't support your original insight?

To explore this question, let's go back to our fictional airline, Prep Air. Claire, who is in charge of ticket revenue at Prep Air, is doing her usual data analysis. She finds an unusual trend in sales as they suddenly drop. This is serious, and Claire realizes she should explain the situation to her manager, Preet, so he can take action.

Claire starts working on an explanatory chart to show Preet, but the data is volatile and updates frequently: the story could change before she gets a chance to present it. Even if the trend persists as the updated data comes in, any increase or decrease in the measures Claire used might require her to rework the whole chart. Preet has a good level of understanding of data, and therefore Claire feels comfortable being able to talk about the variability in the data with him and how an update to the underlying data might change the insight she's found.

If you build an explanatory view of your data on a data set that can update, do so with caution. If the data will be updated before she shares her analysis with Preet, Claire should ensure that any of the values or annotations she includes in her communication will update as well as the charts. Claire will need to check the analysis to make sure that her original message stays true as the data updates.

So What?

Just sharing your findings is not enough. As the name suggests, explanatory communications should explain your findings clearly and form them into a cohesive message.

Some of the questions I find myself asking when forming an explanatory view are as follows:

- Does my message have more than one part?
- If so, which chart(s) tell the different parts of the message clearly?
- Do all of the categories and time periods you've included fit the message you're trying to convey?

- What do I want the audience to take in first? In what order should I tell the story? Should the most important chart go first or last?

- What is the audience's most important takeaway message, and how can I make sure they remember it?

- Why is my message important? So what?

Being clear with the "So what?" is crucial. What action do you want your audience to take?

If you overlook this aspect, why build the work in the first place? Sometimes just providing information for context is useful, but often you'll want to achieve a certain outcome. Make sure you drive your audience to take that outcome.

If your "So what?" is for your audience to take a measurable action, like clicking a link or filling in a survey, you can easily track that activity to see how effective your work has been. More often than not, the action will be shown in a future analysis if, for example, more staff are added to the rotation or a price change occurs to generate more revenue. Although this isn't as simple as counting clicks on a link, a traceable difference is still being made, showing the effectiveness of your communication.

If your "So what?" is less measurable, test your communication. Have you ever asked a colleague to look at an important email you've drafted, to make sure your message is clear and you're striking the right tone? Find a few members of your audience who are willing to help. Show them the work, without guiding them on how to interpret it. Then ask what they're taking away from it. What do they see as the most important points? What do they remember? What do they click first? What was confusing?

As you deal with data more constantly, you'll sometimes run into the *curse of knowledge*: it can be challenging, when you are familiar and fluent with various aspects of the work, to set that knowledge aside and see the work from the perspective of someone who doesn't know what you do. This makes it easy to skip over important contextual information or make incorrect assumptions about what readers will infer or conclude. Pay attention to the questions your test readers ask: they can indicate where important information or context might be missing.

Exploratory Communications

The second style of data communication is exploratory. *Exploratory data communications* allow your audience to navigate through the data visualizations themselves, providing interactive options for them to find, filter, and focus on what they particularly care about.

Gathering Requirements

You've seen that explanatory views are all about meeting the audience's needs, which gives the work a clear scope. Requirement gathering for exploratory views is a little more challenging, and sometimes vague.

Claire's manager, Preet, wants multiple views of the same sales data for Prep Air. She notes his goals:

> "I'd like to see the sales over time but also be able to see it by country or by product."

> "Can I look at sales for each of the last few years separately?"

> "We need to show each region only their own sales, but I need to see them all."

> "My boss's boss said that the CEO wants to be able to sort sales by region, but they didn't give me specifics."

Such requests are where exploratory analysis really shines.

This sounds easier than meeting specific requirements, right? Well, not quite: now Claire needs to choose the best ways to show all those views. She'll need to carefully consider factors like what style of chart to use, how to format labels, and how to word and place titles for each slice of the data.

Exploratory views can also be useful when you aren't certain of the end user's requirements. You should always try to meet with the end users of your work, but this isn't always possible, as with Preet's directive from very senior executives. Exploratory views create flexibility.

Flexibility and Flow

Exploratory communications don't have the same straightforward flow as explanatory analysis. Rather than controlling the order in which the audience consumes the work, you want to encourage them to explore different views and options. Although techniques like the Z pattern (discussed in Chapter 6) can still be used, you'll need to provide *signposts*: ways to tell or show users what they can click, filter, or otherwise interact with. These might include the following:

- Filters
- Hyperlinks
- Clicking one chart to update another

- Changing parameterized values
- Hovering over an area of interest

You can use written instructions or symbols to represent the actions your audience can take. Written instructions can be precise, guiding the user through each element and what it provides:

- Click here to filter
- Hover over to select
- Choose the Top N amount

Figure 7-2 has the first and last element built into the view. The user can pick an individual route to filter the contextual numbers (in this case, London is selected) or select how many routes to see at once.

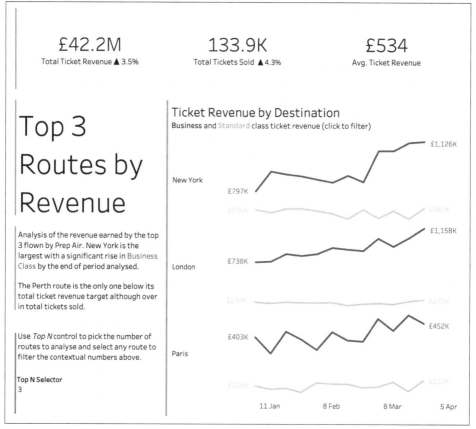

Figure 7-2. Chart with written exploratory instructions

Remember, though, that even when your instructions are short, each word adds to the cognitive effort you are asking your audience to make—as well as taking up precious space. An alternate approach is to use symbols and a simple legend to let your users know the types of interactions that are possible with each chart (Figure 7-3).

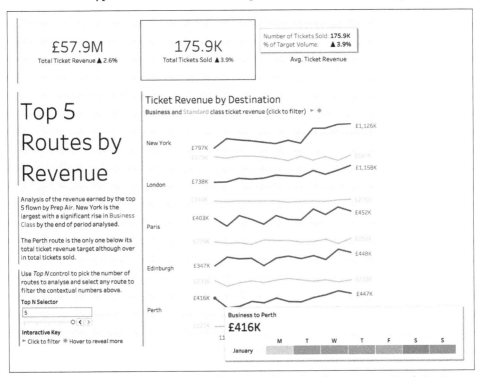

Figure 7-3. Interactivity key (bottom left) with tooltip when hovering on Perth Business Class

If you produce work regularly for the same audience, use the same symbols and meanings consistently for the same interactions so that they become intuitive over time.

Another option is to provide a video walk-through of your work so that you can present it as you might in person. The downside of this technique is that the video is likely to be stored in a different location and may not be easily accessible because of bandwidth or access issues.

Now that you understand the differences between explanatory and exploratory communications, let's look at the medium in which you're communicating. Are you creating a report, a dashboard, an infographic, a live conference presentation? The rest of this chapter looks at how the medium affects your message.

Methods: Dashboards

Preet walks into Claire's office with *The Big Book of Dashboards* in his hand. "I think I need you to build me a dashboard," he says. He reads the book's definition aloud: "A dashboard is a visual display of data used to monitor conditions and/or facilitate understanding."[1] "That would be so helpful!"

Claire is familiar with dashboards; they're one of the most common requests she gets. She knows that dashboards are many things to many people, and she stays on top of new techniques and styles as they evolve. To help Preet, she'll need to know the conditions he wants to monitor and what he needs to understand.

Monitoring Conditions

When most of us think of dashboards, we think of cars. Motor vehicle dashboards show information that allows the driver to monitor and assess a range of conditions, such as these:

- Speed
- Fuel level
- Engine temperature
- Lights
- Indicators
- Outside temperature
- Engine revolutions
- Distance traveled
- Warning lights

That is a lot of information to take in, especially when you need to focus on the road. An effective dashboard communicates pieces of information to the driver in small chunks, alongside each other, so they can be considered together. That's why dashboards are so helpful for monitoring conditions—and this holds true for your organization's dashboards too.

Let's say you are driving at night. The dashboard displays some information that you'll want to check frequently: how fast are you going? Are your headlights on bright, potentially dazzling other drivers? If you have a manual transmission, do your engine revolutions show you're in the optimal gear? You might need other information only occasionally: has the temperature fallen below freezing, meaning there

---

1 Steve Wexler et al., *The Big Book of Dashboards* (Hoboken, NJ: Wiley, 2017).

could be ice on the road? Do you have enough gas in your tank? Are there any warning lights?

If you know exactly the piece of information you need, you should be able to find it quickly. The most frequently checked pieces of information are often larger and in more prominent positions on your dashboard. Rarely used warning lights and the fuel gauge, however, are usually much smaller and on the periphery of the dashboard. Take this into account for your own dashboard design.

A vehicle dashboard is a snapshot of the exact moment you look at it. As soon as you look away from the dashboard, something might change: you might slow down, for instance. The organizational dashboards you create will likely also provide a live view of a situation, which means they need the latest data. I discuss the challenges of that in the next chapter. You might see this in, for example, a dashboard for call center workers, which might display the number of calls waiting to be answered, the number of call handlers available, and the number of calls answered that day.

Claire makes a list of what she'll need to ask Preet:

- What does he want to monitor?
- What does he need to check frequently, and what does he refer to less often?
- What data sources need to feed into the dashboard?

Facilitating Understanding

Most of the dashboards Claire has built focus less on monitoring conditions and more on the other part of the *Big Book of Dashboards* definition: facilitating understanding. Few organizations keep all of the information they need for decision making in live data sets.

Usually, what Claire's stakeholders want are views that will assist them in longer-term strategic decision making. Those dashboards are all about facilitating understanding by providing context and by answering multiple questions at once.

Context

As you learned in Chapter 6, large, contextual numbers reflecting key metrics are a great way to provide context. For Preet's dashboard (Figure 7-4), Claire decides to use triangular indicators to describe how the metric compares to a previous measurement. Did sales go up or down? Are things OK, or does the situation need urgent focus? In Figure 7-4 the comparison is to a target. Both options are possible, so you need to be clear to your audience. I use a tooltip to clarify this when the audience hovers over the values.

Figure 7-4. Setting context by using contextual numbers

Frequent consumers of this information may remember what is good and what isn't, so they're likely to focus on the values rather than the indicator arrows. Claire positions the contextual numbers much like the key dials on a car's dashboard. The contextual numbers sit at the top of the page or screen, since this is where the audience's attention is likely to be focused first (Figure 7-5).

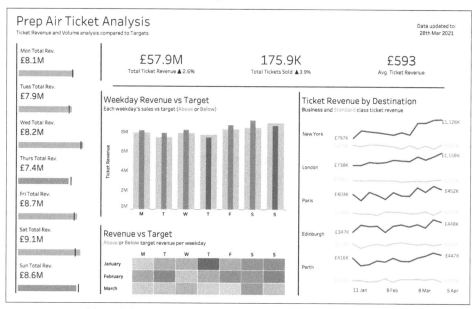

Figure 7-5. Dashboard showing ticket revenue data for Prep Air

The charts alongside the contextual numbers provide additional detail on revenue by weekday, versus target, by destination, and over time (Figure 7-5). Breaking the dashboard into sections chunks the information into more-digestible pieces. The differing charts also allow the audience to dig deeper.

Answering multiple questions

Designing a dashboard to answer multiple questions at once can save a lot of repetitive work and change requests. When you are working with data, you will frequently find you want to go beyond answering the key requirements. Including multiple charts allows you to articulate additional points that may solve questions before your audience can ask them.

Adding interactivity can take this approach even further, allowing your audience to focus on what they care about. Figure 7-6 shows the same dashboard as Figure 7-5 but filtered to focus on Paris.

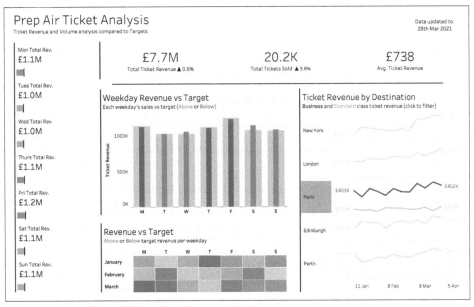

Figure 7-6. Dashboard filtered to focus on Paris

The interactivity in Figure 7-6 means Preet can start from an initial question and answer additional questions that might come up. Here's how the flow of questions might go:

1. What's the revenue for Prep Air this quarter?

2. What about for our new destination, Paris?

3. Are there any days of the week that are weaker than others?

4. Is the below-target performance for Monday, Thursday, and Friday a new phenomenon, or has it happened throughout the full quarter?

The dashboard shows particularly poor performance against the target for Mondays in March. It would be difficult to design a dashboard that would allow Preet to find out why Mondays in March are particularly poor, but Claire has saved herself three revisions to this dashboard by allowing Preet to learn about the issue and identify instances more specifically. Focused questions like "What happened in March on Mondays for Paris?" help analysts identify important issues in ways that probably wouldn't have been possible with the dashboard alone.

The point of a dashboard isn't to answer every question your audience will have. It's to allow them to answer more than just one question by using interactivity. As you gain more experience, you will become better at studying the requirements (sometimes imprecise ones) and thinking about what else your audience might want to understand or explore. Be prepared to iterate your initial work, and know that when you do, it's because your communications are facilitating an even deeper understanding of the data.

Dashboards Summary Card

✔ Monitors various metrics alongside each other

✔ Well suited to exploratory analysis, as you can apply filters and assume the audience will interact

✔ Provides lots of design choices to create something memorable

✘ Requires user testing to ensure that people find the information you intend

---

Methods: Infographics

Infographics use multiple charts within a single view to tell a specific story. They are often used to share information in a basic but digestible way with people who are new to a subject. Whereas dashboards are usually exploratory communications, infographics are explanatory communications.

There are many definitions, but I like this one by Ben Jones: a "style of data display [that] includes a series of facts about a specific subject, often orientated in one tall column."[2] I would add that an infographic displays data visualizations prominently (by which I mean at least half of the metaphorical data-ink on the page, as covered in Chapter 3) alongside text to communicate a focused point or story.

It can be difficult to get the balance of data and text right. Jones highlights the challenges:

> Unfortunately, many infographics are merely tall posters full of cheesy images and individual percentages or figures. Often the figures are accompanied by an ill-advised attempt at a visualization that skews proportions horribly.[3]

Remember that the data in your infographic must support the story you're telling in the communication. The right charts, conveying the right information, can add a lot to written communications.

---

2 Ben Jones, *Communicating Data with Tableau* (Sebastopol, CA: O'Reilly, 2014), 233.

3 Jones, *Communicating Data with Tableau*, 233.

In a business context, infographics are useful for interdepartmental communications, when the audience in one department needs to understand a point but might not be familiar with the other department's field. This is also true for sharing information with customers. Keeping the visualizations simple and easy to understand is especially important.

Figure 7-7 uses the same data as the dashboard in Figure 7-5 but in a format that's much easier to read and includes much more explanatory text. Although Figure 7-7 isn't oriented in a long column as per Jones's definition, the view has been developed for a single screen and to fit with the waterfall chart that runs through the middle of the view.

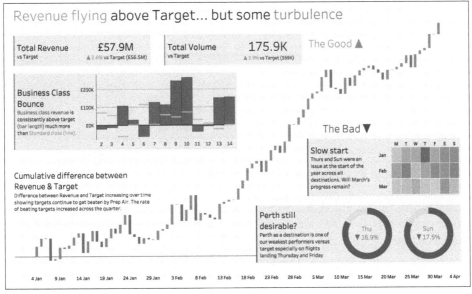

Figure 7-7. An infographic on Prep Air's revenue

While the dashboard in Figure 7-5 will help Preet do his job, this infographic would be good to share with the rest of Prep Air's employees, to help them understand what has happened to ticket revenue in the first quarter.

Infographics frequently use nondata imagery to help establish the theme for the work; these must still support the story you are telling. Remember, too, that overloading the work with too much text or too many images or charts can turn audiences off.

Long-form infographics—the tall, single-column style Jones describes, designed for scrolling down, allow much more detail than can fit on a single computer screen. In Figure 7-8, for example, dividing lines separate the sections of the work: you could easily make each section fit the landscape orientation of a standard computer monitor.

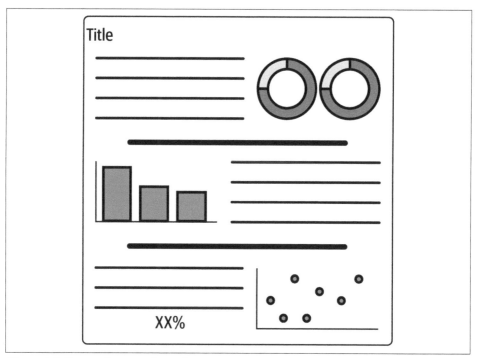

Figure 7-8. Layout for an infographic

The Z pattern you learned about in Chapter 6 applies to infographics too: the audience reads across, then down the page. This clearly structured flow, which guides the audience from beginning to end, is especially good for explanatory work.

Infographics Summary Card

✔ Can be eye-catching.

✔ Useful method to tell a clear story.

✘ Take care when updating data sets that your story doesn't change.

Methods: Slide Presentations

Dashboards and infographics are fantastic media for communicating data with your audience when you are not there (for example, while working remotely). If you work in an office, though, you are likely to have more opportunities to communicate directly to your audience in person.

PowerPoint and other slide software programs are popular for these styles of presentations. The challenge with this format is its static nature: yes, you can add animation to your slides, but your audience won't be able to hover over interesting data points for more details. To make up for that lack of interactivity, you serve as a guide, walking your audience through what you want them to see. You can show the details you want them to focus on. You can add more context if your audience needs it. Stakeholders are comfortable with receiving information from presentations of slide decks. They are likely to expect the following:

- A title slide stating what the presentation is about
- A slide offering an overview of the current situation
- A set of slides outlining your proposed solution
- A slide stating next steps

Best of all, though, you can answer questions. Answering questions about your data can be a whole new challenge. Say you're presenting to senior stakeholders: you show a profit chart, but an executive might ask what the profit ratio was that year, or want to compare it to the previous year. You can't memorize the whole data set, so it's impossible to prepare for every question.

Here's my advice: think about how the slide deck will be used *after* your presentation. Stakeholders will often ask you to send them your deck so that they can refer to it later, and they are likely to share it with others who did not see your presentation. They often expect the deck to include an appendix of data visualizations, which is an opportunity to present all of your charts. Presenters are often advised to use as little text as possible in their slides so that the audience will focus on the visualization, but this advice does not account for the slide deck's second role as a supporting document. Without your words, it's easy for someone reading the slides outside the context of a presentation to misinterpret your points.

For this reason, I recommend that you include additional informational text *within* your visualizations, not just alongside them. This will also help you answer questions on the spot. You might even consider sharing a dashboard with your audience after the presentation, to allow them to further validate your points or challenge their own assumptions.

Slide Presentations Summary Card

✔ Good for a lower-level data-literate audience

✔ Good when delivering the message inperson

✘ Difficult to update as data changes

Methods: Notes and Emails

Researcher Joseph Johnson estimates (*https://oreil.ly/Pky7o*) that by 2020, 306 billion emails were sent and received every single day. That number is expected to grow to 376 billion in 2025. That's a lot of email. How can you get people to read *yours*?

The first step is to become known for sending meaningful and insightful messages. If recipients know that your emails are worth reading, they'll open them. If you send too many messages that are boring, pointless, unsupported by evidence, or tough to consume, you can lose that reputation quickly.

One of my first data roles in a large organization was to audit all of the team's reports to see what people were actually reading. My manager took a radical approach: stop producing *everything* and see who notices.

Instead, we sent emails that didn't contain the report but just a link asking whether the report was necessary. Over 60% of the team's work never received a single click. The radical approach worked: once we identified what wasn't being used, we could focus on who *hadn't* clicked and why. It turned out that people were treating the reporting emails like spam: filtering them out of their inboxes and ignoring them. Obviously, that wasn't effective communication—or a good use of anyone's resources.

It's also important to think about how your emails are distributed. Who are they reaching, and who is being left out? The Information Lab founder Tom Brown (*https://oreil.ly/l1HqF*), in an interview with *Forbes*, notes, "The To box masquerades as an opportunity to include people, but in fact it's an opportunity to exclude people."

You can't embed interactive data communications into your email, so consider email as a way to *navigate your audience to the work*. Use snippets or small screenshots of your work to show your audience why they should take the time to follow the links to the actual work. Make it interesting, and then watch the numbers to see what works.

Notes and Emails Summary Card

✔ Most common form of organizational communication, so don't ignore this method

✔ Data can be added in screenshots, so not possible to be interactive

✖ More likely a conduit to other methods of data communication

---

Summary

Bringing multiple charts together into a single communication can help you tell a more compelling and rounded story with your data. Getting it right, though, is a tough balance. If you use too few charts, gaps will occur in your analysis—and your audience might infer that there are also gaps in your conclusions. Use too many charts, however, and you can overload your audience. Their eyes will glaze over, and they won't even attempt to expend the cognitive effort to decode and assess your message. Communicating with data is a skill, and it takes practice to get a feel for that balance.

You've also learned about explanatory and exploratory communications and how to determine which you need, based on the requirements and scope of the work. Neither approach is better; they're useful in different situations, and it's important to develop your skills in producing both.

Dashboards are a great form to help your audience develop understanding of a subject. Humans are fundamentally intelligent creatures with a natural inclination to dig deeper, so enable that instinct and give them the tools they need to explore the data.

Explanatory communications walk your audience through the data and toward your conclusions. To make them effective, be sure you have a clear sense of your audience's data-literacy levels; their prior knowledge of the subject, if any; and how much time they'll have to understand your communication.

If you can create compelling and attractive communications, you'll fare much better in the battle for audiences' attention. To develop your skills, I recommend that you read and analyze examples of great data communications, just as aspiring novelists should read literary classics. Many of the examples in this chapter draw on the fantastic style of my colleague Ellen Blackburn (*https://oreil.ly/axFVj*), whose designs capture attention without sacrificing analytical depth. Chris Love's website, Everyday Dashboards (*https://oreil.ly/zXm3i*), allows you to view all sorts of dashboards and views from specific departments (with their data anonymized). It's a great place to look for inspiration.

Now that you're creating strong data communications, Part III will look at Prep Air to discuss how to implement data communications in your actual workplace, with real people, teams, and departments, complete with conflicting interests and power struggles.

PART III

Deploying Data Communication in the Workplace

CHAPTER 8

Implementation Strategies for Your Workplace

Now that you can put together compelling data visualizations that communicate your points clearly and effectively, you might expect this would be where the book ends. Now, though, we're going to look at how to *use* the products of your labor in your workplace. This is the "people" side of things. How can you make the most of your work and advocate for its importance? How should you justify your choices? This chapter and the next will take you through some challenges you can expect when working with different teams, departments, organizations, and industries, all with different needs and approaches. If you're aware of differing opinions and possibilities, you'll be better prepared to deliver what is required.

No data visualization is ever perfect. Your work can always be changed, tweaked, or adjusted based on the stakeholders' design, as well as analytical or subject-matter expertise. Therefore, do not expect many hard dos and don'ts—just a better understanding of where to strike the balance.

The challenges we will cover include the following:

Tables versus pretty pictures
> Attitudes toward the use of visualization techniques to demonstrate stories in data

Static versus interactive
> How interactive your analytical products can be before the audience might start to miss key messages

Centralized versus decentralized teams
> How centralized data teams and assets pose different challenges than a more decentralized model

Live versus extracted data sets
    Working with current live data or extracted, static data sets

Standardized versus innovative reporting
    Whether you'll be making your data communications by using set templates or crafting the methods from scratch

Reporting versus analytics
    Striking the balance between presenting structured reports and customized analytical visualizations

This chapter shows how these choices affect how you use, access, and share data. Being conscious of them will allow you to pick a more effective path.

To illustrate how to find the balance between all of the challenges, as well as some tactics you might use to improve the situation, I'm going to use our hypothetical companies: Prep Air and Chin & Beard Suds Co. Although you have seen data and visualizations from these organizations used as examples throughout the book, let's learn more about the organizations themselves.

We're going to look at them through several lenses, each representing a factor that affects data communication. I have given each organization a score from 0 to 10 to represent its position on the spectrum between the extreme ends. These organizations are at the opposite ends of most of the spectrums covered in this chapter; yours is likely to fall somewhere in the middle on most measures. The definitions for each factor are discussed in more detail throughout the chapter.

Let's start with our big corporate airline: Prep Air.

Prep Air Fact Sheet

Business: Global airline selling tickets online

Founded: 2000

Employees: 5,000 (head office—500, customer facing—4,500)

To summarize the current use of data communications in each of the companies featured in this chapter, Figure 8-1 is a visual that shows the predominant attitudes across the organization for each of the factors you'll find in this chapter.

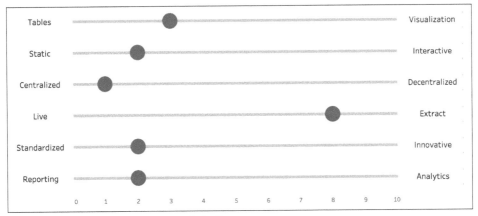

Figure 8-1. Prep Air organizational challenges scores

Like many large, traditional organizations, Prep Air set up most of its reporting early in the company's development and hasn't invested much in more modern self-service tools since. Because aviation regulators must operate worldwide in a range of economies, the airline industry is full of traditional (and sometimes incompatible) data feeds, including paper printouts. All of this makes the leadership of Prep Air hesitant to invest more in data-driven decision making.

Because of movement of staff from other airlines as people change jobs but stay within the industry, a few visual requests do get through to the central data team. The data team is heavily centralized, as the focus of its data work is reporting to regulators and producing financial returns. *Centralized* refers to moving people with a certain skill set into one centrally managed team that supports the rest of the organization. This means the data people work primarily with static views based on extracts so as not to strain the aging data infrastructure. Data is seen as an expense rather than a benefit creator, and, therefore, automation of reporting has been the major focus.

When I've worked with organizations like this before, I've seen the benefit of giving more modern data visualization software to their newer staff members. The data tools they are used to using elsewhere, either at a university or other companies, can help them to communicate more effectively with the high-quality data sources that have been built up over time. Prep Air is likely to have data assets that are well structured, but access needs to be given to subject-matter experts across the organization to make use of the data sets. Modern self-service data visualization tools would be perfect for this job, as they would connect directly to the centrally controlled sources. This would create more exploratory analysis that will complete the baseline knowledge formed through the current reporting. The goal of the exploratory analysis is to find the nuances required to stay with or ahead of their competitors.

The downside of the exploratory analysis is the proliferation of alternate data sets. Proliferation of data sets becomes an issue when data workers don't know which data source to use, because so many have been created by people to conduct their own analysis. You might have come across the phrase *single source of truth*, which describes an existing single data set that is proven to have accurate records for a certain subject. As long as the proliferation is managed, this downside should not cause much of a problem.

Trying to create the energy for the change is the harder part. Often it takes a new member of the executive team or a few subject-matter experts finding a new data tool to demonstrate the benefits that data can offer. A new member of the executive team asking for more analysis creates the drive to provide what they are asking for. If you are used to working with data to drive the organization, you will quickly try to replace it if it isn't there. The new executive doesn't have to come in from the same industry to drive that change, as industries can learn from each other in crossover functions like marketing or sales.

A new tool can empower subject-matter experts in the organization. This can create friction between the IT function and these individuals, but this is where the difference between reporting and analytics is really felt. The IT function is discussed more in Chapter 9. The IT team members will often be involved in many parts of the process when you work with data. They will be the hosts for lots of the data sets your organization will rely on, pick the software you have access to, and may also help you turn your communication into a regular report. As the IT team will have likely chosen the incumbent tool in the organization, the use of the new tool and the work to incorporate it into the existing tasks can be vast, thus creating the aforementioned friction. Empowering the subject-matter experts with software that is easier for everyone to use will enable them to leverage their expertise in a way that the IT team can't for all roles in the organization. You can then share good-quality analytics with the executive team, and other teams are likely to also feel the influence of such a change.

A lot of change will be required by Prep Air to enable an environment where everyone can work with data to inform more decisions. Not all of these things will have to be in place to communicate well with data, but if they are, Prep Air would find it much easier to implement the advice within this book.

Let's now assess how data is used differently by a small retailer: the Chin & Beard Suds Co.

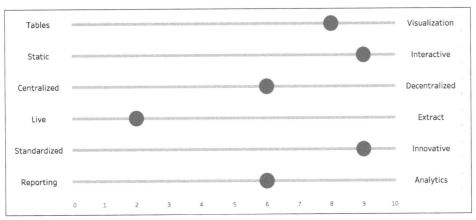

Chin & Beard Suds Co. (C&BS Co.) Fact Sheet

Business: Retailer of soap-based products selling in-store and online

Founded: 2018

Employees: 100 (head office—20, customer facing—80)

Figure 8-2 illustrates how the attitude toward data communications differs in C&BS Co. for each factor.

Tables	●─────────	Visualization
Static	●─────────	Interactive
Centralized	●─────────	Decentralized
Live	●─────────	Extract
Standardized	●─────────	Innovative
Reporting	●─────────	Analytics

Figure 8-2. Chin & Beard Suds Co. organizational challenges scores

As a newer organization and without heavy regulation, C&BS Co. has a lot more flexibility in its use of data and a newer set of tools to work with it. Like any modern retailer, much more business is driven from online sales than in-person, store-based sales. This means C&BS Co. has had to use analytics to monitor competitor pricing and promotions to stay competitive while not overly discounting to the point of losing money.

As C&BS Co. does sell online as well as in stores, it has established a culture of using data early. The store managers are data savvy and enjoy working with data sets to understand their customers. The managers are experienced in using modern applications that utilize data visualization throughout.

However, as a retailer, a lot of the focus on the expenses of the organization goes into the stores and the products sold. This means IT and data expenditure have been less compared to what we saw at Prep Air. This reduced expenditure means centralized data sources are not as closely managed, and various teams throughout the organization have their own data sets. Lots of the data sources are run within the headquarters team instead of by someone at each store, though.

Because of their background of using data, the analysts on the team can be more innovative and try different techniques to share their insights. Being in retail means people are often quite creative and therefore can flex their visual style to make something more memorable and attractive for the teams to use.

We'll keep referring back to these organizations throughout the chapter to see how they respond to the challenges they face.

Tables Versus Pretty Pictures

After specializing in data visualization for the majority of my career, I have lost count of the number of times people have told me, "I don't need pretty pictures, just the answers." This is a clear sign that they haven't encountered data visualizations that communicate clearly. (Some haven't encountered data visualization at all.) As communicators, we have to get people over the perception of "pretty pictures" before they can gain the benefits of visual analytics. So why not just use data visualization for everything?

Sometimes the precision of a table is the best approach. People request a table instead of a visualization for many reasons, but the two I've found most common are that they don't trust visualizations to tell the data's story, and they want to use the data elsewhere. Let's dig into these reasons:

Trust
> Early data visualization software wasn't designed for storytelling. Instead, it often defaulted to visualizations that *hid* the data. This made them easy to misinterpret, leading to bad decisions and undermining trust. As with any form of communication, if you don't trust its source, you are unlikely to trust the findings. Trust also needs to exist between the person who is encoding the data into the visual communication and the recipient. If a stakeholder doesn't trust the data, the format, or the person presenting it, they are likely to request the data in table form so they can "see it for themselves."

Data to be used elsewhere
> Sometimes people request tables because they want to use them with another tool that they may feel more comfortable with when conducting their own analysis. Often the tool people feel more comfortable with is the one they have the most experience on—namely, Excel. The question here is: what are they really looking

for? What answers do they need? If they aren't getting those answers from your visualization, this may indicate a failing in your requirement-gathering process. As covered in Chapter 2, you need to determine what answers the stakeholder is looking for and deliver those. If another process is needed, you can design a visualization to find the right data points to kickstart that process.

When should you respect someone's request for a table, and when should you challenge it? It's all about context, and that is what this section delves into.

Data Culture

How much does your organization incorporate data into everyday decision making? Do your people trust your organization's data? Are they comfortable using it in their daily tasks?

Your answers will tell you something about your organization's *data culture*: how comfortable people are with trusting and using data. If your organization routinely includes data in everyday decision making, that's a sign of a strong data culture. If people are requesting tables instead of visualizations because they don't trust the data or use data only sporadically in decision making, you might have a weak data culture.

If you want users of your analysis to accept the stories your visualizations tell without questioning what you may be trying to hide, you'll need to develop a strong data culture—and that means trust. Don't use visualizations only when you want to convey positive news; you want people to get used to working with visualizations and to have a sense of perspective and context when viewing them.

You can use tables alongside visualization to generate trust in what the visualizations are saying. This process doesn't take years, as clear communication of data in tables and visualizations will soon build the trust you need in both methods. Without that? Try to use visualizations to convey bad news, and you're likely to find your audience blaming the charts for "exaggerating" the message rather than focusing on the causes of underperformance.

Verbal communication is important here as well. You can develop a data culture by meeting people and understanding their challenges and issues. If your audience communicates with you verbally and understands your intentions, they are more likely to buy in to the analysis. Your work will also become much more relevant when you work directly with people, as you will be able to look for what they are struggling to achieve without data.

Once you've built that trust, you'll have more freedom to build the best visualization for the analysis rather than making suboptimal design decisions just to ensure that your point gets across. With better use of data visualizations, you are more likely to be able to articulate the story in the data quickly and clearly to the users of the analytical views. Having a richer set of tools at your fingertips will allow you to understand how different views have different strengths when it comes to the type of data being analyzed. A stronger data culture will not just be better positioned to use the views but will also be open to alternate visualization that may not be as commonly used. Tables will also be less likely to be requested as standard but will still be used where needed within the analytical products.

However, data cultures don't just switch from weak to strong overnight. The development of a data culture takes time and requires a few facets to be present in the organization:

- Data-driven leadership
- Investment in data tools
- Communication

Data-driven leadership

The executive team sets the tone for the rest of an organization. If the executives are looking to make data-driven decisions, they will expect the people they directly manage to be well versed in the organization's data. During my time as a consultant, I was frequently asked to support teams that were trying to get up to speed, to be able to answer the data-driven questions the leadership was posing.

These situations were frequently caused by a change in leadership, as a new member joined the executive team or the whole team was replaced. With the greater emphasis on data, new skills have to either be developed within the existing team members or brought in through new hires.

If you are in this situation and are part of the team being asked to produce more data analytics, you have already made a step in the right direction by reading this book. By understanding where data is coming from, the charting options you have when analyzing data, and how you can communicate your findings through visualizations, you will be able to respond to your leadership's questions.

Adding a new member to the executive board of Prep Air would kickstart this transformation, as it is difficult to create that drive without previous experience.

Investment in data tools

Just being asked for data sets, or answers based on data, is not the easiest path to a strong data culture. Without investment in products to assist in the storage, transformation, and visualization of data, workarounds and resistance to using data are likely, because it will be difficult to achieve the required output. With investment in data tools, the organization is likely to become faster and better at answering questions than otherwise achievable.

You are unlikely to successfully make the purchasing decision for new data tools if you work at a large organization like Prep Air, but highlighting the challenges you face due to the tools you currently have to work with is an important first step. Most leadership teams I have worked with are unaware of the quantity of work being undertaken to deliver even basic answers. By highlighting the effort involved, or where savings could be made, you may prompt investment in tools that will reduce your workload on preparatory tasks and instead allow you to focus on your analysis and communication of the findings.

A lot of Prep Air's investment in data tools was made more than 20 years ago. Therefore, employees are working with tools that do not take advantage of recent technological improvements. In data-rich industries, like travel and transport, being able to form decisions quickly can be the difference between being a market leader or follower. For example, being able to change your ticket prices based on ticket sales to date, website traffic, and pricing by your competitors will allow you to stay competitive. With modern analytics tools being able to connect to live data sources (we'll come back to these later in this chapter), you can base your analysis on the latest position rather than last week, month, or quarter.

There is a commonly applied logic for development of data solution maturity. Most organizations get stuck at Prep Air's current stage, with *descriptive* reporting. At this stage, data is used just to show what is happening. The next stage is *diagnostic* analysis, through interactive reports like dashboards, where you can understand why something is likely to have occurred. Mass production reporting tools don't always have the ability to let their users interact with the reports. The final stages are *predictive* and *prescriptive* analytics, in which different tools are likely to be needed to allow you to first understand what is likely to happen and then what you might want to do about it. Moving from one stage to the next takes maturity in the data culture as well as investment in data tools.

Communication

Like any change in an organization, communication is required to understand the organization's challenges as well as sharing with others why the increase of data needs to occur. Many people in your organization won't know what is possible to achieve with data. You will need to show them what you can achieve with their data and the tools available. By collaborating with your peers, you will be able to understand their challenges and provide data-led solutions where applicable.

One aspect of organizational life that you can save from eroding your data culture is descoping data from projects as budgets get squeezed. Project timelines and scopes can be reduced with a frequent cut, data. When delivering projects, data is often seen as a by-product of the project and therefore is an easy element to cut in favor of reducing the product scope or buying cheaper parts. However, this is a false savings.

As soon as a project is delivered, management will want to measure the impact of the project, and that will require data. Communicating the benefit you can make with data will ensure that data shouldn't be descoped.

Data Literacy

Having a strong data culture isn't enough to harness the value that data visualization can offer when being used in analytical products. To make sure data-informed decisions are being made, your organization needs a base level of comfort with data-based solutions. The skills required to work with and understand data-driven solutions is referred to as data literacy.

Data literacy can be defined as the ability to work with and understand data. Data literacy is commonly regarded as the key element that describes how well data is used in an organization. However, data literacy isn't just one skill, as Ben Jones of Data Literacy (*https://dataliteracy.com*) describes. He articulates that data literacy involves the following:

- Domain acumen
- Graphicacy
- Communication skills
- Technical skills
- Numeracy

Let's focus on two of these: numeracy and graphicacy.

Numeracy is the ability to work with and understand numerical information and mathematical concepts. In your organization, this is likely to include working with percentages and looking at variances. You might even be tested for numeracy by your organization through mathematical reasoning tests before you are able to join, as it is a core skill for many jobs. Many users of data visualization will be used to looking at charts containing these elements, and being able to understand what the percentages or variances represent ultimately means the user will understand what the chart is representing. If you are not comfortable with these elements, then no matter how the data is visualized, you are unlikely to correctly understand the insight in the data.

The numerical elements of the visualization are not the only aspect that requires understanding in order to gain value from using data visualizations. The actual parts of the visualization need to be clear to the reader in order for them to understand what the chart is showing. This is what *graphicacy* represents in Ben's definition of data literacy: the ability to read and interpret charts.

One of the most significant challenges for an analyst is to use charts every day, but remember that not everyone who will view their graphs will have the same amount of exposure to visualizations. Familiarity with any topic breeds comfort. It is incumbent on the analyst to build the skills required for the user to understand their analytics or to not use those techniques in the first place. Many of the most basic chart types are widely taught, but I've found you don't have to develop much beyond basic bar and line charts before some will start to struggle to understand what the chart is showing. However, by adding more explanation to analytical products as you introduce developments to your existing stable of charts or new chart types, you can grow your users' graphicacy.

Without strong levels of graphicacy, your stakeholders are much more likely to ask for tables instead of charts. Domain expertise, technical skills in use of data, and communication skills will obviously also have an effect on the requirements set, but graphicacy and numeracy are the major drivers for a more table-based request. Developing both of these key skills over time is likely to help your organization develop a strong data culture through building trust in the analytical products created and reducing the number of mistakes that undercut the trust and culture you are aiming to form.

Both of our featured organizations should assess their data literacy and graphicacy levels before developing analytical solutions. Progress can be made over time by building on top of the baseline skills. Giving a waterfall chart when people aren't even used to reading normal bar charts is a recipe for disaster and confusion.

Improving the Visualization Mix

Exercises can help improve your organization's visualization mix, depending on its existing data culture and literacy. The *visualization mix* is the variety of methods used to communicate data. This might be a range of charts or the format of visual communications like slides, dashboards, or infographics. From early, developing data cultures to more advanced data cultures, continuing to develop the mix of visualizations used in an organization is important.

It's a process of gradual development and improvement rather than a "once and done" thing you will need to do. Next, we'll look at techniques you can try to help improve the visualization mix in your work, depending on your organization's data literacy levels.

Start with the basics

If the consumers of your analysis have lower levels of data literacy or there isn't a strong data culture, you will need to build basic visualizations into your work to avoid creating even more barriers to people using data. Simple key performance indicators (KPIs), with iconography that demonstrates rising or falling values, can be a simple demonstration of the benefits of visualization (Figure 8-3).

Total Sales

£733K ▲

Figure 8-3. Basic KPI with change indicator

If the visualizations are successful and well received by the audience, building on this concept can involve adding a sparkline to add context to the initial KPI. The sparkline is a simple line chart that doesn't start at zero and shows how the value has changed over time (Figure 8-4). Those who are familiar with the value will know whether the current value is good, bad, or indifferent. For those who do not, the sparkline gives an indication of previous performance. A sudden rise of 10% sounds good unless you find the value had fallen 50% the month before.

Figure 8-4. Basic KPI with sparkline

Using tables is a great way for people to become more comfortable making decisions with data, although they may have to work harder to find the insights. Tables of data, if kept as small and summarized as possible, can provide a view that is similar to data that they will see in their everyday lives in newspapers, bank statements, and sports league tables. Adding visual indicators to the table will help guide their attention to the key changes in the data. Tables will help build trust with the users of your analysis and the data set it is formed from. In Figure 8-5, when more bikes have been ordered than delivered, the red dot indicator draws the reader's attention to the relevant rows where the issue occurs.

Other chart types make it much easier to see the insight in your data at a quick glance, as covered in Chapter 3. By starting with simple bar or line charts, you can begin to get your consumers used to using charts. If these charts are built on a data set that your previous analysis was constructed upon, you can leverage the trust gained. Adding annotations to help people understand the new charts when they are first introduced can help user adoption and understanding (Figure 8-6).

Store	Bike Type	Ordered	Delivered
London	Gravel	355	355
	Mountain	● 1,077	1,067
	Road	● 973	948
York	Gravel	726	726
	Mountain	1,154	1,164
	Road	● 1,037	1,017

Figure 8-5. Table with added indicators

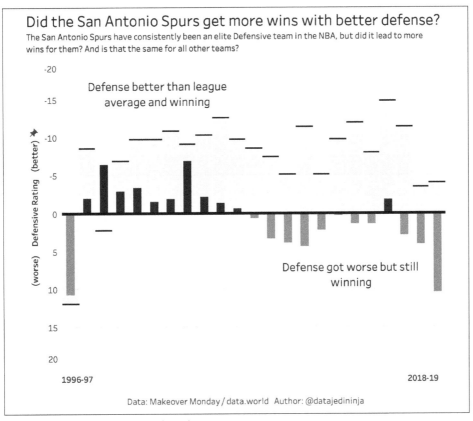

Figure 8-6. Annotations on a bar chart

When introducing newer chart types, small panes of explanation can be used to clarify how to read and interpret a chart. Instead of a small example and extra explanation, you will need to use a lot of text to describe what the user should be taking from the chart. If you don't take care, the chart soon becomes redundant to the text or swamped by the amount of text it takes to interpret the chart. Therefore, using a simple, visual example alongside the new chart might help avoid vast volumes of text.

In Figure 8-7, I used a pop-out explainer to describe how to read the chart where I had layered two elements on top of one another. Extra explanation might need to be added multiple times to help people get used to the chart type and what it is showing within the data.

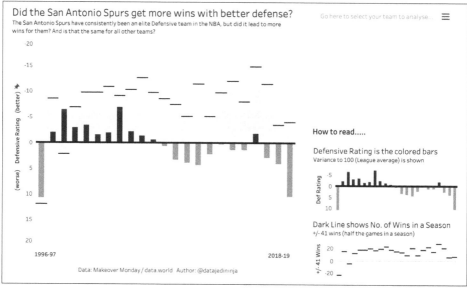

Figure 8-7. Basketball analysis with chart explainer

Instructing your users

For more major pieces of work consumed by a wide audience, you might consider putting together a video walk-through of the analysis or even provide training to users. If your audience is the general public, this will lend itself to a video walk-through, as you won't be able to gather the general public together for training. If your audience is your own organization, the size and geographical spread will factor into whether you can train users in how to use the work in person or not. The benefit of in-person training is that it provides the chance both for the users to ask questions and for the creator to see how the users interpret the visualizations. You should look to complete user testing throughout the build process of your work, but collecting a lot of users together is sometimes a tough challenge to complete earlier in the process.

When using new visual elements, it is better to introduce them via easier-to-read charts. For example, when using average lines for the first time within a chart, it is better to use them on a single-axis chart like a line or bar chart. This allows a user to become familiar with what you are trying to demonstrate with the charting element before using multiple elements in a single chart. Once a user is familiar with the element, you can begin to use multiple elements on a single chart, like average lines on a scatterplot, or a line chart that is broken into multiple years (Figure 8-8).

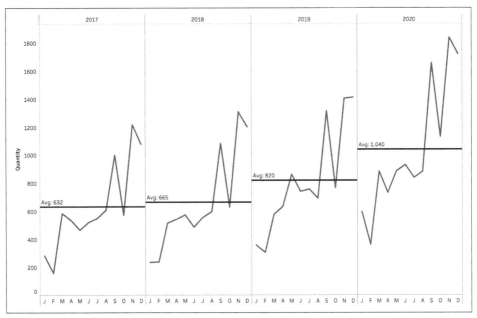

Figure 8-8. Simple reference lines

Building trust through beginning with tables or KPIs is a great place to start when your audience has lower levels of data literacy or you are operating in an organization with a weaker data culture. Trying to gradually develop data visualizations rather than add too much novel complexity is a key consideration. If successful, you will soon be able to have an engaged audience for your visualizations. If unsuccessful, you'll need to take multiple steps backward to reengage the audience and develop the trust from scratch once more.

Static Versus Interactive

For many organizations, static reporting is the main method of viewing analysis. The main forms of static reporting are covered in Chapter 7. As a recap, most data professionals have heard the request "Can I get that as a slide?" Ensuring that the analysis is in a form that allows the audience to make best use of the work is important, but an interactive visualization opens up a number of possibilities that static visualizations do not. Despite championing many forms of interactive data communication, using static reporting will be the favorable option for you in several situations.

Let's Talk About PowerPoint

A book about communicating with data with a focus on how to effectively communicate in organizations has to mention the *P word* at some point. For many, being able to communicate clearly through PowerPoint is one of the most important skills to develop. Mastering the tool you use to design your slides, whether it is PowerPoint or Google Slides, is something that takes a lot of time and practice. But why are slides such an effective communication method?

Many of the elements that make a slide clear and understandable also make data visualizations effective forms of communication:

Simplified messages
Slides should contain as few words as possible, so they require key concepts to be concentrated into simple points.

Clear titles
Like data visualization, the title of a slide should make clear the question being answered or the point being made, and what you are showing on the slide should be easily obvious to your audience.

Visual clues
The imagery, font, color, and theme all can add visual clues about the message within the slide.

Because slides share these elements with data visualizations, it's not a surprise that visualizations are often fit onto slides. Data analysis is often requested to be added to the slide deck in order to fit into the communication of the rest of the supporting points. Slide decks are frequently used to communicate to the managers in your own organization or leaders of other organizations. By designing for slides, you are likely to be designing for communication to leadership teams.

By including data analysis into the rest of the slide deck, the analysis is being actively used in the support of the points being made. All of these things are beneficial to the use of data and the growth of an organization's data culture when done well. However, that is the challenge: it is difficult to make effective visuals that fit in the small space of an image on a slide alongside the slide title and text. Data visualizations are often not specially made for the slides and therefore are cut and pasted into the slide deck, often taking the work out of its original context. If the work is specifically made for the slides and to fit the spacing, it is difficult to sum up complex, multifaceted points into a single image.

More Than Just PowerPoint

Static visualizations need not be used only in slides, though. There are many reasons to use a static visualization to demonstrate clear findings in your data without having to output them as slides.

Easier production

Building a static visualization is much easier than an interactive one. Planning how the user will see and view the visualization is much more straightforward when building a static view by sketching the output. A sketch will allow you to plan what data you need to form the analysis while ensuring that the output will meet the requirements set (Figure 8-9).

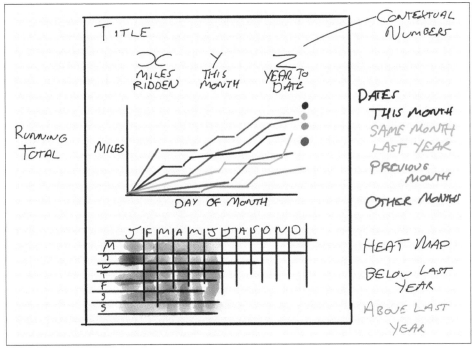

Figure 8-9. Sketch of static view

This is much harder to do with interactive visualizations. The sketches are more challenging to piece together, and you can determine how users will actually interact with the work only via testing. Sitting next to someone and observing how they use your analysis is an important step to take whenever you get the chance. Watching without interrupting or correcting the user will help you understand how they access and interact with the visualization as well as what they miss. Clearly, after you've made your observation, you can correct them on what they missed, but asking them why they missed that interactive feature or explanatory text will help you refine your future outputs. Thinking all of this through as you produce a visualization is why static work can be much easier to conceptualize and produce.

Easier to use

Static work isn't only easier than interactive views to produce but also to consume. For the viewer of the analysis, the work can be much easier to digest when you don't have to hunt for the insights. Many stakeholders will be time poor, so being able to get straight to the point is an important requirement. A common aim in the data visualization field is to design your views so the audience easily sees the message within five seconds of opening the work. Static visualizations require more care to show the message clearly, as it's less likely the user will be able to form it themselves. If you needed to compare some key states' profits, as in Figure 8-10, it would take longer compared to simply having the values highlighted based on a search box.

Figure 8-10. Searching for data points

Easier data storage

The data the visualization is based on should also be considered when deciding how it will be stored. With a static visualization, this thought process can be much easier to decide on the best approach. Take, for example, a data set based on everyone's salary in your organization; you don't want to pass the unaggregated, individual data points widely around any of the divisions. Creating a static visualization that can export just the image and none of the underlying data points will save having to worry about the data storage. If this same visualization was made interactive, careful aggregations of the data have to be made to ensure that sensitive information isn't revealed while filtering or drilling into the information.

Data governance is an important aspect of any data work, to ensure that data sources are used in the manner they were intended. This is covered more deeply in "Centralized Versus Decentralized Data Teams" on page 268. On a more personal level, you can ensure that your work is stored correctly by making sure that those who have access to it are clear on how it should and should not be used. Controlling access to your work and the data it contains is a necessary part of data work.

In many organizations, data source access is controlled and linked to a certain job role. This might seem like a bureaucratic hurdle to overcome when you want to get access to a new data source, but it's a necessary restriction to ensure that the right data is shared and used in the right way. The way in which data is held and governed is often a regulatory requirement that is not negotiable; this is discussed more in "Data Sources" on page 269.

Taking time to think about how your audience could use your data communication or the data it contains is a must, especially when that work is interactive, as it is likely to contain much more granular data to allow for the interactivity.

Interactive User Experience

With so many benefits of the static method of communicating with data, are interactive visualizations ever worth the extra effort to create? Very much yes. While creating interactive visualizations means more planning, more effort in production, and more data management, the process can actually create less work in the long term. To assess how, first let's look at the various forms of interactivity commonly found in workplace reporting:

Filters

Common across most data tools, from spreadsheets to specialist visualization tools, filters allow the analyst and user to remove irrelevant data points to the questions they are attempting to answer. You will find many types of filters, but the two major types are *sliders*, which allow you to choose the range of values returned, and *drop-down selections*, which allow you to pick categorical values to analyze.

You or your audience can use filters to tailor the data visualizations more specifically to what you are interested in. You might focus a map to your local area or change the time period being shown, for example. For C&BS Co., each interactive report could make the reports relevant to each store by allowing the team members to filter out other stores' data points. Without this functionality, a separate report would have to be produced for each store. This interactive report would then allow each store to investigate what the other stores are doing well on and to learn from those producing the best results.

Tooltips

These visual or text objects that pop up when you hover over a mark on a chart are useful for extra contextual information or an additional chart that adds more detail to the mark being hovered over. In more complex visualizations, or when the data contains specific terminology, tooltips can provide definitions or descriptions to help the user understand what they are looking at.

Links

Links can redirect the user to a more detailed view, change the visualization type being shown to offer a different perspective, or send the reader to a nondata web page to add context to the interpretation of the data.

Altering a value

Allowing a user to enter their own value or pick a value in a range can allow for visualization to be used to model "what if" scenarios—to demonstrate not just what is happening now but also what the results of an $n\%$ change would be.

Each of these interactions can allow a user to answer not only their initial questions but additional questions they form from their first analysis. This is one reason interactive visualizations are much more likely to be created: to allow people to explore the analysis for themselves rather than have you present the work to them. Creating a clear storyline in a format that allows the user to explore the subject themselves is a harder task. However, interactive visualizations offer time savings that can be created for those producing the analysis—as without the interactivity, you are likely to receive three or more requests before you get to the same point:

"Is the trend the same as last year?"

"Is the trend the same across each department?"

"Is the trend the same if we ignore the executive team?"

If these questions haven't been set as initial requirements, it is difficult to predict that they will be asked as follow-ups. These questions could be built into static reports, but the static view could quickly become difficult to consume. Allowing many of the categorical data fields in the analysis to be interacted with can allow the user to explore what they are intrigued about. Interactivity can remove the need to show all these potential trends at once and allow the user to show these facets when required. Enabling these options saves the analyst from having to rework the initial visualization each time the user wants to explore another question. Eventually, the user will have refined the questions they are asking of the work to the point that no matter what interactivity is built into the initial work, the user will require a customized piece. As someone who ran a business intelligence team, this deep, unexplored analysis is what makes the team's role much more interesting.

As your audience begins to work with the interactive data communications more, they will begin to ask better questions in their initial requirements. This is a great sign that data literacy levels are increasing and the data culture is developing well. Creating data analytics when there are lots of clear requests with the right question being asked the first time is a good situation for the organization. Less rework and iteration means you can produce more pieces of analysis, answering more questions. The data sources powering this work can be developed more succinctly if it is also focused on the right questions the first time.

By developing the line of questioning from the audience about the subject, the questions might go beyond the initial data source. Sourcing and having to add more data sources to answer deeper questions can be a challenge. This is why it's important for anyone completing data analysis to be confident and comfortable with adding their own data sources through joins and unions, as covered in Chapter 2.

 Joins and unions are covered in greater detail in my first book, *Tableau Prep: Up & Running* (O'Reilly).

The use of interactivity can pose more challenges to newer users getting used to the reporting. Often greater interactivity can come only with greater complexity in the way users need to interact with the view. If someone is new to this style of reporting, they rarely will be able to fully utilize the work as intended, so you must ensure that all of your audience will be able to understand the messages conveyed.

It is therefore important to monitor the usage of the interactive work to make sure you are reaching the intended audience and that they are getting the answers they require. Once the audience is used to the interaction and the options available, interactivity can create much deeper insights and flexibility for users to make the work relevant for them. Determining whether the additional planning and testing is worth saving time building iterations is very much dependent on the context of the request and experience of the users.

Centralized Versus Decentralized Data Teams

Whether you can work with data visualization tools or even access data is heavily dependent on how centralized your organization's use of data is. By the *use of data*, I mean the data sources, the products made from that data, and the individuals who work with the data. In large organizations, there may have been multiple cycles of centralization and decentralization of data work. So what is centralization?

Centralization simply refers to how a certain skill—in our case, working with data—is held by a single team. *Decentralization* occurs when that skill is spread across multiple teams and departments across the organization. The capabilities covered can include subject specialization, management of the task, or control over the infrastructure used for the capability, like the governance and storage of the data.

The battle between centralized versus decentralized is not a simple one-or-the-other option. A blended approach should be adopted to take advantage of pooled skills and knowledge. However, to reduce the normal frustrations that arise with centralized data, access to customized reporting and self-service tools can meet the needs of many.

The Data Team

One reference I make throughout this chapter is the difference between a centralized data team and those who work with data in the differing lines of business instead. By a *data team*, I mean a centralized team that pools data knowledge, skills, and experience to create a focal point for data work. These teams were traditionally in charge of storing data and producing reports from those repositories. Depending on the size of your organization, this team could involve hundreds of people or just a few. There isn't always a clear separation of data from a central IT function, especially in small organizations.

Prep Air has a large data team that has been pulled together from across the organization. While pooling data workers can facilitate sharing skills, it also can remove advocates for using data from within the different teams. With 5,000 total employees, the data team at Prep Air is about 20 people specializing in different areas of data, from storage to governance and visualization. Specialization can actually create barriers to building a great data culture if the specialists are protective of their skills and do not teach others.

Chin & Beard Suds Co. has only 20 people in head office roles, as most of the staff are store-based. Therefore, a centralized data team the size of Prep Air's is not possible for C&BS Co., as it would take up all the head office roles. Only two central data roles in C&BS Co. are looking after data storage and coaching other team members in the stores to create their own solutions. C&BS Co. will have a challenge to keep up with any regulatory changes and then apply them while still supporting all the other teams.

Just because a centralized data team exists doesn't mean individuals in disparate teams can't specialize in data too, but this poses different challenges. A centralized team has to make its work relevant to the specific needs of each team, whereas the decentralized individuals know their own challenges more acutely but may struggle to scale their solutions or get the technical investment they need to deliver their solutions. You are likely to recognize one of the options to be more prevalent in your organization than the other.

Like the other organizational challenges covered in this chapter, there is no perfect way to manage data resources in an organization, but there are significantly different impacts to you depending on your organization's setup.

Data Sources

An important aspect of data work in an organization is the way data is stored and maintained. Data is likely to be stored and managed in many states.

The rawest data is extracted from operational systems into a data store that is commonly called a *data lake*. This often holds data that hasn't been prepared or cleaned. These raw data feeds are often set up by those with more expertise in conducting these tasks, which may require coding of API queries or setting up access through firewalls. Because of the skills involved, you are likely to need specialists in your organization to help you set up any data sources where these feeds don't already exist. These individuals are usually in centralized functions in most organizations.

Data often goes through multiple stages of cleaning and preparation to make it more easily usable. As the data gets more processed and further refined, the processes are more likely to be found in decentralized teams than centralized teams. However, most data sources start in a centralized data team, which creates and governs access to those sources. In an organization, these data sources normally sit in a central team as their data sources and systems are used by many individuals and teams across the organization. If different versions were created for each team, different answers likely would begin to appear for the same questions.

Control of data source access and use is called *data governance*. This involves tasks like controlling access to, updating, and deleting data from sources. With the greater collation and use of data, more regulations have come into place to protect consumers' data. These regulations differ across the world, but in Europe the *General Data Protection Regulation* (*GDPR*), which began in 2016, details a lot of the fundamentals applied all over the world. Here are some of the regulations:

- The individual whom the data is about has the right to be forgotten and their data deleted.
- The data is used in a manner in line with the permissions granted to it.
- The data is retained for at least a minimum time if required for audit or legal purposes.

If data is poorly stored, all subsequent work based on that data will likely be flawed. Forming your conclusions on incorrect data runs the risk of the wrong choices being made on any number of decisions, from what investment to make to how successful the organization is.

Good control of data sources means that the source can be trusted and that any constraints or gaps should be clearly documented. For many organizations, having control over data sources has sometimes created tension between the uses of data and control over the original sources. For many data analytics projects, the original data source may need to be filtered or restructured to allow for easier analysis. This restructured data can create additional data sources that others then work from if they are not carefully named and stored. By having most of the data work created by the stores of C&BS Co., a proliferation of data sources is likely. This can create confusion over which data source to use.

Having a clear process in place to store new or revised data sets is a key part in the analytical process. Sometimes you may hear this referred to as *productionizing* the work. This normally involves setting up the data sets to be refreshed on a schedule, stored along with other key data sets, and having the analytics checked. This work often needs to fit the organization's data rules and processes, if your organization has developed them, and therefore the work often involves a centralized team. Decentralizing this work often creates a range of differences, from slight changes in naming conventions through to completely different use of tools.

The structure Prep Air has created over time may be off-putting at first for new data users, as they have to navigate more controls. However, by being clear on what data sources to use and controlling access to them, the data communications derived from them are likely to be more highly trusted.

Reporting

Data storage of information sources isn't the only aspect that should be considered for centralization. Reporting is a common task that is centralized as part of the productionalization process. By *reporting*, I mean the regular production of a piece of analytics that gets shared to stakeholders in the organization. Reporting will often involve measuring changes in performance versus a previous time period or giving a snapshot in time of the current performance. Lots of reporting is produced to give the audience information rather than to act on a specific issue. Some examples that you are likely to see on a daily basis might be stock reports for a retail store, student attendance in college, or precipitation levels when monitoring the weather.

Because of the regularity of reporting, the amount of effort in producing reports can be substantial, depending on the tools involved. By centralizing this effort, the central teams can ensure that the best tools available can be deployed. Central teams are much more likely to be able to have access to a wider range of tools, or deeper knowledge in the selection of tools available, to optimize the workload.

Once the reports are set up, the task isn't over, as frequent amendments will be required as the business changes or the audience's questions evolve. Chapter 2 has already demonstrated how collecting and communicating requirements can be a challenge, to ensure that the analysis delivered actually meets the needs. Subject-matter experts can make sure the reports are telling people what they need to know. Those same experts can also help develop the reporting when understanding of the field of expertise changes or knowledge becomes embedded and, therefore, the reporting needs to go further.

The significant challenge that arises from centralizing reporting is that updates do not happen as frequently as required. This lack of updates is often due to the time it takes a central team to understand the request, make the change, and then re-productionalize the data source and report. If the subject-matter experts had access to the tools and skills needed, the changes would more likely happen in a timely manner. To ensure completeness and retain data accuracy, the work to update a report often goes beyond just that report. For example, any change to a data source needs to be assessed, as it is likely to affect any other report that shares that data source. By pooling together the reporting to achieve economies of scale, the work is also pooled, and thus the requests can quickly pile up.

If the reporting is not updated, the reports will quickly be ignored, and other "uncontrolled" methods of reporting will arise. By not receiving the analytics needed, *cottage industries* will begin to pop up across the organization to form the reporting. All of the hard work on setting up strategic data sources is eradicated, as people will cobble together the piece they need. Over time, the pieces add up to the point where people are hired and resources consumed in maintaining the additional reports. For Prep Air, this could be a significant issue across such a large organization. If lots of cottage industries arise, the volume of extra reporting will increase dramatically, and it will be harder to keep it aligned with the centralized team.

Pooling expertise can therefore create a lot of benefits, but as per centralizing reporting, care must be taken to not ignore the wider organization in case it stops using the centralized functions. If teams in the business start producing their own custom work, it can be difficult for central teams to regain control of the work.

If you are on a decentralized team, you might be the data worker who, by showing increasing competency, builds some custom work for your team that utilizes your subject-matter expertise and clear communication with data. To regain the work, your role may be centralized through strategic decisions made by the organization's leadership team. This means you might end up in a different team and use your skills to communicate other subjects than just your initial subject-matter expertise.

By giving a disparate group of analysts and subject-matter experts a process to submit changes with an expectation of how long the change will take, you will help prevent the uncontrolled decentralization you might experience otherwise. This is the strategy C&BS Co. should take to maintain a controlled set of data sources and communications despite having such a small central team. If the cottage industries grow, typically you will find differing tools or versions of the software, less adherence to data policies, differing versions of the truth, and duplication of effort.

Pooling Data Expertise

Data tools are forever evolving, and staying aware of these changes can almost feel like a full-time job in its own right. One advantage of a centralized data function is to disseminate these changes and deploy them en masse. Facilitating software changes is not the only benefit of collecting a lot of your top data workers together. Centralizing the data function carries a few other benefits that cover the people, the tools, and the data.

Analyst community

Creating a team or community of analysts will help create better analytical outputs, as each analyst will ask different questions of the requirements and data. With modern technology, those analysts do not have to be located together, but channels of communication and collaboration need to be in place to allow people to share ideas and feedback. Having central coordination of this community is needed even if the community doesn't sit within just a single team.

Tool expertise

With ever-improving and increasing user-focused data tool interfaces, expertise in the tool can add a lot of benefit to the data work conducted. Pooling data expertise can share performance improvement tips for dealing with large data sets as well as best practices for those tools. Centers of excellence have sprung up in many organizations as a way to share the expertise on particular tools used widely in the organization.

Knowledge of the data

Subject-matter experts are useful when setting context for why findings might be what they are, but without getting the right data, these will still be gut-instinct opinions. The perfect data set rarely exists, so having knowledge of multiple data sets across the organization means the individual likely will know what is possible to use and combine for richer analysis.

Self-Service

As a result of the benefits of centralized data work detailed in the preceding section, it is of little surprise that many organizations have taken advantage of centralized data teams. Yet, most people in an organization have seen their roles evolve to include increasing amounts of data work. You might be reading this book because of this exact evolution.

This growth of data work is reconciled by the growth of data software that allows for increased self-service. The tools have increased self-service by reducing the barriers to use that previously existed. Those barriers included coding requirements as well as seeing the output of your work only when executing a query. With more drag-and-drop tools, as well as those that allow you to iterate rapidly, self-service has increasingly become a way to reduce the waiting time on getting hold of the information needed.

Tableau is the tool most synonymous with the growth of self-serve business intelligence. It was the tool that allowed me to go from being a history and politics student to writing this book on all things data. While requiring some initial training to get started, Tableau Desktop has become an enabler for many people to begin creating their own analysis rather than putting in requests to central data teams. This faster time to analysis has changed how many people work with data. The expectation of many people in organizations is that they should have the access to the data sources and tools to enable them to conduct their own analysis. Many organizations will have only so many licenses to the software to share around. This may restrict you from getting access to the easiest tool to do the job. More web-browser-based data tools are appearing, and this has helped with proliferation of giving access to more people, as licensing is often much cheaper than desktop-based applications.

The key benefit of self-service data analytics is that it pairs together lots of the benefits of both the centralized and the decentralized model. Centralized data sources can be connected directly to the self-service tools to prevent the most technical part of the process from stopping those who are learning to use data. Centralized knowledge can be shared through creating teams of people using technology to allow newer users to learn from those more experienced teams. The knowledge that is harder to share is the subject-matter expertise of all of the folks in the organization. This is the power of self-service tools, as the experts on the context of data can form their own views and iterate rapidly. With such a small central team at C&BS Co., this is how the organization can have a strong data culture.

Once self-service data visualization becomes more common, the focus of data visualization can rapidly become making something look attractive as well as informative. For many stakeholders, the need is for the answer, and not for a beautifully formatted report. Applying the pragmatic approach—that aesthetics aren't as important as the message being conveyed clearly—can prevent overwork.

Self-service can also assist with the validation of the answer. As discussed in "Tables Versus Pretty Pictures" on page 252, one challenge of communicating with data is the stakeholder trusting the findings. Gaining trust through a visualization is harder, as it is a more refined output than a table. Therefore, if the stakeholder is building their own visualization, they receive the benefit of using visualizations while also developing trust through processing their own work.

Live Versus Extracted Data

Whether the data sources you use to form your analysis are centralized or decentralized, you will need to decide whether to link your analysis to live data sets or use an extract instead. Across your organization, you are likely to use both types of data sources.

A *live data source* means the tool you are using to form your analysis is connected to the data source directly. As the data source updates and changes, the visualizations of the data will change also. An *extract* is a static snapshot of data: any change to the original source of the information won't be reflected in the extract. To form an extract, you can take a copy of the live data set. This section covers why you want to carefully consider the storage of the data you are using for your analysis.

Live Data

Live data is a frequent request you will receive from many stakeholders, but this means many different things in different situations:

Direct connection
This is as live as data can be. As the data is entered into the system, the data will be available instantly for analysis. The data analysis tool will read data directly from the system where it is stored.

Analytical data store connection
Connecting to an operational system can create issues if the data analysis queries slow the responsiveness of the system. For this reason, regular data loads occur from the operating system to a data store. The data store is then used for

analytical work. To avoid performance impacts during peak operating times, the data loads often occur overnight.

Being clear on which type of live data is required can dramatically change the type of analysis possible, as well as which tools can be used. Only when decisions are likely to change with the latest few seconds of data points does the first definition of live data fit the need. For example, a stock broker needs to see the latest price to make the right decision, or they will be deciding whether to sell or buy based on a previous price. Most stakeholders want the latest view of the data but are still looking for longer-term trends. Therefore, data connections into a data store is the most common real requirement when a stakeholder asks for a live connection.

Using Prep Air as an example, it will have lots of live data sets that are essential to ongoing operations. Each of these next examples will be a truly live connection into the latest data available from operational systems. Let's dive into a few specific cases to show the importance of live updates:

Ticket sales

The number of tickets sold has a huge impact on all the services involved in running the airline. By knowing the number of tickets sold for each flight, the correct fuel levels can be provided, meals loaded on board to avoid waste, and ticket prices updated to ensure that the revenue earned per flight is optimized. Without having a clear view on who is flying or how many people should be on a plane, significant issues can arise, including overselling tickets or wasting advertising if the flights are already sold out.

Departures and arrival times

As an airline, you are not just reliant on your own operations but on the airports you operate out of too. If a gate isn't available for your passengers to disembark a plane, or ground crew to load the cargo onto the plane, you will experience delays as well as impacts to the next flight for that plane. By having a live view of the latest information, your operational crew will be able to highlight potential problems for subsequent flights as well as warn passengers as soon as possible to prevent frustrated people waiting at the departure gate.

Weather

As commercial aircraft can now fly halfway around the world at a time, it's not just the weather conditions at the departure or arrival airport that need monitoring. Wind patterns need to be monitored to ensure that a sudden prolonged headwind doesn't create an unexpected late arrival at the destination with all the support services not being aware.

Extracted Data Sets

Seeing the latest data is going to help give the most up-to-date information so that is always preferable for making the right decision, correct? Well, not quite. Creating an *extract*, or copy of the data that won't update unless you refresh the extract, can help fix the data to a point in time. This allows the analysis to be formed without having to try to stay on top of changing data points. Analysts are frequently asked to assess certain situations to understand why something may have occurred at a given time. This means that live data just isn't needed in these situations. Data lakes and warehouses frequently hold extracts of data for analytical use at a later date.

Using extracts can be particularly useful as the data in operational systems and data stores refresh in different ways. One of the key benefits of working with an extract rather than a live connection is the ability to use a *cache* of the data. Software loads the data into a cache once but then refers to the same data multiple times to ask different queries of it. With a live data set, you will want the data to continually update to ensure that you are seeing the latest results. In contrast, the ability to get faster answers by refining the questions being asked against the same data is significantly beneficial. Some data loads can take 30 seconds plus, depending on the tool, so removing this wait time can help encourage iterations.

Some data sets do not store the full data forever, and therefore data can be lost if not moved to a data store. The extract can act as a data store for the sake of analyzing the data. If the extract is added to each day, it will form a data set often referred to as a *history table*. These are important when regulations require you to maintain full transactional details. Extracts can be updated through incremental or full refreshes:

Incremental refresh
> Data is added in small additions known as *increments* based on a set field—usually an integer or date. The increment added is based on an ordinal or numeric data field to allow the refreshing tool to identify the maximum value in the extract and therefore know what values need to be added subsequently. For example, C&BS Co. sequentially numbers its transactions, so to create a record of all of their transactions, it wouldn't want to refresh the whole data source every day. By incrementally adding the transactions made each day, the loading time will be kept to a minimum while keeping the data set up to date.

Full refresh
> Everything in the extract is completely updated by removing the previous data and replacing it with whatever is in the current data source.

Therefore, if the data is updating over time and is removed from the original source, an incremental update is what is needed as the old data, potentially no longer in the tool, is not removed. The full refresh is useful if rows of data could be updated; for example, if analyzing a sales pipeline of opportunities, the value of sales could change as the opportunity progresses.

Getting a static data set can be beneficial when sharing the results with others if you have a set story you've found within the data. Presenting your findings to your organization's board would be more challenging if the data was going to potentially change. Imagine preparing for a meeting to share the latest sales numbers without being sure that the data feeding your analysis might change as you are presenting. Therefore, having static data sets can be useful when you want to be assured that the data won't change after you have completed your analysis.

An extract can also open up the number of tools you can use to analyze the data. For example, Excel doesn't directly connect to operational systems, but that might be the tool you feel the most comfortable with. By taking an extract, more tools are able to read common forms of extracted data, like a CSV file. Being comfortable with a tool will allow you to make the most of the tool's ability to find and communicate the message in the data as clearly as possible and not be dependent on having to connect to a live data set.

What type of data source should you use? This is very much an "it depends" situation based on the questions you are trying to answer, the tools you prefer to use, and the way the data updates in the source over time. Being conscious of the choice you are making is the most important part. Figure 8-11 is a decision tree that covers the questions you need to ask when picking the type of data connection to make.

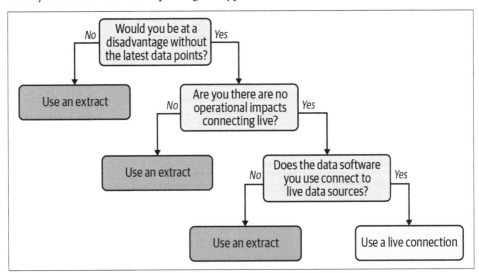

Figure 8-11. Decision tree for deciding when to connect to a live data source or extract

Standardization Versus Innovation

With data literacy levels varying across most organizations as a data culture develops, surely anything to help data literacy is the right thing to do, right? Templates for data visualizations have become much more common as a method to make production easier and more consistent. The templates give a structure for newer users to either choose a chart, collate multiple charts, or guide user interaction on their communications. The consistency that templates offer make the consumption of data communications much easier as well.

However, before you rush off to start developing your organization's template, you should understand that templates create constraints too. This section explores the benefits and constraints of analytical templates in organizations.

Importance of Standardization

Communicating data is all about how you encode the message in a form the receiver of the information can quickly understand. Any technique that reduces the effort to decode the information is more likely to encourage the user to spend time in understanding the work.

Having most of the data communications formatted in a similar way can help overcome the first-glance familiarization challenge. Creating a template can create consistency between different communications (Figure 8-12). This familiarity means the user spends less time scanning the work to understand where they need to look.

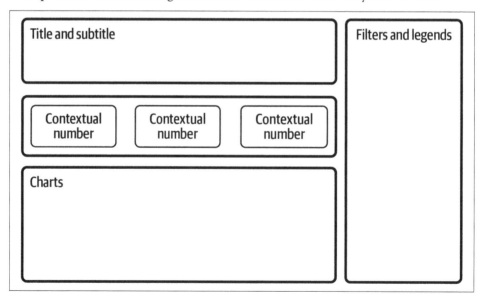

Figure 8-12. Example of a template layout

In an organization with lower levels of data culture, using a template can begin to create a common data language. A template can include numerous elements that can help develop this common data language:

Color

Many organizations have a brand-related color palette that needs to be used on any visualization shown externally or to the executive team. Consistently choosing a color for a positive metric and another for a negative value is a good idea. Choosing corporate colors can become a challenge when they clash with common visual concepts. For example, a corporate color scheme may be dominated by red, which is the color typically associated with poor performance or negative values, as discussed in Chapter 5. Repeated data communications may be required to get past the instinct that red can actually be a positive thing.

Yet corporate colors are not the only option when deciding on a color palette. Many organizations choose the traffic light as the default color scheme, with green representing good and red representing poor performance. This concept plays on the visual cue of green for go and red for stop on a traffic light. Other visual metaphors are used when communicating with data, like red and black in financial data. Being "in the red" is common accountancy language for having a negative value, and "in the black" as having a positive measure. This language comes from traditional representations of the data in financial reporting, so more visual representations can use the same color palette as traditional reporting, making it easier for users to know what the color represents without having to refer to a color legend for an explanation.

Layout

Having a clear layout can not only facilitate interpreting the message being shared but also encourage the user to interact with the work. The layout template will likely dictate how titles and subtitles are used while also positioning the work. A good layout can encourage whitespace and remove a lot of the uncertainty that a lack of a template can create. A set layout can create the greatest amount of visual consistency among various reports. Simply placing filters and legends in a consistent place can help users get straight to the analysis while knowing what filter options they can make in seconds. If the template isn't there, the user may spend time searching for filter options rather than interpreting the information being shown.

Icons

Small icons used consistently can direct users in multiple ways. From showing help instructions to highlighting whether you need to click or hover to interact with a view, icons can make a significant difference to encouraging users. If these icons are used consistently across the majority of analytical work, the familiarity will not require much cognitive work to deduce the options available.

These supporting factors can make a significant difference to the overall ease of interpreting the work, but the individual charts themselves can fit templates too. The use of axes, size of marks, and choices of chart types for certain use cases can all make the visual language easier to read. If different analysts have different styles for the same chart type, the user can misinterpret key elements that may ultimately change the message being communicated.

The use of templates can have benefits that occur not only when developing the visualizations but also in the preparation work. Knowing the structure of data that feeds certain charts or filter options used within the templates can simplify the data preparation stage. Knowing the required structure of data can ensure that time isn't wasted iterating among options. This is especially important when the data preparation is not completed by those building the analysis. Imagine how frustrated you'd be if you spent hours cleaning data fields to make sure they are easy to use when they weren't needed at all.

Overall, the use of templates can save time and effort for everyone within the process of building the product. Creating against a number of known, controlled elements makes production more efficient as less variability exists throughout the process. However, the standardization can stifle the creation of innovative and unique work that is more memorable.

Importance of Innovation

Because so many messages are being communicated to us each day, your communication of a message requires something particularly special to be truly remarkable, and therefore memorable. Advertising is no longer on just billboards or newspapers but everywhere we look. The art of advertising is to get your message across in a way that stays with the consumer long after they look away. The same can be said of data communications, as the message needs to be not only clearly communicated but also memorable. A memorable message is much more likely to result in the desired action, as the communication will stay with the audience for longer.

The challenge with templates and standardization naturally leans toward less memorable visual messages. If everything looks similar to make the message easier to read, creating a strong emotive reaction becomes much harder. This is where innovation shows its importance. Using different visual techniques, themes, or chart types can not only grab the attention of the consumer but also leave a lasting impression.

Innovation allows for, and actually encourages, the analyst to explore the data set more thoroughly. By trying different methods to communicate the data, analysts will often find insights within the data they may not have been looking for. Rather than creating cookie-cutter visualizations, trying different techniques is much more fun for the analyst. Insights come from analysts thinking about what the data is showing rather than just following a step-by-step process.

If you can form your template from a consensus across your analytics community, you are more likely to get adherence to the template. Without consensus, you are likely to find that the template will soon fall by the wayside, and you'll have to develop a new template and transform all the existing work to the new one.

If you are leading the data teams in your organization or a team focused on data, you will need to choose how to strike the balance between standardization and innovation. The balance will largely be decided based on the skills of the individuals on your team. Just because someone has strong data skills does not mean that they should ignore templates. Templates will allow those individuals to deploy solutions more efficiently, as they are not having to make design decisions. As soon as you or your team sees the templates as restricting their work with data, they should be dropped in favor of allowing for innovative, free-flowing analysis. Therefore, having templates to provide a starting point without forcing their use is as good of a balance you will be able to create.

Creating memorable visualizations is much easier when trying different techniques and exploring the data further. However, finding the right balance between creating something unique without having to make the consumer work too hard to decode the message being shared is the aim. Templates should give a solid framework to build from without stifling all innovation.

Reporting Versus Analytics

Reporting versus analytics is the final piece of the battles you face when using data solutions in your organization, as it draws together several of the factors discussed so far. *Reporting* is the term commonly used to describe the mass production of data products. *Analytics* used in this context describes the seeking of deeper insights rather than just basic information.

The choice of data tools available to data workers largely determines whether they are likely to create reports or analytical products. The data culture level sets the requested requirements, as less-established data cultures are likely to ask for more reporting than deeper analytical studies. Because of the more complex, time-consuming nature of analytics, the stakeholders making the requests need to be confident that the longer production time will be worth the investment.

Reporting: Mass Production

Using reports to analyze data has become a typical method of data analysis in an organization, but the onus is placed on the receiver to find the key findings in the data. Reports are typically generated to show the latest position or changes in trends over time. A benefit of reports is that they don't frequently change format, so once they are established, reports in most modern tools do not take much effort to refresh.

Choosing to communicate with data through reporting is a blunter tool than analysis, as it is frequently targeted at a wider audience than analytics. Creating data communications via reporting will likely involve using parts of the report to demonstrate the point you are looking to portray. Reporting does offer many in the organization the opportunity to access data they wouldn't have the skills or permissions to access directly from its source. Serving up data in a simple and easy-to-consume manner begins to let people get more practice with understanding various elements of graphicacy.

But reporting can be quite limiting for users. If their questions go beyond the original scope, an avenue to answer those questions needs to exist—but it rarely does. Remembering my basic premise that humans are intelligent means that as they learn something from the report, they will naturally want to ask more questions.

Let's take the stock reports that I used to receive at a clothing retailer, and one that we'd expect Chin & Beard Suds Co. to have too. These were simple item-by-item reports of the quantity the store was expected to have. While my first question might have been to ask whether we had a particular item, I would have many follow-up questions that would be impossible to answer in the report:

- How many of those items in stock had been held for customers already?
- How many were likely to be delivered this week, this month, or this season?
- How many customers have we left frustrated with a shortage in a certain item?
- Why is the head office still sending us certain items that aren't selling?

No matter how good your reporting or analytics is, you likely won't always be able to answer all the questions the audience of those reports will have. However, ensuring that the report will be able to answer many of them will help the report fit its purpose. If you and your organization are going to use reporting, you need to ensure access to more analytical tools and teams in order to be able to answer these follow-up questions. Chin & Beard Suds Co. is likely to be able to optimize stock levels, therefore minimizing sunk cost, if the stores are able to answer the questions generated by the reports and change the company's buying decisions because of it.

If the channels for further questions are not available, cottage industries are likely to spring up to cobble together disparate data sets to answer those next questions. If the data sources are not gathered from the proper sources, the proliferation of data sets is likely to lead to confusion and mixed messages down the line. What if Chin & Beard Suds Co. allows stores to feed back into the buying decisions by the head office, but a store's opinions are based on incomplete or inaccurate data?

When key decisions are being made from data sets formed by individuals and are not reconciled to validated sources, mistakes can always creep in. In the C&BS Co. stores, imagine one of the stores manually capturing a list of the items sold. The store would probably use a spreadsheet tool to capture the items and the quantity sold. It's easy to mistype a value or have a calculation not include all the records needed. The store's employees would be likely to use this data source to form opinions that they then share back to the buying teams. The potential is high to accidentally point the buyers to a nonexistent trend or miss some key sales made. In a small retail chain, it doesn't take many data points to lead to an inaccurate conclusion. Ensuring that key decisions are based on reconciled and controlled data sets is a must for all organizations.

Analytics: Flexibility but Uncertainty

Analytical data products have almost the reverse issues to that of reporting work. The majority of the effort comes from the analyst preparing the data, finding the insights, and sharing them through a series of charts and graphs. You produce an analysis to enable the consumer to understand why the findings you're sharing are the key insights they need to see, and hopefully spur them into action.

It is much harder to scope and articulate the time it will take to form the views that are required when producing analytical work. Analytical outputs are often the first time questions are posed, so it is difficult to know what it will take to answer the questions within the context of your organization. Organizations that have a lower data culture may struggle to understand why the timescales can be uncertain or why it might not be possible to be very prescriptive with the requirements. Organizations with better levels of data culture will be more used to knowing that fixed deadlines are not possible as well as having more data sources at hand to solve the questions in the first place.

Analytical work is much more likely to be customized through the visualizations used to communicate the message as well as the insights that are going to be found. Creating good data analytics often feels like a chef breaking away from standard recipes to create something they know the customer exactly wants, no matter what is on the menu.

Taking the example from the previous section, imagine the Chin & Beards Suds Co. staff having to form a view from scratch each time they wanted to understand stock levels. With analytics, they might be able to give a customer inquiring about a product's availability a full picture of the history of the product's sales, when it is likely to be ordered into the company's warehouse and finally delivered to the store. Yet this isn't the information that the customer is likely to care about. The customer wants to know when they will be able to get their hands on the product. They'd also probably be unhappy to wait for the answers. Answering common key questions in reports is a necessary part of most businesses to prevent overwork and ensure that the right data is available at the right time.

Even if analytical products exist to answer the question being asked, the communication's unique views are what makes the work harder to consume. Analysis often comes in a greater variety of forms. This can make analysis harder to consume for those who are less data literate, as not only do they need to absorb the information but also work their way through the format. By breaking away from the templated format, not only are the original requirements answered, but the analyst is likely to propose answers to the follow-up questions a user might ask.

The C&BS Co. stores are unlikely to provide an environment conducive to allow the team to form its own analysis. Producing a good piece of analysis can take quite a lot of mental labor. The task is possible only if the skills actually exist to be able to complete the task in the first place. This is why analytics is often more prevalent and suited to non-customer-facing roles. Creating a fixed, uninterrupted amount of time to dig into the data can be tough. This is why, despite how good a self-service functionality setup you might offer your peers, they might not be in a position to take advantage of it.

One of the biggest challenges of analytical work is maintaining the custom data sources that arise. I've mentioned throughout this book that you should tailor your data source to the questions you are attempting to answer. Although this helps focus on the task in hand, if you answer hundreds of questions, you will end up with hundreds of data sources to maintain. Being able to reuse data sources or amalgamate those with a lot of crossover in the columns used or time period covered can save a lot of work.

The productionalization of analytics is much more challenging, as the charts are not the only thing that needs to be updated, but also the annotations and text articulating the findings. Reporting is intentionally designed to be updated and run on a regular frequency, but this doesn't mean your analytical work can't be. The difference between reporting and analytics remains: the former is informative, but the latter addresses particular questions that you are looking to act upon.

When communicating with data, both reporting and analytics have a place in sharing the insights found. Sharing work in a consistent manner can help consumers work through the findings faster. Reporting can help establish a wider data culture by creating familiarity with data in an organization. Analytical work is what takes that basic data culture and really allows you to share deeper, more powerful findings. A combination of both techniques should be used to create a well-rounded experience. Both products should be used to encourage more data-driven decisions, which creates the virtuous cycle of data. Reporting offers the team in the C&BS Co. stores the chance to get the basic answers required to complete the majority of their day-to-day tasks. Giving the same team a way to go further with data and answer more customized questions will allow them to communicate their points with data to help improve the business.

Finding the "Perfect" Balance

Whichever organization and industry you work in, all of these competing challenges will affect you and the data work you use. Finding a balance among all of these factors can feel like walking on a tightrope at times, as no organization has just one set of individuals who all have the same views on where the right balance is. Some organizations will have a rich data culture, favoring innovative visualizations for their quick insights, built from well-controlled centralized data sources. Other organizations may have less experience with data, relying more on tables of data used to help steer decisions. In these cases, data may be used in small pockets of the organization in a decentralized manner, so creating single sources of truth is difficult. (As noted previously, a *single source of truth* refers to data sources that have been validated across the organization as being accurate.)

To help find the perfect balance for your organization, I thought it would be useful to share some tips for each of our challenges, to allow both sides of the argument to get what they need from the data products:

Tables versus pretty pictures
This really doesn't have to be a single-sided answer. Understanding what your audience requires to answer their questions is the most important point here. If you are unsure of the balance between tables and visualizations, use both. A visualization or two to add context to a communication can help steer the audience to look at, or filter to, the right part of a table.

Static versus interactive
Chapter 7 offered lots of ways to pull tables and visualizations together into a single communication, but ensuring that these are interactive to allow the audience to focus on what they care about can make the work more trusted and relative to them. Static reporting still has its place when your audience doesn't have the ability to interact with the views (like on a factory floor). Driving up the amount of interactivity can help encourage the audience to ask their next questions that are based on the original views.

Centralized versus decentralized
Data sources and governance should be controlled from a central team, but the ability to work with data should exist in all teams. This balance enables the right controls to exist, but no one is prevented from trying to answer the questions that they need to.

Live versus extracts
About all the guidance I can offer in this section is to know when you will need to use extracts instead of live sources. The choice of tools to form your analysis and make the communication should be a key factor rather than the inhibitor to

this decision, but you are unlikely to have control of which tools you have to work with, especially in large organizations.

Standardization versus innovation

Facilitating the audience's task of interpreting your message is one of the major focuses of this book. Standardization of your data-based communications can absolutely help that to happen, up to a point. As soon as standardization feels like it is restricting the message being shared clearly, you should feel free to innovate with how you represent the data. Freedom to innovate will also ensure that your work is more likely to remain memorable to your audience. Innovation takes skills that you should feel you have after reading through this book to this point.

Reporting versus analytics

Very much like static versus interactive, reporting can offer a solid baseline to ensure that many of the basics are covered, but analytics transforms data to become much more valuable. If you are answering the same question time and again, it's unlikely you will find anything new. If you are able to ask and answer different questions in different ways, you'll be much more likely to find new insights.

Summary

No single formula for handling all of these challenges exists, as this chapter has hopefully shown you. By being aware of them, you'll be ready to negotiate the challenges as they arise in your organization. As you work with data more, you will inevitably come across each challenge, and in all likelihood, more than once as the organization evolves as people change roles.

No matter where your organization lies on the spectrum of challenges, you need to be cautious about various aspects in order to prevent the balance from going too far one way or the other. Developing a strong data culture with people who are comfortable with all elements of data literacy is an important step. This can be centrally driven or bubble up from nondata teams using new tools that emphasize self-service. Different organizations have different needs, but even within the same organization, different departments have different needs, which is what we will explore in our final chapter.

CHAPTER 9

Tailoring Your Work to Specific Departments

When you get good at communicating with data, opportunities will open up. You might well find yourself working on bigger and more diverse projects with new teams and departments.

The new people you work with will have new terminology, different data sets, and different stakeholders. As you've seen throughout this book, understanding your audience is crucial, and with new departments, you may not know the full context of every situation. You can address this problem by using the requirement gathering process you learned in Chapter 2.

When you step into new roles or new departments, you might even feel a bit of *imposter syndrome*, the sensation of self-doubt many people feel when they step out of their comfort zone and into new opportunities: *do I really belong here?* Try to ignore this feeling; it will fade as you build more confidence over time by continually proving the value of your work. Just remember: if you are being offered new opportunities, you have earned them. If someone else believes in you, believe in yourself! To illustrate this, let me reintroduce you to Claire, who works at Prep Air. In this chapter, we're going to look at how her new data communication skills open up new challenges for her.

I have been fortunate to work with many types of teams and departments in my career, and I have learned some of their needs and wants. This chapter is a bit of a cheat sheet for you. It won't tell you everything you need to know—every organization is different—but will give you a starting point, by noting some challenges that tend to arise when doing data work with departments like human resources, marketing, and IT, as well as dealing with senior-level executives. If you're prepared for these challenges, you can start delivering benefits sooner and continue your good work.

The Executive Team

"Claire?" Preet pops his head into Claire's office. "I have some news for you. The CEO liked that dashboard you made me. In fact, she'd like you to make her a dashboard so she can monitor the company's performance."

The first team beyond your usual department that you will work with is probably the executive team, or C-suite: the most senior level, which might include the chief executive officer (CEO), chief financial officer (CFO), and—in more and more organizations—the chief data officer (CDO). If you are anything like Claire (or me), communicating to this group can be intimidating.

Claire seeks advice from Wang, a senior coworker who deals regularly with the CEO, Toni. "I'm nervous," she confesses.

Wang nods. "I get it. It feels like you'll be fired on the spot if you make a mistake, right?" Claire nods. "You must remember, though, that you are there because these people are looking for your insight and analysis to inform their decisions. Think of this as an opportunity to make Prep Air better."

"Thanks, Wang; that's reassuring," Claire says. "Any advice? How do I get them to listen?"

Wang smiles. "For me, the challenges are time and scope. Think about what it's like to be CEO. Toni has hundreds of opinions, emails, and reports landing in her inbox every day, and she has to figure out how to consume all that information. Who should she believe? How much does each view sway her opinion? What should she try to solve or improve next? She has so much information coming at her that she can't waste any time. So my first piece of advice is to communicate clearly and succinctly. Get your message across fast."

Just as Wang starts to walk away from Claire's desk, he turns and reminds Claire, "Make sure you are confident you are using the right data sources, as the executive team will want to understand that they can trust what you are showing them."

Claire is already forming a plan. She decides to start with a quick overview that clearly indicates what the executive team should focus on. She decides to create a dashboard for Toni, starting with a *landing page*: the first thing the audience sees when they open a dashboard. It gives an overview of the subject, then steers the audience's attention toward the most important areas. This way, Toni will be able to quickly find crucial issues and information in the data, instead of having to scan dozens of reports, hoping to unearth the details.

As Wang noted, Claire will need to put her effort into thinking about scope. What should the landing page include? How can she cover the whole company's performance broadly, without missing anything important?

Claire doesn't want to bother Toni with lots of requirement-gathering questions, so she decides to use the company's KPIs as her guide. The executive team sets the company's KPIs, which are important measures that, taken together, form a picture of how the company is performing in relation to its goals. Prep Air's goals, as present in the last all-hands meeting, are as follows:

- Increase revenue
- Increase profit
- Improve customer experience

Executives spend a lot of time trying to understand the best ways to measure these key drivers; when they decide on the right measures, they designate those as KPIs. One way you might end up working with them is by having a lot of experience in one of these drivers. An increase or decrease in a KPI will trigger the executive team to ask what's causing the change. They know that a lot of additional detail underlies each of those measures. That's where you come in: you are likely to have metrics and qualitative information that can help them understand such changes.

Let's take a look at Claire's landing page (Figure 9-1).

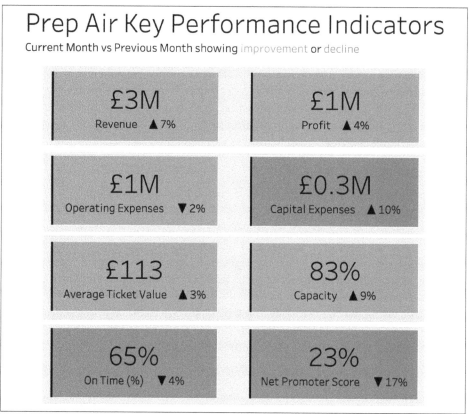

Figure 9-1. Landing page example

Three areas instantly jump off the page: Capital Expenditure, On Time (%), and Net Promoter Score. Note that Claire has used purple for these—here, purple doesn't indicate a decrease or increase but any change that is for the worse. As all of the metrics are on a different scale, using a diverging color palette would take a lot of cognitive effort to understand the schema. The CEO can spot the issues and focus on them quickly, without having to dive into the details of other areas.

Of course, the data includes a lot more there than just a number. A set of reports needs to sit behind each of the tiles on the landing page so the audience can click through to find supporting data and investigate the issue. If Toni clicks the Net Promoter Score indicator, she'll arrive at the screen in Figure 9-2, which dives into the details.

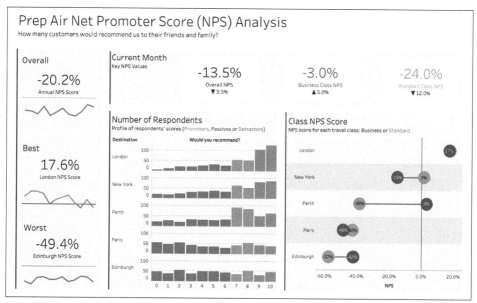

Figure 9-2. Detailed page example for NPS

A lot of information is here, and pulling it all together requires a lot of collaboration across the business. The stakes are high too: this information is going to provide the basis for decisions that could change the whole organization, so its accuracy needs to be spot-on. Finding the right data sources can be done correctly only by collaborating with other data users across the organization.

Claire, realizing this, returns to Wang. "How can I make sure everything is right when I'm not familiar with how all of these departments work?"

"You can't," Wang replies. "You'll need help." Collaboration, he explains, makes the difference in these situations. "Here's what you do. Draft some visualizations and share them with people in the relevant departments. They'll spot your mistakes. They might also disagree with you about what the best measurements are or how to read the data. It's all valuable, and getting those departmental perspectives is really the only way to know what you might be missing."

Claire designs the landing page to provide the executive team with a useful overview of the organization's performance. She submits her work and waits nervously. A few days later, she finds a thank-you email from the CEO herself. "I appreciate what you've built here. This makes it easy for me to identify areas of poor performance and find the information I need to take quick action. Great job." Claire forwards the email to Wang, who congratulates her and adds, "Don't be surprised if you find yourself doing this more often!"

Finance

After Claire's success at providing the CEO with a dashboard, word spreads. It's not long before she receives a similar request from the CFO, asking for a dashboard the finance department can use to track ticket revenue.

Finance teams require lots of timely and accurate data. They're constantly analyzing data sets on income, expenditures, and more. Claire, whose financial experience is limited to doing her taxes, finds herself intimidated once again. "The financial team has so much experience and expertise," she tells Wang. "How can I help them?"

Wang smiles. "Let me tell you something. I've worked with many financial teams, and there's a grain of truth in the stereotype that all they want to work with is tables. No, it's not everyone, but they like to see the data points as clearly as possible so they can dig in."

"So…they hate charts?"

"I wouldn't go *that* far, but finance people do tend to be skeptical about data visualizations. There's a balance. They usually want to see the rawer data even if you also give them charts—I'd lean toward tables if I were you—especially since they're going to ask for reconciliation."

Claire grimaces. "What's reconciliation?"

"It's when you compare the values you've created to values that you know are correct. There are different ways to do it, but it often comes back to checking values against what has previously been reported in tables. They're going to use this for regulatory reporting, taxes, and statements to investors, so you'll want to triple-check all of your numbers."

Claire considers this as she ponders how best to share her message. If they want this much detail, how can she make sure the message comes through clearly? She'll also need to make sure the audience can follow—and check—her logic.

Claire decides it's important to convey the main message *before* adding detail—otherwise, it might get lost in a sea of numbers. She decides to utilize the Z pattern (discussed in Chapter 6), placing contextual numbers and charts at the top of the page and then showing the detail further down. She creates Prep Air's ticket revenue dashboard (Figure 9-3) with a table at the bottom of the view that allows users to validate the visuals and calculations.

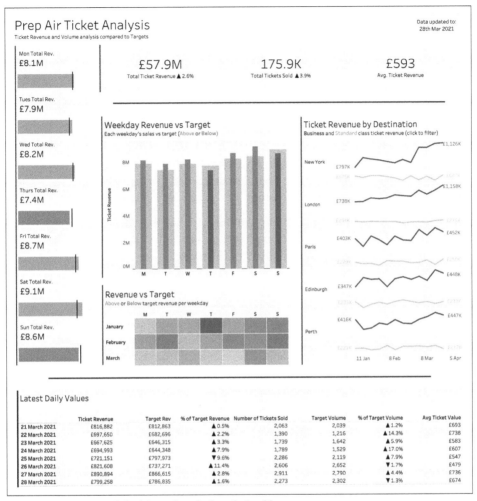

Prep Air Ticket Analysis
Ticket Revenue and Volume analysis compared to Targets

Data updated to:
28th Mar 2021

Mon Total Rev.
£8.1M

£57.9M
Total Ticket Revenue ▲ 2.6%

175.9K
Total Tickets Sold ▲ 3.9%

£593
Avg. Ticket Revenue

Tues Total Rev.
£7.9M

Wed Total Rev.
£8.2M

Weekday Revenue vs Target
Each weekday's sales vs target (Above or Below)

Ticket Revenue by Destination
Business and Standard class ticket revenue (click to filter)

Thurs Total Rev.
£7.4M

New York
£797K

£1,126K

£1,158K

Fri Total Rev.
£8.7M

London
£738K

Paris
£403K

£452K

Sat Total Rev.
£9.1M

Revenue vs Target
Above or Below target revenue per weekday

Edinburgh
£347K

£448K

Sun Total Rev.
£8.6M

Perth
£416K

£447K

11 Jan   8 Feb   8 Mar   5 Apr

Latest Daily Values

	Ticket Revenue	Target Rev	% of Target Revenue	Number of Tickets Sold	Target Volume	% of Target Volume	Avg Ticket Value
21 March 2021	£816,882	£812,863	▲ 0.5%	2,063	2,039	▲ 1.2%	£693
22 March 2021	£697,650	£682,696	▲ 2.2%	1,390	1,216	▲ 14.3%	£738
23 March 2021	£667,625	£646,315	▲ 3.3%	1,739	1,642	▲ 5.9%	£583
24 March 2021	£694,993	£644,348	▲ 7.9%	1,789	1,529	▲ 17.0%	£607
25 March 2021	£721,151	£797,973	▼ 9.6%	2,286	2,119	▲ 7.9%	£547
26 March 2021	£821,608	£737,271	▲ 11.4%	2,606	2,652	▼ 1.7%	£479
27 March 2021	£890,894	£866,615	▲ 2.8%	2,911	2,790	▲ 4.4%	£736
28 March 2021	£799,258	£786,835	▲ 1.6%	2,273	2,302	▼ 1.3%	£674

Figure 9-3. Financial dashboard with detailed table

The dashboard she creates is interactive: the financial experts can use the charts at the top to filter the detailed table below. This way, they won't have to search through a large table to reconcile the values shown with known comparables. The charts themselves can act as a filter: they can simply click or hover over the marks. For instance, if they click Paris in the Ticket Revenue by Destination visualization in Figure 9-3, the table at the bottom of the dashboard updates with figures specific to that city, as well as the other charts too (Figure 9-4).

Latest Daily Values							
	Ticket Revenue	Target Rev	% of Target Revenue	Number of Tickets Sold	Target Volume	% of Target Volume	Avg Ticket Value
21 March 2021	£92,234	£78,540	▲ 17.4%	191	196	▼ 2.5%	£812
22 March 2021	£95,191	£101,713	▼ 6.4%	328	286	▲ 14.6%	£822
23 March 2021	£92,901	£93,758	▼ 0.9%	156	171	▼ 8.9%	£573
24 March 2021	£84,477	£87,011	▼ 2.9%	224	194	▲ 15.4%	£850
25 March 2021	£105,068	£100,057	▲ 5.0%	283	219	▲ 29.5%	£1,158
26 March 2021	£121,840	£114,633	▲ 6.3%	343	304	▲ 12.9%	£578
27 March 2021	£112,724	£97,570	▲ 15.5%	181	187	▼ 3.4%	£1,018
28 March 2021	£90,334	£85,174	▲ 6.1%	288	209	▲ 37.8%	£652

Figure 9-4. Updated table accessed by clicking Paris in Figure 9-3

The charts that can steer your audience to the filtered tables can also offer more context. Charting makes the stories in your data stand out, as you've learned. The same is true when trying to reconcile data points.

Claire decides to ask for feedback, as she did with the executive dashboard, before finalizing her design. Finance users are likely to have a detailed understanding of the subject and can identify potential outliers or mistakes.

Human Resources

Claire's financial dashboard is a success. Before she knows it, Toni, the CEO, is back in her inbox. She wants *all* of Prep Air's departments to have dashboards of their own. HR, operations, marketing, sales, IT—everybody wants one! Claire is thrilled to see that the whole company appreciates her data communication work, but she also knows she'll need guidance on working with such a diverse range of departments.

She schedules a meeting with Wang. "Can you give me some tips for each of these departments?" Wang congratulates her on her excellent work, and they dive in, starting with HR.

"In my opinion," Wang begins, "the biggest challenge with human resources is the data sets themselves. You've got to be very careful with using and sharing sensitive personal information. Imagine how you'd feel if someone was careless with your private data! And of course you need to respect regulations like GDPR." Data sets can contain many sensitive data points, he notes, and many of the most sensitive lie in the hands of the HR team. Prep Air, like any organization, keeps records of every employee's pay, age, home address, and number of dependents, to name just a few.

One common technique for visualizing sensitive data is to *aggregate* it, or show only summarized data. In other words, instead of showing individual data points, you might take information from five or ten individuals (at minimum) and then use the median of that information as a data point. If you do this before beginning your analysis, it is known as *pre-aggregation*.

Pre-aggregating your data makes it much harder to identify the individual people from whom the data is drawn. Although this grouping technique won't give you exact accuracy, it will allow you to share messages more widely than you would be able to otherwise (Figure 9-5).

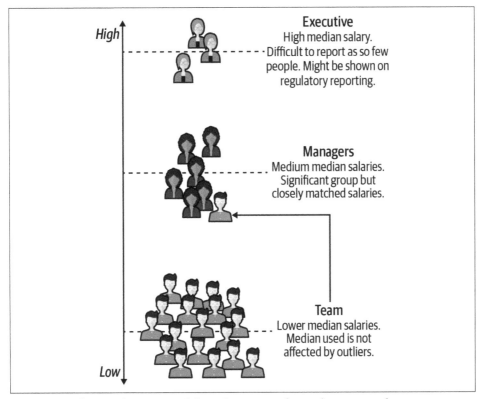

Executive
High median salary. Difficult to report as so few people. Might be shown on regulatory reporting.

Managers
Medium median salaries. Significant group but closely matched salaries.

Team
Lower median salaries. Median used is not affected by outliers.

Figure 9-5. Chart with aggregated data showing median salary per grade

Especially if your data is not pre-aggregated, take care. When you are filtering data for multiple characteristics, it can be challenging to ensure that you don't inadvertently leave individual people identifiable. In the grades shown in Figure 9-5, you can see the number of individuals who were grouped together. The groupings for Managers and Team are sufficient that the median salary won't reveal anyone's individual details. You'd need to take care with the Executive details, as there are so few people in this group.

However, if you broke each of these groups into individual departments, and you know who manages which department, identifying the salaries would be easy. In addition to potentially violating privacy laws, this could bring up morale issues, such as these:

- Individual employees could see their pay relative to that of their peers. If their peers are making more, they could feel undervalued and request more pay (or leave). If they don't see salaries higher than theirs, they could infer that their potential growth in the organization is limited and could begin looking for opportunities in other companies.

- If employees see disparities among departments, this can create resentment.

- If some individuals at lower job grades who have unique experience and skills are paid more highly than other employees at senior grades, this too could create resentment.

The chart does not provide any context that would help employees understand such cases.

One technique you can use to avoid this problem is to set a minimum count of individuals on the filters you use for each item shown—for example, so that the value will be shown only if the group includes at least five people.

Wang advises Claire to account for how her audience might interact with her work to ensure that the messages shared don't reveal individuals' details or create interpersonal conflict. Claire is likely to be asked to share only the dashboard, and other visualizations she might be asked to produce for the HR team, with certain people in the HR and executive team rather than widely publishing the data to provide reassurance over how this sensitive data might be shared.

Operations

"And then there's operational data, which has exactly the opposite challenges," Wang says. "Getting into the details is the only way to find out what's happening, what can be improved, and what kinds of investments that will take."

Of course, operations departments are all different, depending on what the organization does: operations might focus on servicing vehicles, teaching classes, or manufacturing products, for example. At Prep Air, the operational teams handle everything from cleaning planes to selling tickets to handling customer complaints.

Everything an organization does generates data. Communicating that data clearly allows managers to measure operational processes and identify problems (or potential problems) before they get out of control. Those managers would have to talk to hundreds of people every day to achieve the kind of high-level overview that a good data visualization provides. Talking to those on your organization's front line is hugely beneficial, of course, but understanding the data will help managers know where to start those conversations.

Let's take an important operational task as our example. To understand how many people you need for each function, you'll need to measure how long it takes to complete each task. If you don't hire enough people, your team will get stressed and might not be able to complete the required tasks. And if calls aren't answered or planes are messy, customers will quickly become unhappy. If you hire too many people, you might have happier customers, but your team won't have enough to do, and you'll be paying too much in wages and salaries. Operations is all about that balance. So how can you use data to measure how long a given task will take?

Back in Chapter 5, you learned about distributions, including control charts and box-and-whisker plots. These are really important techniques for sharing operational data. They use standard deviations to show not just the median or mean but also the expected values. That's the data your operations team needs for planning. Claire's control chart for this team, shown in Figure 9-6, provides an overview of the data as well as allows for closer inspection.

Claire's control chart shows that typically the team can expect to receive up to 80 complaints per week for each department. The average number of complaints increased weekly until week 19, when the operations team had to take urgent action to address the ever-increasing number of complaints. The operations team added more people to each of the three departments to ensure that customers were receiving better service across their interactions with Prep Air. Adding extra people was a response from the operations management team as it saw the number of complaints rise. When making these types of decisions, this chart would be one measurement to monitor along with resolution times and capacity of the team.

The onboard team might have been particularly worried about week 19, but as the value sits outside the control limits, Claire should ignore that data point in her analysis as being an outlier. In her communication, Claire should highlight to the operations team to not employ so many people as would be needed to cover the outlier amount of complaints on a regular basis.

For project managers, data is especially important: it allows them to measure progress, find blockages, and celebrate successes. Most organizations will fund only projects that include a clear time frame for stages of progress and deliverables, and to set that time frame, managers need data.

The source of data for operations departments is likely to be a project management system. Large organizations often use specialist project management systems to track progress and hold project data, whereas small organizations might simply keep it all in Excel. Either way, you can use that data to look at project overruns, predict that your team might have conflicting priorities on different projects, and plot out schedules, among other things. Project overruns can be costly, by either missing out on new product revenue or not making resource savings from efficiency projects. The cost of project management is often worth the initial investment.

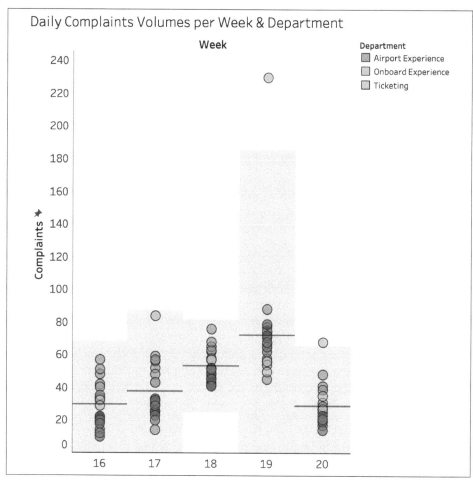

Figure 9-6. Control chart of complaints at Prep Air with faded data points

Using data from Prep Air's project management database, Claire creates the visualization in Figure 9-7, which looks at projects that are overrunning their estimated schedules. From these charts, we can see that some managers are delivering projects on the weekends—a sign that their capacity might be stretched. Ideally, projects would be completed during a weekday, so people are not being forced to work on weekends if that isn't typical behavior.

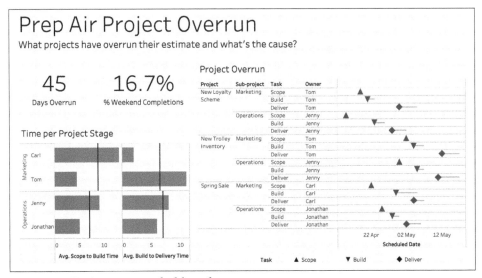

Figure 9-7. Project overrun dashboard

Claire adds interactivity to this view, so her audience can focus on individual task owners or departments. The chart on the right of Figure 9-7 is a Gantt chart, which shows milestone dates for each stage of a project and estimates the time those stages will take to complete. Claire knows all too well that these time estimates are constantly changing, so she builds a dashboard using a data source that refreshes regularly. Updated information helps decision makers know whether they need to add resources to a project or investigate delays.

Marketing

To understand how she can help the marketing department, Claire turns to Alex, Prep Air's head of digital marketing. "How would you say data affects marketing?" she asks.

Alex lets out a low whistle. "You could just ask how it *doesn't* affect marketing. Honestly, the rise of digital marketing creating more data has transformed the whole field. It's so much more crowded and busy. It's harder to make your brand stand out. When I started out in this field, we used to have to rely on focus groups and surveys; marketing research could really only happen one individual at a time. We still do some of that, but now we also collect and track data on social media engagement, web traffic, you name it. You can learn a lot about how customers perceive your brand before you even talk to any of them."

"Where does all that data come from?"

"Good question," Alex replies. "The biggest challenge you'll face when working with us marketers is collecting and collating all those data sources. It's a vast amount of information with different sources having different naming conventions and definitions to merge and clarify."

Alex explains that Claire will need to pull together information from data sets like census records, web traffic reports from Google Analytics, and social media sites like Facebook, LinkedIn, Instagram, and Twitter to create a consistent view that links the most important messages from each. Tracking web traffic on specific campaigns is important too.

"When you click an ad or a link in an email," Alex elaborates, "you'll see a specific URL, or web address, flash on your screen before you're redirected to the product page. We can track which clicks came from which URLs, so we know which ad or email you clicked. Now we know what got your attention and led you to our site. Then we can track your session on our site, so we can see how you navigate around and whether you buy anything."

The ultimate goal is to link customers' accounts to their actual purchasing behavior. This not only allows marketers to understand who is buying what but also lets them reverse the data flow to see what those customers are saying about the brand on social media. You can also find out if others with similar profiles might be interested in your product (or not). This lets you find the people who are most likely to want to purchase your products, so you get the most bang for your marketing buck.

To create those links, Claire will need to match up the fields from each data set: for example, the Name field on a census form should be linked to the Name field on Twitter. Claire, an avid Twitter user, knows that this could get tricky fast: her government name is Claire, but the name she uses on Twitter is different, as Claire was already taken. She quickly comes up with several other potential problems:

Facebook
> Facebook uses real names, mostly, but someone's Facebook name might leave out a middle name, include a former name to help old friends find them, or add a nickname.

LinkedIn
> LinkedIn uses real names, too, but people who change their names when they marry often still use the old name at work.

Census records
> Government census records include lots of details, but at the household level. It can be difficult to tie an individual to a specific household and to differentiate each adult in that household. In addition, people's official government names don't always match the names they use—for example, transgender people sometimes have difficulty obtaining an official name change when they transition.

Web traffic

You might ask customers to enter their email address on your website, but if they don't log in or you don't hold their email address, it's difficult to see what other websites they have visited.

These data sources are just the tip of the iceberg. You can see how linking them all together to form a profile of one identifiable person can be difficult to do. You will likely need to complete a lot of data cleaning to make the values you find from each of the data sources consistent with each other. Just identifying how to link the data sets together isn't enough to form a perfect data set for your analysis. You will inevitably need to spend a lot of time forming the data set suitable for your analysis. Building profiles of customers and potential customers, though, is well worth the effort, because they allow you to target your marketing campaigns much more accurately.

For example, Prep Air would like to focus on individuals who fly frequently for business. This group spends frequently on plane tickets, so it's a great market. Alex and the Prep Air team hope to identify those fliers' preferred destinations by using the geographic data in their social media posts. To do that, they need Claire to link a data set of customers enrolled in the Prep Air loyalty program with a data set of their social media accounts. Alex would love to be able to know who the fliers are and where they go to add special rates on those flights to ensure that they continue to fly with Prep Air and not potentially go for a competitor. Social media is a great way for organizations to see changing consumer behavior as it happens, so the Prep Air team might even notice new destinations becoming popular or emerging. Specialist organizations can form these comprehensive views of activities for you, as this is no easy task.

The challenge, as Claire surmised, is lining up the information in all those data sources to find common fields. Depending on how many data sources she needs to draw together, the task could be one she's able to take on or one that requires her to bring in specialist support. Just picking up the individual data sources can reveal a lot of information, and that would definitely be the key starting point, like understanding customer flow through the website, along with sales conversion rates.

Sales

"I love data!" says Michiko, one of the sales leads at Prep Air. "In sales, we're really driven by targets. We have to make our sales quota if we want to make money. And I don't know if I'm doing that unless I have data. I can't wait to see your dashboard, Claire!"

Sales monitoring systems, also called *customer relationship management (CRM)* systems, contain a lot of data, but that doesn't mean their data is easy to communicate. Many CRM systems offer built-in visualizations, but these usually can't be customized to answer specific questions. "*That's* where you and your data skills come in," Michiko tells Claire.

The sales team members measure their success by the progress they're making against their targets, but what they really need to know is *why* they are (or aren't) hitting those targets. Depending on the product, a single large deal might be enough for a salesperson to make their annual target. So the sales department needs to understand the *pipeline*, or the list of potential deals and how they are progressing toward completion. The sales pipeline has multiple stages, from initial prospecting for clients to closing the deal (Figure 9-8).

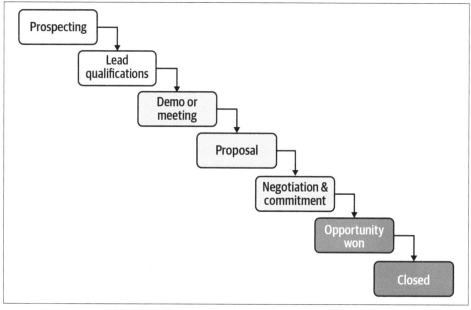

Figure 9-8. Diagram based on Salesforce's sales pipeline stages (https://oreil.ly/mmoYN)

Not every opportunity moves successfully through every stage of the pipeline. The sales department wants to track the progress of each opportunity and identify any issues or blockages it needs to address in order to complete the deal.

We can visualize the sales pipeline in many ways, but all of them need to communicate a few key pieces of information:

- The value of the pipeline as a whole
- The likelihood that each opportunity will *convert*, or create revenue with a sale
- How long each opportunity takes to convert

- Any changes in these measures compared to the previous period
- How each salesperson's pipeline compares to those of their peers

If Claire tried to build all of these elements into a single visualization, it would likely be too complex and difficult to understand. She decides that a dashboard is a better form to share this information (Figure 9-9).

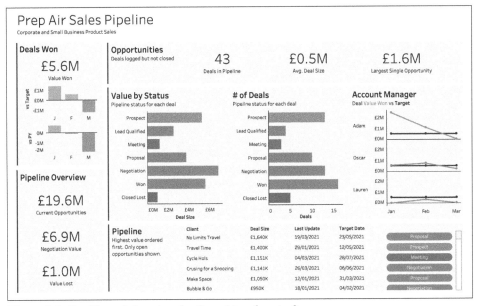

Figure 9-9. Dashboard showing the Prep Air sales pipeline

Monitoring an account's progress through the pipeline is a lot like tracking a journey. It involves understanding how long it takes for an account to progress to sale or rejection, and what happens along the way. Tracking trends in this data can generate a useful analysis of customer behavior. Sales leaders need to know the efforts their team is making and the effectiveness of those efforts.

For Prep Air, Michiko explains, "If our sales team is spending a lot of time focusing on landing large accounts and neglects lots of other accounts, the business might suffer overall. We celebrate large sales, of course, but we have to balance that effort and resources to make sure we're focusing on the right accounts."

To make this analysis, Claire will need records of all previous statuses of each account and when those statuses changed (Table 9-1). To be able to measure this, Claire needs to take regular copies of the table to create a history table. While she can remove rows that haven't changed at all, any change in status is needed to analyze the time it takes for deals to progress.

Table 9-1. Useful data structure for sales data

Account	Account owner	Product type	Estimated value	Status	Data update date
PA-302818	Jenny	Corporate	350000	Prospect	19/12/2020
PA-302818	Jenny	Corporate	290000	Quote	23/01/2021
PA-302818	Jenny	Corporate	290000	Invoice	08/02/2021
PA-302818	Jenny	Corporate	290000	Purchased	21/12/2021
PA-193842	Tom	SME	34000	Prospect	02/01/2021
PA-193842	Tom	SME	34000	Quote	08/01/2021
PA-193842	Tom	SME	34000	Invoice	11/01/2021
PA-127492	Tom	SME	12900	Prospect	13/02/2021
PA-123428	Tom	SME	12400	Prospect	17/02/2021
PA-387492	Jenny	Corporate	125000	Prospect	19/02/2021
PA-387492	Jenny	Corporate	140000	Quote	13/03/2021

This structure doesn't always make it easy to measure the time elapsed between each stage, but it does capture the changing value of each deal. This helps predict the likely conversion rate of the deal and how much of the original estimate is converted. Most of the data sets shown in this book so far have been *event based* (such as the plane tickets bought from Prep Air). The history table in Table 9-1 is a *temporal table*, in which you are likely to have multiple records per event. This style of table makes analysis slightly harder, as you can't just count the number of transactions. You have to apply a lot more logic through calculations to answer the questions you are assessing.

Information Technology

"You couldn't do any of what you do without us," Jamie, assistant to the CTO, tells Claire. "You wouldn't have any data sets if it weren't for the IT department. We built the systems this organization runs upon. We capture the data they produce. Without that, the executives would just have to rely on gut instinct and experience. You need us, and without my permission, you won't be able to get access to the data."

Claire's dashboards have been so successful that department heads are now requesting monthly visualizations they can distribute to their teams. Building all these dashboards is too much work to repeat over and over. If she's going to need to do this for every department every month, Claire needs to *productionalize* her data; that is, she needs to be able to produce it on a regular schedule without too much time and effort. She's talking to Jamie because she knows that the IT department has procedures to carry out each part of the process and ensure that the data is robust. This includes identifying the sources of data, preparing a clean data set, and producing the actual communication.

For example, Claire has been working from extracts of database queries, but Jamie has access to all of the organization's databases. He also has the coding skills and powerful software to move that data from certified sources into a feed, which will make it much easier to update the data sets that power Claire's communications. His process will look very different from Claire's, and it will take time to develop, but it will make producing the analytics faster in the future.

Jamie will need to break down the logic Claire has used to form her data sets through filtering and calculations and then build it into the same software he uses to run similar productionalized work. The same is true for visualizations: using different software may change some of the aesthetics, but Jamie and Claire agree they'll need to take care not to lose the key messages their audiences need to understand. They refer back to the questions Claire listed when she was generating requirements, to make sure the new version of the work still answers them.

"Now, once we productionalize the data communication process," Jamie mentions, "you're going to have a lot less control over how to iterate the work and adapt it to changing circumstances." This is a slightly old-fashioned view of working with data but still has elements of truth. Jamie will want to ensure that Claire doesn't change anything that will impact others' work. Jamie intends to make the data set Claire has formed available for others, and this will restrict how many changes Claire can make if she needs to iterate more. Claire should have the ability to update the visualizations as she needs to, as her stakeholders develop their requests further.

Jamie adds, "Once we've certified that these data sets are sourced correctly, we don't want anyone messing around with them." Claire is happy that she is getting support with the data set but feels like she has lost a little bit of control. In your organization, you might be more actively involved in productionizing your work; it doesn't have to be the domain of IT, but be ready if that's not the case.

The final part of the production process is knowing when to decommission your work. As the author, Claire knows the purpose of the work, so she'll probably have a sense of when it isn't relevant anymore. Since IT has limited resources, Jamie doesn't want them working on data feeds or communications that are no longer required. This decision shouldn't rest on only Claire's shoulders, though: she'll need to talk to her audience to see if they still find the work relevant and useful.

IT also needs data communications to demonstrate many aspects of their own performance and activity. Jamie's job isn't just waiting for others to produce data communications. The IT team will likely have many tasks of their own, like handling support tickets, delivering projects, and measuring system errors. As Claire has done a brilliant job of communicating the challenges across the business, these are similar pieces of work, even though it's a different department she is working with.

Claire has built a support ticket analysis to show the number of tickets the IT department has to deal with and how well they are doing against their targets (Figure 9-10). With this dashboard, Jamie should be able to manage his team more effectively, thus creating time to help out Claire more as she supports Prep Air's other departments.

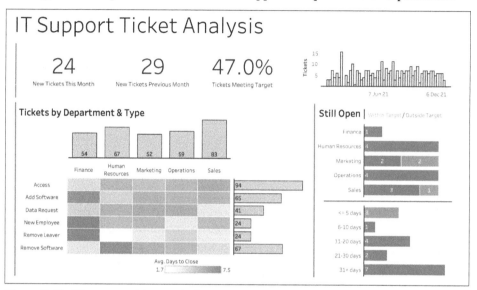

Figure 9-10. IT support ticket analysis

Summary

Working with various departments is an exciting opportunity and one I've always enjoyed. When your data skills shine within your current role, you'll likely be asked to interact more widely with departments and teams across your organization.

When you understand the needs and challenges of your colleagues in other departments, you'll be prepared to give them what they need quickly and effectively. Remember that your colleagues are probably already working with data to some extent, at different levels of data literacy. You will need to be highly agile and fit your approach to each situation, just as Claire did.

This chapter has shown you some of the challenges, terms, and requirements you are likely to encounter, but it is most definitely *not* an exhaustive list. It's also not a comprehensive list of the departments or the characters you might interact with either but has shown you a range of the challenges that you are likely to face. Knowing the unique challenges of each department will also inform your decisions about how best to help them, how best to structure and store their data, and how to spot the broader questions underlying each question they ask you.

The skills you have learned throughout this book, if you use them well, can open new opportunities to you. When you build your knowledge of other departments and foster collaborative relationships with your colleagues there, you'll find that all of your work develops and deepens in ways you might never have expected.

CHAPTER 10

Next Steps

Being a great data communicator is a lifelong pursuit. There is always more to learn, and the benefits you reap will only increase as you do. You can take many paths to progress through this journey and use many tools and resources to help you along the way.

Since every path is so different, it's hard to say exactly what you should do next. Instead, I'll finish by offering some next steps that can take you and your data communication skills in all sorts of directions.

Step 1: Get Inspired

The challenge of data communication is to keep your message clear while also getting and keeping your audience's attention. You've learned about several ways to create eye-catching, informative visualizations, but to keep your eye for design fresh, it's important to keep up on what others are doing in the field. Looking at lots of data visualizations made by skilled practitioners will keep you thinking creatively.

I find I need to take inspiration from others' work and then experiment with similar techniques or approaches on my own. Without the inspiration of others' work, you might quickly find yourself in a rut, using the same old techniques over and over. Just as writers must read great literature and artists visit museums and galleries to fill their creative well, you should immerse yourself in the best work you can find.

Here are some of my favorite places to turn for inspiration:

Social media
> Sites like Twitter are a useful place to find professional work and personal fun projects alike. The Data Visualization Society (*https://oreil.ly/AtzSZ*) is a great account to follow to see work across lots of technologies and sectors.

Tableau Public

Tableau Public (*https://oreil.ly/WfNjV*) is a free version of Tableau, but more important, it's a place where people share their work, personal projects, and new concepts. You can follow specific authors (my profile (*https://oreil.ly/3BFt3*) contains a lot of the visualizations from this book) or scan a collated set of dashboards in the gallery. (*https://oreil.ly/y8luW*)

If you do take inspiration from others, make sure you reference their influence—not only to give proper credit but so others can learn from their example too.

Step 2: Practice

We all know that practice makes perfect. I feel strongly that data practitioners—new and experienced alike—must constantly practice.

But it's hard to practice data preparation if your data sources are closely controlled. That's why I co-created Preppin' Data (*https://preppindata.com*), a weekly challenge that offers a safe space to learn and practice fundamental data preparation skills, such as reshaping, cleaning, and merging datasets. It is mostly focused on Tableau Prep, but you can complete the majority of the challenges in any tool. The challenge is posted every Wednesday, with the solution posted the following Tuesday.

On the visualization side of things, my colleague Andy Kriebel runs Makeover Monday (*https://oreil.ly/QJ0BB*). Each week it provides a not-so-great visualization that could really use a makeover—challenging you to visualize and communicate the data and data set more clearly. Participants post their solutions on Twitter and share feedback.

Learning outside the workplace can be a great way to test out skills and techniques you wouldn't get the chance to otherwise.

Step 3: Keep Reading

This book is about the big-picture concepts, so I haven't taught you any technically specific skills here. Getting started with various bits of software can be tricky and expensive, but books are a great place to start.

Jack Dougherty and Ilya Ilyankou's *Hands-On Data Visualization* (O'Reilly) covers many free tools, showing you how to install them and use them to form compelling data visualizations. Once you've checked out the options and decided on the tools, look for books that focus on those specific tools and do a deep dive.

Ben Jones's *Avoiding Data Pitfalls* (Wiley) is an excellent place to learn about common mistakes and how to avoid them in your data visualizations.

If you want more real-world examples, look to *The Big Book of Dashboards* by Steve Wexler, Jeffrey Shaffer, and Andy Cotgreave (Wiley). You're likely to be asked to produce lots of dashboards, and this is a great way to get to know the options open to you.

There's a rich literature on data visualization and analysis, and it grows every year— so keep reading!

I hope you now feel comfortable communicating with data and embracing the challenges of this exciting, rewarding, creative field. I look forward to seeing what you do with your new skills.

Index

sum of values
    aggregation technique used in columns, 49
    aggregation technique used in rows, 23
    in tables, 190-192
summaries, 192
surveys, 31-32, 35
symbol maps, 131
synchronizing axes, 181

T

Tableau, xi, 273
Tableau Prep Up & Running (Allchin), xi
Tableau Public, 310
tables
    how to read, 72-76
    limitations of, 77
    optimizing, 76-78
    totals/summaries in, 190-192
    usefulness of, 12
    versus visualizations, 252-261
    when not to use, 78
templates, 278, 279
text
    annotations, 201
    text boxes, 202, 218
    text formatting, 203
text files (.txt), 37
thematic iconography, 213
themed charts, 174
themes, 166, 213
tick marks, 81
tile maps, 135
title case, 27
titles
    main title, 196-198
    placement of, 198, 217
    role in data communication, 196
    subtitles, standfirsts, and chart titles, 199
tooltips, 220-223, 266
Total Quality Management, 4
Toyoda, Sakichi, 57
transmitters, 5
transparency, 117
treemaps, 149
trend lines, 112
true/false values, 28
trust
    assessing data for bias, 34
    data without sources, 28

inherent in tables, 77, 252
    role in data communication, 17
Tufte, Edward, 81, 100
2D positioning, 10, 95
.txt (text files), 37

U

unioning data, 64
unit charts, 175
unit indicators, 75-76
unsquare shapes, 177
up and down arrows, 209
upper control limit, 188
uppercase, 27

V

validity, 28
values
    altering in interactive visualizations, 266
    defined, 72
variance analysis, 78
vertical axis, 94, 101
views, 40
visual context
    background and positioning, 216-219
    contextual numbers, 205-206
    iconography and visual cues, 213-215
    interactivity, 220-224
    legends, 208-212
    text and annotations, 201-205
    titles, 196-200
visual elements
    color
        avoiding unnecessary use of, 168-171
        choosing the right color, 166-168
        types of color palettes, 160-166
    multiple axes, 179-183
    reference bands, 187-190
    reference lines, 184-185
    size and shape
        challenges of using, 175-177
        limitation of uses, 178
        themed charts, 174
        using carefully, 172-173
    totals/summaries
        in charts, 193
        in tables, 190-192
visualization mix, improving, 257

W

waterfall charts, 91-93
weak correlation, 114
Western cultures, 94, 119, 167
Wexler, Steve, 311
whiskers, 189
whitespace, 218, 279
whole numbers, 25

X

x-axis, 101, 116

.xlsx file extension, 37
XML (Extensible Markup Language), 42

Y

y-axis, 101, 116

Z

Z reading pattern, 217
zero line/zero point, 82, 136

About the Author

Carl Allchin is a Tableau Zen Master, multiple-time Tableau Ambassador, and The "Other" Head Coach at one of the world's leading data analytics training programs at The Data School in London. After over a decade in financial services as a business intelligence analyst and manager, he's supported hundreds of companies through consulting, blogging, and teaching on market-leading data solutions. Carl is the cofounder of Preppin' Data, the only weekly data preparation challenge on Tableau and other data tools. He published *Tableau Prep: Up & Running* in 2020 with O'Reilly.

Colophon

The animal on the cover of *Communicating with Data* is a parti-colored bat (*Vespertilio murinus*). Also known as a rearmouse, this species of vesper bat can be found across much of temperate Eurasia. The name of its genus is derived from a Latin term meaning "evening," and as such these bats and their close relatives are sometimes called "evening bats," and were once known as "evening birds."

The parti-colored bat gets its name from its fur; its back is a reddish dark-brown, while its underside is white or gray. It has relatively narrow wings and a wingspan of 10–13 in (26–33 cm), and a body size of approximately 1.9–2.5 in (4.8–6.4 cm). These bats hunt their prey primarily during twilight above streams, lakes, and forests, or near street lights in more urban areas. Like other vesper bats, they employ a wide range of ultrasonic sounds for echolocation and communication. They feed on mosquitoes, caddisflies, and moths. Parti-colored bats are often found living in groups, but have been observed to hibernate by themselves between October and March.

The current conservation status of the parti-colored bat is "Least Concern." Many of the animals on O'Reilly covers are endangered; all of them are important to the world.

The cover illustration is by Karen Montgomery, based on a black and white antique engraving from *British Quadrupeds*. The cover fonts are Gilroy Semibold and Guardian Sans. The text font is Adobe Minion Pro; the heading font is Adobe Myriad Condensed; and the code font is Dalton Maag's Ubuntu Mono.

O'REILLY®

There's much more where this came from.

Experience books, videos, live online training courses, and more from O'Reilly and our 200+ partners—all in one place.

Learn more at oreilly.com/online-learning